Living in Godless Times

Living in Godless Times

Tales of Spiritual Travellers

Alison Leonard

Floris Books

First published in 2001 by Floris Books

The publisher would like to thank Bloodaxe Books
for their permission to reproduce extracts of poetry,
published from the collection *City Psalms* by
Benjamin Zephaniah (Bloodaxe Books, 1992).

British Library CIP Data available

ISBN 0-86315-341-0

Printed in Great Britain
by Biddles Ltd, Guildford

Contents

Introduction
The decline of religion and the rise of spirituality

All things are changing; nothing dies. The spirit wanders, comes now here, now there, and occupies whatever frame it pleases.
> Pythagoras *(c.580–500 BC).*

This is my church. This is where I heal my hurts. Not an exclusive church. An all-inclusive church.
> Faithless (rock group), *God is a DJ, 1999.*

Open a newspaper at random and you will read news of God's funeral. Survey after survey shows the decline in church attendance in Britain. Over a single decade, the last one of the twentieth century, the Church of England saw attendance fall by five per cent.[1]

Desperate measures are needed. A report commissioned for the Methodists even proposes they admit non-believers so as to boost membership. Yet the same survey that reported the decline in church attendance then tossed the seesaw down on the other side: during the same period the proportion of people believing they had a soul went up by five per cent.

A.N. Wilson, the latest enquirer into the death of God, quotes Hegel:

> "God has died, God is dead — this is the most frightful of all thoughts, that everything eternal and true is not, that negation itself is found in God ... However, the process does not come to a halt at this point."[2]

No indeed, says Posh Spice/Victoria Beckham. Religion is not about going to church, religion is between herself and God. "People don't want others to take control," says the Methodist Rev Dr Stephen Mosedale, who made the radical suggestion quoted above about inviting non-believers into church membership. "They don't want organized religion getting in the way of their relationship with God."[3]

Religion used to deliver God. Now it is seen as getting in the way of God.

I have been part of this movement myself. "In order to own what my spirit was," I wrote in *Telling Our Stories,* "I had to step out of the power structure of the church. The key seemed to lie in being true to myself. But I had no idea who that self was."[4] Someone thrust into my hand a copy of *The True Wilderness* by H.A. Williams, where I read about true power being the strength that comes from wholeness within. "More light, deeper perception, a less clouded vision of what life is about. How am I to get it? Only in the ancient school of experience, by trial and error, by pain and joy, and, most of all, by faith, by confidence that, in spite of all appearances to the contrary, life is on my side and not against me."[5]

The faith that Harry Williams speaks of was sought by earlier generations within organized religion. It is still sought there, and sometimes found. But larger and larger numbers are seeking it elsewhere.

An end to certainty

This is a massive social shift as well as a spiritual one. Tabloids and serious television programmes link plummeting moral standards with the decline in religious authority. If we cannot be policed by priests and commandments, they seem to say, then we must be policed by surveillance cameras in our streets and GCHQ trawling through our e-mails, and the old religious certainties were so much pleasanter.

But we cannot return to those certainties. Globalization of manufacture and trade, the advent of the Internet and e-mail, the pervasive power of popular culture, all ensure that freedom from the old standards of religious and moral authority is not an option but compulsory. For instance, as a parent you can tell your children to stay off drugs, and your stance will be supported by strong words from teachers at school and from the elders of your religious community if you belong to one. But the markets have brought in the substances from around the globe, the Internet which contributes to your children's education also supplies them with information about, and access to, drugs, and the exchange of substances for cash is made around the corner from their home or school. As they tell you, "Everyone is doing it."

A couple of decades ago Fay Weldon made the point in a television debate with a bishop about authority and adultery: "But the impulse to be good has to come from *inside.*" A more recent commentator, the journalist Ekow Eshun, makes a similar point: "We may not be obeying orders, but we're asking more questions."[6] The only tool with which we can face the pluralistic (or chaotic) scene outside is the development of personal resources within.

As outwardly visible, acceptedly authoritative religion declines in the face of a pluralistic society, so the movement that comes "from inside," the movement that we call spirituality, rises and grows. It cannot be quantified; it cannot be hailed as "the new moral force in our society." No one has yet done a sociological analysis of meditators on weekend courses, Spiritual Discovery house groups, Wicca covens, religious and non-religious retreatants at Catholic and Anglican abbeys, mourners and celebrators at outdoor New Age funerals and weddings, consumers at the Mind-Body-Spirit shelves in bookshops, rune-readers, Living Art workshoppers, shamanic dancers and journeyers, people who grow organic vegetables in reverence for the land, people finding stillness or forgiveness at a Buddhist monastery, people visiting their spiritual director, people who devise rites of passage for themselves or their children so as to make a chain-link with the past and the future. There is no overall authority to vet them or control them. They contribute both to craziness and to sanity, to citizenship and to subversion.

The necessity for discernment

We can deplore these movements, as Jacob Bronowski did thirty years ago:

> "I am infinitely saddened to find myself suddenly sur-
> rounded in the west by a sense of terrible loss of nerve, a
> retreat into ... what? Into Zen Buddhism, into extra-sensory
> perception and mystery."[7]

A better way, it seems to me, is to evolve skills of discernment towards them. This isn't easy. With religion the issue was relatively simple. If you wanted to leave the faith of your childhood you could read books and ask questions to ascertain the vital aspects of other faiths. What did they require in terms of belief, what were their religious practices? There were forms of words and outward acts. There were bodies of people to be observed, fixed times and places of worship as examples of the faith concerned.

With spirituality the whole picture is more fluid. You can delve into *The Good Retreat Guide,* follow the small ads in *Resurgence* or *Kindred Spirit,* key into the shamanic network or join an e-mail correspondence group on the meaning of mythic symbols or nature of spiritual healing. But all the time you have only your own discernment to rely on. Try, and see. That is the only way.

What the spiritual field lacks more than anything else, I think, is a collection of role models, guides, companions on the way. Religiousness can be tested in the outward observance. Spirituality can only be tested in the living out of a life.

But to whose lives should we turn?

When I began to look for people to tell their life stories in this book I had only a hazy idea of what I was about. I set out in a spirit of open enquiry. I had been brought up a Christian in the Anglican and Methodist churches, I had become a Quaker, and I was developing interests in Buddhist meditation, Ignatian-style visualization and Goddess stories. My personal criterion for discernment was "As the spirit moves." But the spirit could move in very mysterious ways, and I longed for people whom I respected to say to me: "Look, I followed my inner promptings and this is how it's turned out for me. It'll be different for you, no doubt. But maybe there's something in my story that will help and support you."

Promptings and questions

I wrote to a selection of people I knew or had contacts with, supplemented them with others whose voices I had heard or read and whose views and life journeys excited me, and when I next reviewed the situation I realized that I had in my bag a range of people who could be, for me and others, just such companions, inspirations, role models.

I wanted my collection to include:
— people who were still within a faith community as well as those who had left one;
— people who had travelled, physically and spiritually, and had lived through doubt as well as conviction;
— people who had faced the worst of life's challenges but who could also articulate joy, love and vital energy;
— people who, while representing no one other than themselves, could bring a wide variety of culture, and of spiritual and world view.

I also felt, quite personally, that four aspects of the spiritual life had been missing from my own religious upbringing, and that it was this sense of lack which propelled me out of the mainstream Christian faith and into a lifetime of seeking. These four are:
1) the path to a still centre within;
2) a realistic look at suffering, evil and death and their place in our lives;
3) an awareness of spiritual community and how to maintain and develop it;
4) ways of rediscovering a sense of the sacred.

Some well-wishers urged me to concentrate on first-rank-famous names. But I decided against that. Those who are permanently in the public eye cannot speak openly; they must always watch their back. Others encouraged me to include fanatics — "Try that man ... that woman ... They'd condemn themselves out of their own mouths!" But I decided against that too because I wanted to like my interviewees, and to be honest and not feign fascinated attention where I felt none. I finally chose individuals who showed an interest in spirituality and had an eminent c.v. in their own field, or who had unusual and vital experience on which they'd reflected in a spiritual way. When I made my invitation I asked whether they would welcome open-ended questions, and whether they were willing to offer the deeper aspects of their lives for inspection by the spiritually curious.

My letter invited them to talk to me, personally and autobiographically, about their lives as a spiritual journey. Their responses were heartening.

> I'm excited by the prospect of exploring spirituality and religious experience in people's lives without starting from preconceived answers. Faith is *not* knowing the answers, but moving forward into new awareness and new vision. (JR)

> This seems like a creative and original attempt to respond to the spiritual yearnings of thousands of people who can no longer find a home in institutional religion. By presenting some radical and very different struggling souls it seems to me that the message of "We are because I am and I am because we are" might have resonance even in this individual- obsessed culture. (BT)

> I like your emphasis on processes. I judge processes to be too often ignored and overlooked — so many people are end-goal orientated that people aren't often thoughtful about how things came to be. (JBB)

> The search for meaning is lifelong and I prefer company on the journey. I'm inspired by the concept of collaborating with a collection of God-questioners from such diverse backgrounds on a contemporary search for a spiritual centre. (NG)

> *The true method of discovery is like the flight of an aeroplane. It starts from the ground of particular observation; it makes a flight in the thin air of imaginative generaliza-*

tion; and it again lands for renewed observation rendered acute by rational interpretation.
Alfred North Whitehead (1861–1947), *Process and Reality.*

The process

I decided against asking specific questions such as "When did you first experience God?" or "Have your feelings about spiritual reality altered over the years?" Instead I asked each person to tell the story of their life in the way that best revealed its own truth. Some told the story chronologically. Others started from how things are now and worked backwards, or moved from theme to theme rather than age to age, or gave mostly their childhood awareness ("Everything else stems from that"), or just sketched in a brief background before concentrating on the overwhelmingly important experience.

The selection of contributors couldn't be entirely my own. Some I passionately wanted were unable or, for different reasons, unwilling. In the end I contacted and/or interviewed more people than could possibly fit into a book of this sort, and my gratitude to those who went through larger or smaller amounts of the process only to find themselves in the end omitted is profound.

I particularly wanted to interview people who had remained within their original faith but who were prepared to speak out or step out in the process of being true to their individual spiritual search. June Raymond took leave from her Catholic order for purposes of discernment and then returned to a different relationship with her religious house; Jocelyn Bell Burnell moved steadily from one part of the Quaker world to a different part; Raficq Abdulla and Naomi Gryn wrestle painfully with aspects of Islam and Judaism but remain at the heart of these communities.

In deciding how to conduct the interviews I took on board the principle of absolute collaboration enunciated by Mary Loudon: "'You won't get the truth if you promise the contributors the right of veto,' a friend said to me. 'I won't get anything at all if I cheat them,' I replied."[8] The wisdom of this principle was entirely borne out in practice. In deciding not to be the journalist in search of a hatchet job I knew I ran the risk of sounding reverential. Indeed,

in the face of some of their stories I *felt* reverential. But I didn't
duck chances to pose a challenge, from a mild "That's an unusual
thing to do, isn't it?" to a forthright "Don't you ever think 'I'm an
arrogant bastard'?" or "Has anyone suggested that you visit a
good psychiatrist?"

Optimistically, I took note of Adrian Cooper's experience in his
writing of *Sacred Nature:* "These interviews began with the
intention of discovering and celebrating the richness of personal
experience. All these people brought a sustained enthusiasm and
creativity regarding the aims of this book.[9]

My optimism, too, was continually confirmed. From first to last,
each contributor opened up not only to my tape-recorder but also to
the editing process. I suggested that we give their chapter as much
time as it needed to get the resulting portrait absolutely right and,
like Mary Loudon, I let them delete anything they felt uncomfortable with. They had friends and family and employers to consider;
I'd asked them to be truthful, yes, but I hadn't asked them to hurt
people or to subvert the rest of their lives. They all offered their
time, their commitment, their honesty and enthusiasm to the task.

The interviews were generally carried out in two half-sittings,
with a substantial break in the middle for relaxation and reflection. Occasionally we needed another shot at it, either because the
milieu was unfamiliar to me and required clarification or simply
because there was too much material and we hadn't been able to
find a clear line through.

I usually ended up with about five times as many words on tape
as I had room for as text. In editing, the choice of incidents was
usually mine while the words were the interviewee's. Exceptions
came when long incidents needed to be condensed or the interviewee felt that the final version needed later tweaking to avoid
giving a false impression.

One pitfall was entirely of my own making. It's the failing
common to biographers who also write fiction and plays, as I do:
the tendency to over-dramatize. So there arose a dialogue
between the one who had actually experienced the event and saw
it in the context of a whole life, and the other who, as audience,
stood outside and felt the fresh impact of its drama. A lengthy and
careful editing process allowed us to reach a point somewhere
between the needs of these two opposing points of view.

Experience and response

In shaping the chapters into a book I chose to group them into those four original themes for which I had felt a need: those who were discovering a still centre within; those who inspired me by the way they have faced evil, suffering and loss; a third group who have a strong relationship to a spiritual community; and lastly a group whose life path rediscovers a sense of the sacred.

This categorization was much more difficult than I anticipated. All the elements were there, certainly, but the categories overlapped to such an extent that I wondered whether my groupings were meaningless. I'd anticipated that Raficq Abdulla's relationship with his faith community of Islam would be the key aspect, but in fact he came over as someone who through poetry had found his still centre. I knew Anne Gray as someone who had lived with the suffering of children with multiple disabilities and even more closely with her husband's disability, but it was her insights into community living that pushed her chapter into that group. Gordon MacLellan's spiritual practice of trance might place him in the "still centre" grouping, but his shamanic vision provided an overwhelming sense of the sacred. Benjamin Zephaniah's experience of racism, family breakdown and imprisonment might put him in the group facing suffering and evil, but in the end it was his inward stillness that was the inspiration.

So the groupings are signposts, not maps. The signposts will lead into the labelled territory, but they are also invitations into other territories and even into other landscapes altogether. The interviews will propel the reader, as they propelled me, out of *terra cognita*. Readers' life experiences will vary as widely as the experiences in this book, but these sixteen journeys can give shivers of amazement as well as glimmers of recognition: Gordon MacLellan trance-dancing till he bleeds; collision between Mehr Fardoonji's ideals and her physical capacity to sustain them; Marian Partington literally losing a sister; Rose Hacker dancing goddess-like on Crete at the age of ninety; Dayachitta, young and alone and looking cancer in the face; Benjamin Zephaniah's reconciliation with his father; Jocelyn Bell Burnell's rejection of fame.

What shifts these experiences into the spiritual arena is not the events themselves but the individual's response to them: the refusal to ignore complexities, the willingness to set aside energy for reflection, the vision of wholeness into which the best and the worst can, in time or in eternity, be fitted. Each chapter contains experiences which scientists of consciousness call *qualia:* what C.J.S. Clarke, formerly a professor of Applied Mathematics and active in the Creation Spirituality movement, describes as "deepest emotions ... even certain aspects of the external world such as the particular subjective experience of a certain colour ... experience[s] that cannot be broken down into any smaller or elementary components or described in terms other than [themselves]."[10]

> *When I examined the way of development of those persons who, quietly and as if unconsciously, grew beyond themselves, I saw that their fates had something in common. Whether arising from without or within, the new things came to all those persons from a dark field of possibilities; they accepted it and developed further by means of it ... But it was never something that came exclusively either from within or without. If it came from outside the individual, it became an inner experience; if it came from within, it was changed into an outer event. But in no case was it conjured into existence through purpose and conscious willing, but rather seemed to flow out of the stream of time.*
> C.G. Jung, Commentary on *The Secret of the Golden Flower*

Self-deception and lightness of heart

The need for discernment lies at the heart of this book. But of course we can exercise all our available discernment and still be duped. As Eric Maddern says, "Making stories about ourselves is how we find, and make, meaning in our lives." This raises the fundamental question: if we're finding it for ourselves, is that meaning false or true? Naomi Gryn's account complicates the situation further. Faced with the apparently senseless death of a close friend, she found that by fictionalising it she was actually presaging her own fate: "My story was told in the first person and I had to envisage my own death. How did I do it? I had a truck turn over on me. I pre-empted what was to happen to me. Maybe we write our own stories."

The truth is that we can never be sure, when we tell our stories, whether or not we are deceiving ourselves. "Memory," says Holocaust novelist Anne Michaels, "can be a ceremony of restoration."[11]

But it can also be a ceremony of self-justification, of settling old scores or of seeking personal sanctification. One reassuring aspect of these life stories is that they are well-rooted in other spiritual stories of past and present. Teresa of Avila, Thérèse of Lisieux, Julian of Norwich,* Carl Gustav Jung, Joseph Campbell, James Hillman emerge from these pages. Ancient and contemporary myths are engaged with, like Kathy Jones with Ariadne and Green Tara, Eric Maddern with legends of Britain and Australian Aboriginal myths, David Banks with the Cyberman of Doctor Who. They also have a sense of wider purpose: of imaginative ways of meeting social need; of personal change in order to relate better to society and to those closest to us. Marian Partington uses her grief to help her understand how the extremities of pain brutalize people; Gordon MacLellan treasures his relationship with animal spirits and then shows children how to strengthen their relationship with the world around them; Naomi Gryn tells the story of the Holocaust and goes on to link the lives of Muslim and Jewish women.

> For my own part, I have also a horror of being duped; but I can believe that worse things than being duped may happen. Our errors are surely not such awfully solemn things. In a world where we are so certain to incur them in spite of all our caution, a certain lightness of heart seems healthier than this excessive nervousness of their behalf. In all important transactions of life we have to take a leap in the dark. William James[12]

Finally, it's important to emphasize that these sixteen people are just that: sixteen people. They are not gurus or saints; they do

---

* Anchoress and mystic who lived 1342–*c*.1416, author of *Revelations of Divine Love,* a document of religious experience.

not have *The Answers.* They are living the questions rather than grabbing at answers. June Raymond, as a child, realized that "it wasn't that adults *wouldn't* answer my questions but that they *couldn't.* So I knew I had to work things out for myself, and if it took forever, well, it took forever." Each reader's answer will probably take forever. But, as you leap in the dark, these sixteen companions will engage you in dialogue to lighten the way.

Finding the Still Centre

Jocelyn Bell Burnell

My assistant for no apparent reason said quite urgently, "The woman in blue on the back row." I called the woman in blue, and she spoke about evil and suffering from her own experience and it called the whole gathering to an immensely deeper level. Helen just knew it had to be her. That was God working in a way that was dramatic, and scary.

There's always been a base for me in Meeting for Worship, in the encounter with God. It's a continuity which has always been important to me. I've been on and off about whether I call myself a Christian. Sometimes Christ plays a relatively small role in my outlook, sometimes I feel comfortable calling myself a Christian. One's spiritual life evolves.

Spiritualizing everything

Jocelyn Bell Burnell was part of the team of astronomers who discovered pulsars in 1967, for which Antony Hewish and Martin Ryle were awarded the Nobel Prize for Physics in 1974. Born in 1943, she grew up in Lurgan in Northern Ireland, and was educated at an English Quaker boarding school and at Glasgow and Cambridge universities. "When Burnell was appointed Professor of Physics at the Open University, the number of female professors of physics in the UK doubled" (Britannica 1998). She has been a member of the Religious Society of Friends (Quakers) all her life, and for five years was Britain Yearly Meeting Clerk, chairing their 800 to 1500 strong annual gathering.

Jocelyn is briefly back home in the UK from her visiting professorship at Princeton University, USA, to check on her house in Milton Keynes and to help her son Gavin move his gear to Cambridge. Our conversation is punctuated by odd thumps from the latter process and by amiable negotiations about keys, cars and lengths of journeys. Princeton Physics Department seems a long way away, as does the Radio Telescope Committee near Gothenburg, Sweden, which she's due to attend in a couple of days' time, and next month's lecture tour of Australia. There is nothing overfacing about Jocelyn Bell Burnell, astronomer and near-Nobel prize-winner. She talks about her spiritual life in the manner of someone who thinks about it every day.

I had heard her on the radio in discussion with novelist/political commentator Norman Mailer and geneticist Steven Rose, and regretted that there wasn't time for her to answer Norman Mailer's insistent question: "But how does all this science fit in with your Quaker beliefs?" *What would her answer have been?*

"The answer's very simple," she says, "but it's not short enough for a soundbite. It's that I find a similarity between the methods of scientific research and methods of religious exploration. Both start with a hypothesis, a model, a picture, which you revise by experiment in the case of science, by life experience in the case of theology. If it works, you go with it. If it doesn't, you go back to the drawing board. Both hold ideas provisionally and are prepared to revise them."

Not a common view of the religious enterprise?

"Maybe not. But I can never quite understand why people see such conflict between science and religion. People are always asking me to speak on that subject, and I tell them I have nothing to say."

She may have nothing so say about this conflict, but she has plenty on how the scientific enterprise is undertaken, on how she personally, and the community of Quakers of which she is a member, undertakes the spiritual journey, and on the connections between the two.

Complicated Quaker roots

"Yes, I was brought up a Quaker and am a Quaker still. That sounds simple, but it's not! There is a tension in Northern Irish Quakerism — a tension between a liberal wing and a more fundamentalist and evangelical wing, and as a child growing up in this community I was very aware of this tension. Looking back I can see myself as a liberal at heart, but I did value the God-centredness of those who perhaps felt that the liberals were in league with the Devil! That is said with the benefit of a lot of hindsight, though. At the time I found it confusing."

Was she always of a academic bent? "No. I failed the eleven plus."*

We both laugh at the irony of that, and I recall a comment she recounted to me from Norman Mailer: "Well," he said after the BBC mikes were turned off, "it's been a pleasure to be in discussion with people more intelligent than myself."

Did it hurt, that early failure?

---

* The English educational test which divides eleven-year-olds into grammar school entrants (approximately sixteen per cent) and the rest.

"Yes. It did. I've only recently realized how much. It's only since I became a professor that I've actually admitted to failing the eleven-plus. But my mother was very eager for us girls to have a good education, because her family's resources had all gone into her brother's education while she was trained to be a secretary. And my father agreed. He had phenomenal general knowledge; he was three times Northern Ireland finalist in *Brain of Britain.* So my parents persuaded the grammar school to take me on for the two years between Junior School and going to The Mount Quaker school in York, England.

"One day I was sent along to Domestic Science with the other girls, but I said, 'No, I think I'm meant to be along *there* ...' in Science proper. My parents had no problem with that, but Friends in Lurgan Meeting tended to reject science because of the conflict with Genesis."

What was English Quaker boarding school like?

"Hard, at first. I was the eldest in the family, the first to go, and there were a lot of adjustments to make. But I built up quite a life there. I was glad to get out of Northern Ireland, not be seen only as my parents' daughter, not to get told off by school-friends for wearing a green jersey!*

"The Mount was a community and I got dug in. I liked the Quaker aspect of it. The Quaker Meeting was precious to me: the expectant silence and the spontaneous spoken ministry. During the holidays I caused problems for the family by preferring to go to Meeting rather than going boating with them." *Did she feel that God was there, at Quaker Meeting?* "Yes," says Jocelyn carefully. "I think that's the language I would have used.

"At the Mount we had an RE teacher, Dorothy Webster, who was a considerable influence. She was an unprepossessing-looking woman, slightly dumpy, not very elegantly dressed, but she was very widely respected and a lot of what she taught us has stuck: Quaker history, sixth-form excursions to the Lancashire-Cumbria '1652 country' where Quakerism began, and the human side of Quakers. She was very realistic about Quakerism: she'd tell funny stories about what had happened in Meeting. And the Bible, I remember doing the minor prophets, Amos and Hosea,

---

* Green is the colour of the Nationalist, i.e. Roman Catholic and Republican, Irish.

and she managed to bring out the issues, which are still around today even if the context has changed."

How did she, at that age, take in the Quaker way?

"Every evening we had Evening Meeting. We were read to from a book with moral and spiritual content — no, not exclusively Christian — and then we had a good chunk of silence. And we maintained the silence as we went to our bedrooms, to give us a chance for private prayer. Some girls knelt down but I just sat on the bed and used the time for reflection. The public Meeting for Worship was less good because there were too many pupils there in proportion to adults. One or two Sundays a term we could visit other churches, but I liked the Quaker Meetings on those Sundays because the people who were there *wanted* to be there. I could sense the difference that made."

Becoming a scientist

"In those 'proper' Science lessons in Lurgan we were taught some physics and some astronomy. Yes, it's astonishing that they included astronomy! But during my teenage years it wasn't clear that I would go into science. I was good at Latin and Maths as well, and I was interested in architecture because my father was an architect. Then in the run-up to O levels I used to spend a lot of my evenings explaining Physics to girls at the Mount who were struggling with it. We had a very good teacher, Mr Tillett, who'd come out of retirement for the second time because Physics teachers in girls' schools were so hard to come by. But for a very long time I lacked confidence: I was not at all sure of my own capabilities.

"My interest in astronomy started in my teens with some library books that Dad brought home. What fascinated me was stellar structure, the physics of a star. It was around 1957, the era when the Russians launched the Sputnik, which meant that there was a great push for science because the West wanted to be in front again. There was also the feeling that science could provide the solution to all the world's problems.

"Because I was a girl there was pressure for me to go into teaching." *Here she pauses to ponder the position of women at that time.* "Our generation was a turning point, I think. My mother's generation didn't work when kids came along, and maybe even stopped work when they married. And after us, young women expect to have careers. Our generation were the in-between ones. Our career advisers were anxious to send us to work, but into jobs that were *of service."*

This brings her back to the main story. "At Glasgow I was fascinated by geology, but I was very firmly told that geology was not a suitable career for me. Travelling the jungle ... rugged ... Not for a woman!

"I ended up being the only woman doing Honours Physics in a class of fifty. The male students, whenever a female entered, stamped and thumped their desks. The noise! The din! And the lecturers did nothing." *Jocelyn has already told me how, when she first went to Glasgow University, she would go to the Quaker Meeting but slip out before coffee because she was so shy. How did she cope with this barracking? She smiles.* "You can teach yourself not to blush. I've forgotten it now! But the course was hard, I didn't want to waste my energy on this kind of struggle, I wanted to put my energy into the science."

Did she use her spiritual self?

"Well, it may have been stubbornness! But, yes, there was the Quaker witness: *they shall not win this situation.* I can remember people saying after the first lecture, 'You'll be changing course, then, Jocelyn.' But I would not.

"I got a good Second in my degree, and wanted to do radio astronomy. Again, the woman problem came up. One application was said to have fallen down the back of a desk, but I heard later that their one woman researcher had had an affair with another student, so 'Never another woman.' But I applied to do a Cambridge PhD, not expecting to get in, and they accepted me."

In Cambridge she set to work with a sledge-hammer and a soldering iron to make her own radio telescope. She describes the discovery of the pulsar as 'accidental' in the course of her PhD research on quasars. *

"In my final year I was operating this telescope, surveying all the sky that was visible from Cambridge, measuring the sizes and

* Pulsars: pulsating radio star — a rapidly spinning neutron star formed when the core of a supernova collapses inward. Quasars: quasi-stellar objects, discovered in 1963, they are powerful sources of radio waves and other forms of energy.

strengths of quasars, looking for the fluctuations. I picked up some funny-looking signals in the middle of the night when we wouldn't expect it. I noted it with a question mark, and when a few more came I showed them to Tony Hewish. Then it vanished! But that's how it behaves, it comes and goes. Eventually it came back and we checked to see it wasn't stray signals from a satel- lite, or my precious home-made radio telescope going wrong — that was my dread, that all these bright brains of Cambridge were being led astray by my bad wiring — and then we knew it was something new."

I want to get to the truth about the discovery and the 1974 Nobel Prize. Britannica *states:*

> "Although Burnell shared the prestigious Michelson Award
> with her former graduate advisor Hewish in 1973, the
> Nobel Committee the following year did not acknowledge
> her role ... Many distinguished astronomers including Sir
> Frederick Hoyle, have expressed the view that Burnell
> should have been awarded the Nobel Prize."[1]

How did Jocelyn feel about it?
"I remember the day the news came out. I was working in X- ray astronomy, which you do from satellites. Our satellite was launched that morning from off the coast of Kenya, and we were listening to the launch over the radio link, and when we heard that the launch was successfully in orbit there was a terrific atmos- phere around the lab. Then at about noon someone came rushing in — 'Have you heard the news?' I thought it was about the satel- lite, but no, it was about the Nobel Prize for Tony Hewish and Martin Ryle. I was absolutely delighted that the Physics prize had gone for astronomy for the first time. Nobel didn't institute a prize specifically for astronomy, and this was hugely important as a political statement. And I was very pleased it was pulsars that got it. John who'd come rushing along the corridor to tell me was quite disappointed that steam didn't come out of my ears. I was- n't in the least miffed that I hadn't got it myself."

She didn't even have to fight down that feeling?
"No. I think I saw the broader issues. The real flak started about a year later, when Fred Hoyle made what he claimed was

an off-the-cuff remark about the prize being 'filched from Joce-lyn Burnell.' I had to be very diplomatic and calming."

But, surely, wouldn't she have liked the situation to have been different?

"No, actually. Years later, in 1993, another Nobel prize-winner for pulsar work, Joe Taylor, another Quaker, invited me to Stock-holm for his prize-giving. That was a tremendous week, a week of parties. But I saw it was incredibly demanding actually to *get* the prize. I do wonder how I would have coped back in 1973. I was getting over my shyness ... It's incredibly high profile, and you can spend the rest of your life being a public figure rather than a scientist.

"And again, there was the woman thing. At the time of the dis-covery journalists just couldn't handle a woman being a scientist. In interviews they'd ask Tony about the scientific significance and me about the human interest. I was asked for my vital statistics. How many boyfriends did I have? Was I taller than Princess Mar-garet or not quite so tall? Would I please wear something low cut?"

How did she handle it? Had the Quaker world sheltered her too much to help in this situation?

"I think so. And the academic world, too. I handled it rather badly. I forgot my vital statistics. I wore what I wore. I remember how, when I got engaged to be married in between discovering the first pulsar and the second, people were keen to congratulate me on my engagement but less keen to congratulate me on my discovery. Then people assumed that I would leave academia to be a married woman."

Which she had no intention of doing. But motherhood was a different matter.

"I assumed when Gavin was born that I would stop work and be transformed into an ideal mother. After about six weeks I real-ized I'd made a mistake! It's so difficult to combine work like mine with motherhood. And my husband moved around a lot. I would just have set up child-minding, then we'd upsticks and off and I'd have to start again at square one. The women around me said, 'You've got a husband, a new house and a baby and you say you're *bored?* What's *wrong* with you?'"

How was her relationship with Gavin?

"That was fine. But I did fear that I was a bad mother. And a bad wife, too. I had to learn not to come home and happily report some success or other."

There are a lot of issues here about the feeling of self-worth. "But there was always a base for me in Meeting for Worship, in the encounter with God. There's a continuity there which has always been important to me. Even now, coming to Princeton, it's very important that there's a Quaker Meeting there. Among Quakers I'm accepted for what I am."

Christian, or not?

Quakers have no creed, ordained priesthood or firm theology, so each person finds their own individual position. Would she call herself a Christian? "I've been on and off about that one. Sometimes Christ plays a relatively small role in my outlook, sometimes I feel comfortable calling myself a Christian. One's spiritual life evolves. Coming to a different Meeting can develop a different part of my personality. I wouldn't say 'Jesus is Lord,' I would say '*God* is Lord'."

Does she explore other faiths? "No. Simply because I haven't run out of things to explore in my own faith yet!" *But she has represented Quakers on Christian ecumenical bodies?* "Yes, and my contacts there have been very revealing. I mean that word 'revealing' exactly. I've found myself thinking, 'So *that's* what that puzzling concept or activity means to that Methodist or Anglican or whatever.' When I listen to them, I hear where they're coming from.

"And they must listen to me. I remember the British Council of Churches* drafting a statement on Northern Ireland, and I realized that the wording of it was entirely Protestant and it would deeply upset all Catholics. I stood up and told them it was slanted. It was a very demanding thing to do, but they heard me and redrafted it.

"Another occasion I remember well. It was immediately after the Falklands war, the Malvinas war. An Argentinian delegation came to the BCC to re-establish relations. At the end of that item

---

* The UK umbrella body for non-Catholic churches until 1990.

the chair thanked the distinguished men visiting from Argentina, but failed to thank the female interpreter. I took the lead in having this corrected, and other women afterwards thanked me for doing it — they had felt unable to speak out. Later I realized why I was able to speak in front of bishops and archbishops and they weren't: in my Quaker life I was used to being heard. That's a huge thing."

One of the hazards of Quakerism, she says, is that you can lack nourishment, and she was nourished by the ideas she met and the worship she experienced at ecumenical gatherings. "I've kept some of their worship material and I use some of the prayers for myself. They alienated me sometimes, but they also fed me."

Voices being heard

I was able to speak, and they heard me. *The theme of voices being heard, whether of women in science, or of reconciliation in an inter-church meeting, or of conflicting attitudes from Northern Ireland, is a recurrent one for Jocelyn. The way voices are heard through the Quaker decision-making processes is precious to her.* "Take the Nominations process," she explains. *What's that?* "It's a small committee that looks for the right person to do a job. It happens in the tiniest Meeting in the back of beyond, or in a great national body like the Yearly Meeting. They regard fitting the person to the job as a matter for spiritual discernment. So if they ask me to do something, even if I'm afraid I can't do it I still take them seriously. I don't always say yes, but I respect their leadings."

What does she mean by "discernment" and "leadings"?

"It's sensing what is God's will for that situation." Yes, but how does that work? "The process is set within worship. And it's not done in a rush. At bottom, it's a sort of gut reaction — 'That *feels right*'."

Couldn't that just be prejudice?

"The group guards against that. Not always, but generally. Sometimes the group isn't sensitive enough. Sometimes they're too cerebral, not intuitive enough. There has to be trust, in God and in the Quaker process."

So she was asked to be "Yearly Meeting Clerk." "It came out

of the blue. But I'd clerked the Committee on Christian Relationships, and the work of that group goes very, very deep. Quakers
have no sacraments or set words for worship or hierarchy, so
they're very different from all the other churches, and working
together can be very demanding. I knew I could handle that sort
of thing. But I'd never handled an enormous meeting like the big
annual one of Friends."

*This huge gathering has to become corporately alert to the will
of God, and the clerk must sense what all these people unitedly
feel that God wants. How?*

"It comes in many parts. First there's the careful drawing up of
the agenda. Then there's making sure that all the issues are properly introduced. Then that every side of the issue is heard. In a big
gathering there are the more mechanical things, like monitoring
the proportion of women and men who speak, making sure the
people in the gallery don't feel neglected, listening for the rustles
that mean people are getting restless and tired. That's all part of
the process.

"Then there are moments when God breaks unmistakably
through. I remember one meeting where I was feeling that I'd call
so-and-so over there to speak, but my assistant clerk, Helen, for
no apparent reason said quite urgently, 'The woman in blue on the
back row.' I called the woman in blue, and she spoke about evil
and suffering from her own experience and it called the whole
gathering to an immensely deeper level. Because she was so moving it took over the session. Helen just knew it had to be her."

God spoke to her?

"Yes. 'The woman in blue on the back row'." Jocelyn is moved
now, and has to blow her nose. "That was God working in a way
that was dramatic, and scary."

So God's voice, too, must be heard.

"There was a simpler example in Princeton just the other week.
Not a vital matter, but I could sense the Meeting feeling, 'That's
it. The right thing has been articulated, and we should accept it.'
Sometimes you sense that half of it's right and there's something
wrong with the other half. I don't know what sense it is you're
using, sixth sense or intuition or whatever, but something clicks.

"Yes, there are other times when a Meeting gets totally lost,
and the clerks get lost with it. Sometimes a little group, a like-

minded group, get to reinforce each other — 'This suits us' — rather than listening properly to the leadings. It's a very precious and delicate process, and it's never guaranteed."

Relationship with the stars

For some people, I suggest, their relationship with the stars is almost equivalent to their relationship with God. Is it so for her?

"I gaze at the stars and say 'Isn't it beautiful.' I'm slightly chary about the step that says, 'It's beautiful therefore it is God.' My God is more inward.

"But there's also an issue to do with God the Creator, and whether I mean that phrase literally." *Again, she's speaking very carefully.* "I wouldn't define God as Maker, The One Who Made The World. I'm much happier with God The Creative Spirit. For me God isn't the one who laid out the stars. I'm not convinced God did that." *But, I argue, she did quote Job's God in her book* Broken for Life: "Where were you when I laid the earth's foundations?"[2]

"Yes," answers Jocelyn, smiling, "but I also say that God was pulling rank at that point in the argument!"

So how does God work in her life?

"Through the inward. I see God as standing back from the world. I don't think God interferes in the world ..."

She can speak of God as an entity?

"Yes ... But people are God's agents in this world, through their decisions and actions."

What would she say to those who argue that this leaves us with human beings and no God?

"I'd resort to the Quaker phrase about there being 'that of God in everyone.' There's the essence of God in everybody."

Then is God an essence, rather than an entity?

"I don't know," replies Jocelyn equably, "and to be honest I don't awfully care. God is not a possession. God is a relationship."

Does she have a spiritual practice? "Yes. Unless I'm particularly rushed, I put aside a quiet time each day. I use readings and then have a quiet time of reflection afterwards." *Like Evening Meeting at Quaker boarding school?* "Yes. Very like."

Does she pray? "I tend to spiritualize everything. It's a dialogue with God, it's a relationship with God, it's a being present
with God."

*We're silent for a moment to recognize and ponder the impor-
tance of this.*

Wounded healing

*Clearly Jocelyn has a preoccupation with suffering. Of her own
times of suffering she wrote recently, "The Quaker Meeting for
Worship provides few props and there have been times when the
only thing I could do was attend as a 'passenger'."[3] When she
gave the Swarthmore lecture, of which* Broken for Life *is the
book, she was conscious that many people search for "wholeness" while she recognizes that some things are simply broken,
incurable.*

"Gavin had been diagnosed diabetic, which is incurable. There
were Northern Ireland's troubles, which at the time seemed incurable.

"I also moved among people who were so keen to emphasize
the positive that they were denying the negative. Both scientists
and Quakers. So I wanted to ask, what is the role of the situation
which we cannot resolve? There isn't always cure. There isn't
always wholeness. So it may be that we have to think about 'the
wounded healer'."

*The early part of the book takes all the religious theories about
suffering, starting with "We suffer because we have been bad,"
going through "God has His reasons, maybe he wants to test us"
to Einstein's famous refusal to accept randomness: "God does
not play at dice." It then points up the limitations of each expla-
nation. Suffering does not always lead to healing and rebuilding,
she says.* "We may have to take seriously the idea that some
(much?) of it is not part of a Grand Design and that it will not
come to a purposeful ending unless we work at it to ensure that it
does." *The book concludes:*

"*There is a cyclical nature to many things with breaking
down being a vital part of the cycle; without the breaking
the cycle is halted ... There are things that only the*

*wounded can do, because they are wounded, and those
things are of the most important and costing kinds of
service."*

The very fact of facing these questions has made her into someone people turn to with their pain. "I tend to, so to speak, collect
hurt people. People tell me that they're in pain, that they've got
leukaemia. I can never be properly prepared for it when it happens. But they need to talk, and I listen. I can see that it helps
them."

*The lecture and the book were prophetic for Jocelyn because
within six months of its publication her marriage had broken
down.* "Some of the things I had alluded to began to make a more
particular kind of sense. It was quite striking."

What about the purpose of suffering? In Broken For Life *she
was uncompromising in her demolition of the standard answers to
it. Do we have to face the purposelessness of pain?*

"Yes, in some circumstances we do. But I also take the scientific approach. You go back to the beginning and examine your
assumptions. Religious people tend to start with two assumptions: one, that God is loving, and two, that God is in charge of
the world. When faced with a conundrum like the problem of suffering, what the scientist would say is, maybe one of those
assumptions is mistaken. I feel it's the second assumption, that
God is in charge of the world. Human beings will never grow up
unless we have a God who stands back."

Is she happy with the concept of randomness?

"I see that chance is part of the operation of the natural world.
But equally I feel that God has chosen not to intervene to prevent
the damaging random event."

Here she makes a very specific point. "I think that it's because
I'm a Quaker, and because I'm female, that I'm allowed to think
these thoughts. I recently took part in some Science and Religion
workshops in the States. We were a group of astronomers from
different Christian denominations, together with a Jew and a
Muslim and an agnostic. I was the only woman. I noticed that
they were all working quite hard to make their science fit what
they felt they had to believe as a member of ... whatever they
were. Because Quakers think for themselves, even tend to be

anti-authoritarian, I didn't feel any of that constraint, any fear that I might step out of line. And because I'm a woman and not a man — and women are known to get satisfaction from a wider variety of activities than men — I was less focused simply on my astronomy. So I was able to ask these wider questions."

What is your authority?

Jocelyn quotes John Habgood, former Archbishop of York: "There are three sources of religious authority: there are the holy writings, there's tradition or the history of the faith, and there's continuing revelation." "I think Quakers have an unusual emphasis on the third one. We go with the continuing revelation of God in our experience. That is our authority. But," she continues, "you have to remember that Quakerism is very diverse, particularly if you look world-wide. I am not typical. None of us is typical."

In religion as in science, she seems unconcerned about any Grand Theory. She doesn't ponder endlessly about eschatological questions. I tell her I've noticed her concern about voices being heard. "Not in the sense of Joan of Arc hearing voices. But in the sense of *people* being heard, yes. I want to hear each person, to deny no one's voice."

Would she now say she has a sense of God being with *her?*

"No. Some Friends are very certain of being 'guided,' and I don't feel that. When I was a child people used to stand up in Meeting and were 'guided' to speak for twenty-five minutes and I wasn't quite sure their 'guidance' was true." She laughs, then returns to seriousness. "But I am conscious of some situations being holy situations. Sometimes you know it at the time, sometimes you only realize it later. I try to be alert to the holiness of any situation. I look for the spiritual in everything."

Raficq Abdulla

You can't will it, this intimate, inner experience, this perception that's filled with wonder. Christians call it Grace, Muslims call it Barakah, *God's blessing. It happens if you're open to it.*

Suddenly we're aware of the utter contingency of our lives. The music stops and there's silence. Deus Absconditus. But at the end of the day it's the truth. You don't know, I don't know. We have to live with that not-knowing.

Things that unfold to delight

*Raficq Abdulla was born in 1940 in Durban, South Africa.
His father, a landowner and businessman, was an Indian
whose ancestors came from Hyderabad in South India, and
his mother, a medical doctor, was of Malay parentage. Educated at English prep and public schools and Oxford University, he practised as a corporate lawyer and is now Secretary
to Kingston University, London. He describes himself as a
secular Muslim, a devotee of all the arts and especially
poetry, a lover of pleasure, and a traveller in this life. He has
received an MBE for his community work, especially making
links between Muslims, Jews and Christians.*

Raficq Abdulla's conversation and writings are peppered with words
like chaotic, contradictory, evasive, ambiguous, freewheeling, post-
modern, irreverent. Yet he is a public Muslim: there's the MBE, he
sits on the UK Sharia Law Council, he's legal adviser to the Muslim
College, and he recently broadcast a series of talks on the BBC
World Service on the Prophet Muhammed and the Four Caliphs.

A freewheeling postmodernist with a taste for pleasure, ambiguity and paradox is not the image that the British press gives us
of the average Muslim. "Our image!" sighs Raficq. "Terrible.
Fundamentalist, book-burning. Yes, there's racism and old colonialism behind the construction of the image. But don't we sometimes ask for it? We can bewail it, but shouldn't we also ask why
that image sticks?" *His favourite book on the Prophet is Maxime
Rodinson's biography*[1] *which is prefaced by T.S. Eliot's transla-
tion of St-John Perse's* Anabasis:

> "Not that a man be not sad, but [that] he beholds at the end
> of the fasting sky great things and pure that unfold to
> delight."

Son of his mother, father of his son

Delight comes in Raficq's picture of his mother. A woman of intelligence and dynamism with Sufi healing capacity handed down to her from a saintly ancestor, she specialized in gynaecology and venereal diseases at a public South African hospital until she discovered that her salary was a fraction of that of white doctors. She was outraged at this unequal treatment — "I qualified at Edinburgh University!" she told her employers, "not at some second-rate South African Medical School!" She had a clear sense of hierarchy when it came to higher education establishments. She set up in private practice and was able to give free medical treatment for the poor by charging the wealthy who were prepared to accept her rates out of respect for her medical knowledge. "In this way she behaved more like a socialist than some of her more ideologically correct left-wing friends," says Raficq. "She loved dancing, lovely clothes, perfume. We read widely: not only the Qur'an (in English) but also Mann, Mauriac, Proust and Rabelais."

Raficq sees himself as one in the middle of a threesome: his mother, then himself, and the third is his son Adam. "I tell my son that there is a flow of affinity, a sort of charismatic bond, between the three of us which runs from death into life (my mother having died over twenty years ago) which is really beyond our choosing. Of course, there is love towards my wife, Adam's mother, towards my father, and also towards my dogs. They were my boyhood companions — my family were unusual as Muslims in their love of dogs and horses. My father owned race horses until non-whites in apartheid South Africa were forbidden to own them. Yes, he was a great gambler too! But he still regarded himself as a Muslim and didn't feel guilty about it. I expect it would be a little different in today's climate."

Raficq didn't marry until some years after his mother died, so his only son was born to him when he was forty-four. His wife Marianne and he have shared the child care in every way. Adam is now fourteen, and father and son read and talk together, and love each other and hate each other as people who are really close always do. A poem of Raficq's called "Adam's Evening Chat with Father" speaks from his son's point of view, and ends:

"I need to escape, / see / myself / moving about / laughing, frowning, keeping time / to music outside / me / and / from going mad / next to my Father / who understands nothing."

First God Question: certainty

What are the "God questions" in Raficq's life? To illustrate the first answer — or rather the first question — he tells me about something that happened to him at school. His mother insisted on him being sent to England for his education from the age of ten onwards because education for non-whites in South Africa was so appalling. It was at Epsom College at the age of sixteen that he experienced a revelation so sharp, so upsetting of his assumptions, that he could do no academic work for four days and retreated to the library to read Gone With The Wind.

"An ironic choice of novel! Because the revelation was this: one of my main subjects was history, and it suddenly dawned on me that there wasn't a single History. There wasn't a single answer to anything. Every event was someone's story. I was taught the English version of Waterloo, but there was also a French version, the officer's version, the foot-soldier's version. So *there could be no certainty.*

"I didn't absorb the implications of that revelation for years. I went to Oxford to study Politics, Philosophy and Economics, then I quit because I couldn't stand Economics and decided to study Law. Why Law? Because it was divorced from anything that interested me. It was useful, a good training in cogent, analytical thinking. It was a means to an end, in that it made it easier to find jobs. But my friends were reading history, philosophy, literature, and it was about these things that I talked all the time.

"It was traumatic, then, to realize there was no certainty. An emotional and intellectual crisis. But now, at the age of fifty-eight, I've come full circle.* I thank God there's no certainty. I love ambiguity, I love ambivalence. What impertinence, what arrogance for us human beings to think we have certainty! And there's no fun in it, anyway.

"Take the question of bias. People say writers shouldn't be

---

* Two years elapsed between the interview and publication. See also Adam's age, above.

biased. But of course they're biased! Everyone's biased. What's necessary is to recognize it and take it into account. Take the case of Salman Rushdie. The sort of things he wrote in *The Satanic Verses* were nothing new. The great medieval scholar Tabari, a commentator on the Qur'an, dealt with the 'satanic verses.'* But we don't hear much about it because those intellectual challenges within Islam ended almost completely in the thirteenth century, when the theologians won the battle with the philosophers."

But isn't Islam intended as a universal religion, and therefore certain?

"Sure, it claims to be universal. Doesn't every religion? But what is universality? Look at the language it comes in. Islam is mediated through Arabic because the Qur'an is in Arabic. I don't speak Arabic. Most Muslims, the vast numbers on the Indian subcontinent for instance, don't speak Arabic. So by definition we're second-class Muslims because we haven't got the language.

"Religions are rooted in their geography. Christianity too claims to be universal, but it was only saved from ghettoization by Saint Paul, who Hellenized it. Islam was also Hellenized. The Muslim scholars brought Greek learning to the West through Byzantium and through Spain ..."

Here he digresses about his love of Spain. "I speak Spanish, I love the Alhambra in Granada which is one of the glories of Islam ... Yet I am not entirely a part of the culture that the Alhambra represents. I am a visitor, an honoured visitor but a visitor nevertheless. You see, I am a Muslim but I am more than a Muslim, my culture and therefore my identity is hybrid. It's made up of several elements — Islamic, European (which in itself is more fragmented than we are led to believe), Indian, Malay. Then there's one's upbringing. Mine had great chunks of the Greek and Norse myths, which my Mother read to me as a child." *He laughs at the complexity.* "Yes, I'm the epitome of the cosmopolitan, the kind that Hitler would have liked to kill. As Salman Rushdie says (a tortured and not particularly pleasant character but a wonderful writer), we're hybrid creatures. And we're told by scientists that

* Abu Ja'far Muhammed Ibn Jarir Al-Tabari (*c.*838–923 CE), author of *Jami al-Bayan* or *Tafsir,* a commentary on the Qur'an.

hybrids enjoy a vigour not necessarily found in pedigrees. The entire notion of purity is problematic and probably a myth.

"But to get back to the thirteenth century. All this philosophy, this Hellenism: the theologians stamped on it, and the doors were closed. They wanted certainty. Theology and Law crave for certainty. Philosophy and poetry thrive on uncertainty. Give me philosophy and poetry any time!"

Next God Question: poetry

Poetry is central to Raficq's life. "It's a necessity for me. I write poetry and I read it all the time."

At the moment he's working on the Islamic mystic Farid al-Din Attar, and he has recently published translations of the poetry of the thirteenth century Sufi mystic Jalal ad-Din Rumi.[2]

"Rumi was intoxicated with God. He was a respected religious scholar, a man with a secure following. But then he fell madly in love with another man — very hard for his wife, I can tell you — and that was a mystical experience that made him throw off his learning and become an ecstatic. Listen:

'I was once like you, enlightened and "rational" —
I, too, scoffed at lovers.
Now I am drunk, crazed, thin with misery.
No one is safe! Watch out'."

In response to his translations of Rumi, Raficq himself has written poems that are extensions of Rumi. Here's an extract from one:

"Love is a wounded word ...
But the word I stroke myself against like a cat,
the word I take unto myself in silence,
praying it may bear fruit,
is as sweet as pomegranates, and as cold as stars,
a word which needs no consolation,
a word understood by the fewest few ...
It is called ..."

"So," he finishes, "it's up to you to find your own word. I know what my word is. What's yours?"

These poems, are they his or Rumi's? "I don't know. I don't know where he ends and I begin. There's a real erotic charge in Rumi's poems. He was on the edge of madness. He saw the divine in this man, despite his marriage and family. The man disappeared, he may have been murdered by one of Rumi's sons. Oh yes, it's the stuff of the wildest fiction. But it's true, and the poetry came from that ecstasy and madness."

Rumi's work is full of simplicity, joy, yearning, bewilderment, bliss. "All those things reside both in art and in spirituality. Rumi didn't have a set of beliefs, he returned faith to its proper enchantment through the metaphorical power of his art." *Its* proper *enchantment?* "Yes. Art teaches us the deep, sublime meanings of symbols. It refines our inwardness, the inwardness that's necessary to faith. Faith isn't about absolute beliefs. It revels in paradox, irony, even in doubt. Faith needs to be meek ... that's a Christian term ... or submissive, and that's what the word 'Islam' means: submission.

"We've got to allow ourselves the space both for faith and for art. The world we live in is obsessively rational. It's intent on measuring and analysing. Yet at the same time it's dangerously irrational and self-deluding. The inner life is trivialized, sentimentalized, waxed and polished into an American sitcom. If, as Montaigne counsels us, we make a room at the back of ourselves that's just for us, then we can discover and create meaning for ourselves, and not just have them fabricated for us from outside."

Third God Question: the uncanny

This saint in his mother's background: who was he? "Don't think of 'saint' in the Christian sense. There are two men of great spiritual power in my mother's family who could be called saintly. One was an ancestral saint, a charismatic figure who had healing powers, and people visit his grave to this day. The other was my mother's grandfather, who used books of talismanic Sufi mantras that had thaumaturgic powers, and when he died he told his son to sink his books into the sea off Cape Town."

And Raficq's mother followed in his footsteps? "Not at first.

Oh no. When she was studying in Edinburgh, all illness had to follow the physical model. But later in her life she looked into the spiritual aspects of illness. She had the healing gift, and if you've got it, you've got it. It came out in her sense of the uncanny. She was in many ways a pagan: as I mentioned, she used to read me the Greek and Norse myths. Her sense of spirituality was very, very wide. She had a great sense of place: she loved Chartres because, like the Kaaba in Mecca, the place 'had it.' But the London Mosque in Regent's Park, she said, didn't. And she had a sense of the irreverent. Yes, and of reverence too."

As well as a sense of the psychic and the sacred, perhaps integrally with them, Raficq's mother was an immensely warm person physically. So was his father.

"We were all very touchy-feely. My father and my mother would be all over me, kissing and hugging me. They didn't have any hang-ups about sex. The two of them were always going up to bed together in the afternoon. When my mother was in her sixties she was still an attractive woman. I can remember her telling me how one day she met a younger woman at the opera in London who told her how attractive she was. She thought this admiration from another woman very flattering."

His mother came over to live in England after her husband died when Raficq was sixteen, and after university Raficq lived with her for fourteen years. So when she died it was traumatic for him, and for four years he suffered from psychosomatic stress disorders. His wife, whom he describes as an intuitive, sympathetic and obstinate woman, was an invaluable companion through this trying period of his life.

"I realized it was grief for my mother. She'd told me that her death would be the end, she didn't believe in life after death. But she had a dream a few days before she died of her parents on a bus, and they were urging her to climb aboard." *In the end, he realized he had to live through his grief till he got to the other side. The best help he got was from a Tibetan Buddhist course in bereavement.* "The leader had us hooting with laughter. It was terrifically therapeutic. They know about death, the Buddhists. They live with it, so there's not this Western fear of it. 'I'm going to die,' they say. 'So, I'm going to die'."

He sees the perception of God as something which has to come from one's own experience. "You can't will it, this intimate, inner experience, this perception that's filled with wonder. It happens if you're open to it. Christians call it Grace, Muslims call it *Barakah,* God's blessing. I have a sense of something other than me, greater than me, the God (as Islam says) that brings fear, brings awe, the *mysterium tremendum.*"

Death often brings with it experiences of the uncanny. "A dog of mine died of a broken heart when I left South Africa. He just lay there, wouldn't eat, and died. And my mother's grandfather knew when he was going to die. He said, 'Where's my son?' This son was another dog-lover apparently, and he'd gone off after some dog or other. 'Oh well,' said the old man, 'I can't wait, tell him I love him,' and he turned over and died. He knew that he was going to Heaven. I don't know that, but I'm willing to let go, let myself go into the greater whole."

Fourth God Question: identity

Raficq was recently asked by the Jewish Leo Baeck Institute to give a lecture in the West London Synagogue. "They asked me to talk on 'Assimilation and Acculturation.' My heart sank. So academic, so much hard work! Look, I said, I'll do something impressionistic and personal, and I'll call it 'I belong, therefore I am,' okay? What I wanted to say to them was ... well, I quoted Henry Miller: 'The man who looks for security, even in the mind, is like the man who would chop off his limbs in order to have artificial ones that will give him no pain and trouble.'

"I started from Descartes' *Cogito ergo sum,* 'I think therefore I am.' But, I asked, *what* do I think, and how, and why? We look anxiously at our fellow human beings as we share the telepathy of our common discontent, I said, and we shift self-consciously in our seats and pluck at our *cogito's* like worry beads ... I think we think too much, because we so much need to belong.

"How are we to get to grips with this dispersed and opaque thing we call 'the self'? Kierkegaard said that most men live in relation to their own self as if they were constantly out, never at home. Lacan argued for a de-centred self: 'a privileged symptom, the mental illness of man.' That's bleak, but I still find it persuasive. Our modes of knowing are so complex, so intertwined with our bodies. They betray our desire for stability. Yes, we must belong. But we must always be aware of the politics of the process of belonging. Look at Serbia, Rwanda, Israel, Northern Ireland: they're places of exclusive belonging, fixated and asphyxiating belonging, the sort that destroys rather than creates a way of being. If we belong fanatically, we become over-whelmed with the business of hating."

He sees a constant tension between identity and autonomy. "God so often comes in as a stick to beat you into an identity, a set of rules. God, religion, says No Orgies! But I say, if you're going to have an orgy, have an orgy and enjoy it, so long as you don't hurt anyone." Doesn't God have a right to interfere with the orgy? "It's not my business to enquire. People forget that one of the key sentences in the Qur'an is 'There shall be no compulsion in religion.' Yes, it's submission to the will of God, but you have to be free to choose to submit to the will of God. That's auton-omy."

Final God Question: being a Muslim

Raficq reads the Holy text of Islam, the Qur'an, and the supple-mentary texts of the life and sayings of the Prophet Muhammed, as a "slow reader." "To quote Nietzsche, I read 'slowly, deeply, looking cautiously before and aft, with reservations, with doors left open, with delicate eyes and fingers.'

"As revelation, the Qu'ran was mediated through language, and even though the revelation is said to be beyond history, it's open to discussion once it's within language. The Prophet received the *parousia,* the absolute Presence of Being. But we can see only the shadow of God through the opacity of the Holy Text. Whether we like it or not, sooner or later we enter on a process of reflective critique on what we read. We shouldn't be afraid to use our intel-ligence or our emotional grounding when we look at these texts. *Hermeneutics,* the science of interpretation of texts — now look at that word: the god Hermes was also Mercury, mercurial, quick of intelligence."

In Raficq's telling of his life story and ideas there seems none of the West's preconceptions about Muslim practices. For instance, there's no gender hierarchy. He heartily dislikes the way so many Muslims vilify women as purveyors of sexual immorality.

"Take the rule for a man not to be alone in a room with a woman. If I could speak to the Prophet I'd say to him, 'Why shouldn't I? You were alone in a room with a woman, why shouldn't I be?' It's demeaning for both the man and the woman to have a rule like that. It assumes a sexual relationship when in fact there may be an exchange of intellectual or spiritual worth."

Wasn't his father regarded as a man who couldn't control his wife? "No, indeed he was not. In any case he couldn't give a damn what they thought of him. Of course he was rich so he didn't need to give a damn, he had the right to be arrogant, if by arrogance one means a robust disregard of calumny and specious criticism. Then he was arrogant, and so was my mother. And they weren't alone among South African Muslims in living in this way, Muslim but secular." *But if they'd lived in the Indian sub-continent, wouldn't it have been different?* "Yes, it would, if they'd been poor. But if they'd been rich and influential it would have been similar. Take Jinnah.* Jinnah was not unusual in his secular ways. I have Pakistani friends who drink, who have an irreverent sense of humour and enjoy Western culture as well as being faithful in their own way to Islam. You could say that's part of the colonial experience. Nehru was in the same mould. He was steeped in Hindu culture, but he was educated in England and spoke perfect English. What they're saying is this: we're Indian, Pakistani or whatever, we've been colonialized, but now we're going to make our own choices as far as we can. Yes, we're Muslim, we belong to our religion, but our choices will be wider than that and it's important that our choices remain just that, free choices. My parents made choices, they married each other for a start! My father liked his glass of whisky and made no secret of it, he gambled on the Tote, and my mother gambled also. But she was against drinking alcohol. She was a teetotaller on religious grounds."

When Raficq speaks or broadcasts on behalf of Islam, isn't he very cautious in what he says? "Of course I am. Listen, there are two things here. First I speak to my friend Dr Zaki Badawi, who's

---

* Mohammed al Jinnah (1876–1948), founder and first Governor-General of Pakistan.

a great Islamic scholar, to authenticate what I'm going to say.
Then there's an element of self-censorship, because I'm in a public not a private role.

"But the people who mainly censor me are my BBC producers,
and that's because of *their* public role. One producer was a Northern Irish Protestant who was much more enamoured of some of
the characters in my series on the Prophet than I was. He adored
A'isha, the Prophet's last wife. I thought she was a pain in the
butt, quite frankly. 'You can't say that!' he told me, 'she was way
before her time, a proto-feminist ...'."

Has the Rushdie fatwa *put a lot of pressure on people?* "Yes.
Everyone takes up a position about it. I met a Sufi sheikh recently
(he was a Scottish convert to Islam) who said that there shouldn't
have been a *fatwa*, Rushdie should have been killed outright for
what he had written. Now that was incitement to murder, and I
said so. But lots of people who heard him were frightened to challenge him, because he was their charismatic leader. He sat on a
chair and they sat on the floor, you know? Like colonialism, I
thought.

"A lot of Western liberals walked on eggshells where the *fatwa*
was concerned. They were afraid to condemn it for fear of seem-
ing racist or anti-Muslim. I said to them, and I still say, 'If a thing
is wrong then it's wrong, and you should say so.' Incitement to
murder is wrong, in law and in ethics, and you and I and everyone should condemn it openly."

Where does Raficq stand in relation to religious practice?
"There's the religious life of dogmatism, ritual, liturgy, of right
ways of behaving and limits to what is permitted. That may sound
negative but it's not: it can be enriching. However, too often it's
dogmatic and spurious. This insistent claim to *know* God and *his*
ways ... it's absurd. We don't even know ourselves. It's the religion of closure. I don't want a religion of identity, of what makes
'me' different from 'them.' I belong to another tradition, the tradition of being on an existential path, a religious path that leads
to liberation: the expansion of one's sense of being, the cultivation of a sense of the sacred. There's a strong element of agnostic
doubt in my make-up. I am at home in *not* knowing the unknown,
if you see what I mean. I recently wrote a poem called *'Credo ut
Intelligam'*:

I cannot believe in the life of the trumpeted Word
Nor eat the flesh or drink the blood with knowing faith ...
... there's no way of knowing
If God mediates from the start, whether the glowing
Aurora light is His finger's art that paints the dark;
Whether scripted Adam or Eve, or Noah's infested ark,
Are but infidel words and sounds too pricked with fear
For me to know the Word or hear it sung with faithful ear.

"We don't know the word. And I will be dogmatic, we can *never* know the Word, and if we hear it sung with faithful ear we cannot communicate that epiphany to anyone else. So much of institutionalized religion is humbug.

"The sort of liberation I'm talking about doesn't even have to come through religion. It comes to me through art. Again, Nietzsche said somewhere, 'Art is the only thing that saves us from bestiality.' I draw from that something which Alan White said in his commentary: that we all need a sustaining myth that enables us to behave other than from our own ego.[3]

"For me, art is more potent than religion. Music, for instance, Sufi Qawwali songs, *ghazals* which are love songs, the music of Schumann, Schubert. There are so many composers and genres to choose from, I've only scratched the surface. Music speaks to me directly, through an inchoate, unformed expression. I catch my breath in wonder. Painting, literature, all art: those are 'God places' for me.

"There's an Islamic spirituality of illumination, when you go 'Wow!' You can have it either momentarily, or in a more sustained way. But there's an element of paganism in me as well. I'm not at home with the exclusive monotheistic God. Invariably that God is masculine. Though in Islam, as in Christianity, there's a strong feminine aspect to the Godhead, and in Islam that's expressed in Sufism. Sufi poetry has a deeply erotic element to it. Eros is the powerhouse of the spiritual, it's a place where you lose yourself. And it is energy, it's that strange force which animates all life and keeps it teetering on the edge. It's got loss and it's also got possession: being possessed, and possessing. The losing of limits, structure, the theology of the self, the self as enclosed in the skin."

What about prayer? "Prayer is very important. It's not only the five times a day Muslim prayer for me, and it needn't be a mumbling stumbling petering out of petitions either. Prayer isn't about ritual, but about intent. Muslims are told that without intent there is no worthy prayer, no matter now meticulous the ritual. Judaism too has the notion of prayer as *kavvana,* the intention, the inwardness. Inwardness — though for me it's often *inwaywardness.* The Biblical Psalms talk about prayer as an 'outpouring of the soul,' a 'cry from the depths.' It's an artistic activity with God as the audience. Of course it can also be communal and structured, but the deepest prayer is getting in touch with the higher Self."

With the soul?

"Well ... The word 'soul' maybe too much implies a fixed self. The higher Self is a misty thing, seen through layers of consciousness; an onion if you like, with layers that peel off and you don't know which layer is the final skin before you reach the real onion. The soul may be as immaterial as a quark or a neutrino. I'm embarking on a book exploring the connections between sex and the soul, looking at both religious and secular writers and poets from many traditions. That's a fascinating area."

'A world made up of signs of the hidden God'

Again and again Raficq uses the word "liberation." "What's important in liberation is learning to grow in the moment. Not to look forward, to anticipate a reward in heaven. I don't like the notion of Heaven and Hell: there's something very Disneyland about it, very judgmental, very patriarchal. My aim is to attain a level of awareness, through art, through nature — this morning I got up, the air was so fresh, I breathed it in — not to be locked into the past, into guilt, not to fear the future, fear death or disaster, but to live in the moment. I drive through Richmond Park, I stop to let two deer cross the road, they pause and look around, they're so beautiful, one of them pretends to be nibbling grass because she's not sure ... then off they trot ... A moment of blessing."

And the word God? *Raficq laughs.* "The word pisses me off, quite frankly. The way it's marketed, traded by the religions, it's repugnant. There's another way of looking at God, the one that Eckhart talks of, not trying to pin down the Godhead in words and concepts.* It looks at God negatively: the God of unknowing. As the Hindus say, *'Neti, neti,* God is not this ... not this ...' God is deferred all the time. Saying this is, of course, a paradox or oxymoron. Here I am trying to define or describe the Godhead negatively ... not this, not this!"

But isn't it frightening, this not knowing? "Indeed it is. Suddenly we're aware of the utter contingency of our lives. The music stops and there's silence. *Deus Absconditus.* But at the end of the day it's the truth. You don't know, I don't know. We have to live with that not-knowing."

Religion is in the living, not in the knowing? "Exactly. It's not worrying whether I'm right or wrong. It's not regretting. It's walking on."

But Islam is known for its central tenet: "There is no God but the one God, and Muhammed is his Prophet." Isn't that knowledge? "Look. I was talking the other day with my friend Dr Badawi, and I quoted that to him. 'That's the heart of Islam, surely, isn't it?' 'No no no,' he said to me. 'It's knowing that we all belong to each other. Then, more fundamentally, we all belong to God.'

"Compassion is at the centre: for ourselves, family, friends, but eventually for all living things. Compassion and liberation are indispensable to each other, yin and yang. If we don't have that compassion we won't have liberation: if we don't have liberation we won't have compassion.

"This world is, as Muslims say, *dunya*: a world made up of the signs of God. One of Allah's names is *al-Ghayb*: the unseen, the hidden. If we belong to anything in this *dunya* we belong to the ever-greater, unattainable Whole. In it we may find our being, which is its Being. All else is becoming. Like the blind Oedipus on the road to Colonnus, I'm at home on each part of the way, and I start my journey at each moment I travel."

---

* Meister Eckhart *(c.*1260–?1327), German mystical writer.

David Banks

"Then my father says, 'And what side are you on?' and I say, 'I'm on the inside, you're on the inside, everybody's on the inside — except the Bad Uns'!" Yet he wasn't made to feel a "miserable sinner"? A Bad Un? "Not at all."

"There was a void in me which Jesus left. But the void is all right. It's not blackness or emptiness, it's more like the void before things were, and it seems to me that in that place everything is all right."

Living where the heart is

David Banks is an actor, director, writer and specialist in computer software. He was born in 1951, the only son of fundamentalist Christian parents, and grew up in Hull. Major acting parts have been as the Cyberleader in the long-running TV series Doctor Who *and in the soaps* Brookside *and* Canary Wharf. *His plays include* Severance, *and prose writings include a book on Cybermen and the novel* Iceberg *(Virgin 1993). He decided in his late teens that the Christian faith was not for him and has explored his own path through the Tarot, through Lao Tsu's* Tao *and the* I Ching. *He might now be described as meditative non-religious and practises T'ai Chi.*

Humanity, its origins and perversities

David and I sit by the wall-length windows of his new Islington flat. It's so new that the building still resembles the Greetings Card factory it so recently was, and we're looking through scaffolding at Regent's Canal below us. David's partner, the actor Maureen Purkis, comes in with croissants and news about furniture deliveries while we discuss the best place to start. With *Doctor Who,* with alternative realities and artificial intelligence? Or with his parents' faith?

"Where I'd actually like to start," says David, "is with two words which were fundamental to my thinking in my novel and are crucial to my own (if you like, spiritual) journey. The two words are *heart* and *home.*

"*Iceberg* took themes from *The Wizard of Oz* as well as *Doctor Who,* and Oz's Dorothy was taken away from her home and met up with the Tin Man who had no heart. The people of Mondas in *Doctor Who* denied themselves feelings, heart, because the changes in their environment, their home, demanded it. Acting the part of Cyberleader and writing the novel *Iceberg* threw up questions of what 'God' does, and what it is humanity's 'purpose' to do."

Questions, I ask him, like those the Old Testament throws up, such as God's purpose for Adam and Eve that they should have no knowledge of good and evil?

"Yes. There's an evolving concept of who we are, who God is and what are our origins. In those early myths it was not seen as 'given' to have that knowledge, so Eve was perverse to ask for it. In that story humanity loses the chance of living a simple and good life. Each new generation brings its own challenge of this sort. It's repeated again and again, with the traditional view saying that we shouldn't be doing this or that because it infringes what is inviolable. At the moment it's genetic modification: have we the right to change this fundamental aspect of created life?

"I have a memory of when I was three or four years old. It was round Bonfire Night and the caretaker said, 'I'll make a Guy Fawkes out of you!' I thought he had the power to turn me into something not human, and it was terrifying."

So by the time he began to play the Cyberleader he'd already pondered what it meant to be human or a perversion of human? To have, or not to have, a heart?

"Yes. I read a lot of science fiction, which is a rich crucible for looking at the way we live as human beings. I was also very much into the early personal computers, Sinclair and so on, and I was influenced by an amazing fantasy of a book by Douglas Hofstadter, *Gödel Escher Bach*."[1] *David goes to get the book. He has only a few books here, the rest are in store during the move, but Hofstadter's is one of the few.*

"His argument was that, given enough complexity, you could reproduce human intelligence. By contrast, Cybermen believed their intelligence could be enhanced and made more rational by replacing organic tissue and human sensibilities. Cybermen were human once, but because their environment changed they too had to change, and they changed themselves so that they had mechanical organs and no emotion."

There was no mechanistic process which could replace human feelings?

"Emotion was seen as unstable. There's a classic conversation in the first *Doctor Who* story I did as Cyberleader, when the Doctor tries to reawaken the Cyberleader's folk memory and says, 'But how can you get any *enjoyment* out of life?' And the Cyberleader replies, 'These things are *irrelevant.*' It's the militaristic view: you've got to damp down feeling, you must be totally rational, surviving, conquering. But if you have no enjoyment of life, what is the purpose of living?

"We are driven, as Richard Dawkins says, by our genes.* People say that makes us into robots, but it doesn't. Look at this view!" *David looks through the scaffolding down to the canal below.* "The evolution of those Canada geese was driven by pure DNA. Yet they're beautiful, and they seem to enjoy life. The two things, the persistence of DNA and our enjoyment of life, work on different planes. Both are aspects of reality, but it's impossible for us to look at both at the same time.

"Hofstadter shows, quite beautifully, how the mathematician Gödel proves that given a powerful enough system for manipulating numbers, there'll always be a contradiction within it, always something that's inconsistent. It goes along with Heisenberg's Uncertainty Principle.† We can never know. We can never be sure.

"My question is, what is home? And if home is the place of the heart, how can we find it and live there? Home is where the heart is, not the other way round."

Childhood Eden

This seems a good point to look at the formative years of David's life. His parents were ardent Christians. "Both of them lost their parents when they were young, and they married late. Those words *heart* and *home*: my father lost his home at sixteen when his parents died in the 1918–19 flu epidemic, and he did menial jobs, anything from a coffee house to a tanning factory. Then he

* Author of *The Selfish Gene* and other books arguing that natural selection takes place at the level of genes and arguing also against a spiritual origin of life.

† Werner Karl Heisenberg (1901–76) was awarded the Nobel Prize for physics in 1932 for his development of quantum physics.

worked for an estate agent, collecting the rent, and because he'd been adrift he found a home in religion, in the Trafalgar Street Free Evangelical Church in Hull, which he helped to start up.

"My mother's parents died even earlier, her mother when she was under a year old, her father when she was four, and she was looked after by her older brothers and sisters."

He shows me the autobiography which he helped his mother, Mina, to write. It begins, "I was born prematurely ... My weight was two pounds exactly ... I was baptized in a soup bowl."[2]

"She was fort-three when I was born, he was forty-eight. I'm going to be forty-eight tomorrow and it seems significant that when he was the age I am now, I wasn't even born. I'm reading my father's diaries at the moment, and there's a strong sense that life has the possibility of taking some extraordinary turning however old you are.

"They rejected any notion that another sect or faith could have true value. Those people could be good, even worthy, but they were always on the wrong track and would be damned. My Auntie Marjory — not a real aunt, a close friend who was a missionary — even supported the 'Evangelization of the Jews'."

So his parents' God was always in charge, and whatever horrors might happen, He knew what He was doing?

"Auntie Marjory thought that earthquakes, famine or whatever in India where she worked, were God's action in the world. It was a sort of acceptance that 'this is what happens.' There was no anxiety, no demand for what they might deserve. Both my parents were paid very poorly for the good work they did, but they accepted it. They were borne up by the arms of the Lord. You threw yourself on the Lord's mercy.

"That was the atmosphere I grew up in. In church people witnessed to it Sunday by Sunday. I absorbed the language, it became my own. So these questions, the God questions, like 'Where do we begin and cease?' were important for me from the start."

Did his parents reject science?

"My father loved technical things, mending watches, radios and so on. My mother had attended lectures by Fleming and saw the immense difference that antibiotics made.* Evolution? Well,

---

* Alexander Fleming (1881–1955) who in 1928 discovered penicillin.

that might be one way of explaining the truth of God's word. But if you wanted truth you went to the Bible first and last.

"Christians don't know where we come from, before birth, but they do know where we go after we die. As a child I knew where heaven was. We used to go to Christian conventions at Butlins in Filey, on the Yorkshire coast, and I went on the rides, and for me that was heaven. It was mixed up with that bit in Revelation about 'Worthy is the Lamb that was slain.' Those words had such a resonance for me, the notion of blood, of animals being killed vicariously for our salvation. Because the Lamb was slain I gained the freedom to go on the heavenly rides.

"I actually asked God into my life when I was four. I'm not sure whether this is a real memory or whether I just remember my mother's story about it. I always said my prayers at night and they overheard me saying, 'I want God to come into my life so I can be saved,' and then I turned to them and said, 'Now we can all be together.' I've got a recording of me singing this song:

> One door and only one, and yet its sides are two,
> Inside and outside, on which side are you? ...
> One door and only one, and yet its sides are two,
> I'm on the inside, which side are you?

"I got it a bit wrong, I sang 'And yet its sides *is* two.' Then my father says, 'And what side are *you* on?' and I say, '*I'm* on the inside, *you're* on the inside, *everybody's* on the inside — except the Bad Uns'!"

Yet he wasn't made to feel a "miserable sinner"? A Bad Un?

"In a way my childhood was like an Eden. Settled, happy, secure. I was in the right place. It was home."

The journey out of Eden

During an interval for some more furniture delivery, I've read David's notes upside down from where I'm sitting and seen the words Child in the temple: asking adult-like questions. *Is that David at his next significant point?*

"I wouldn't associate myself with *the* child in the temple," says David, laughing, "because Jesus taught and had great wisdom, whereas I was just poking around. I'd started being interested in science fiction, Jules Verne, John Wyndham and so on. My uncle ran a small private school with a little library; he was a polymath and very interested in science and the arts, and he encouraged me to read a lot. So when I got to secondary school I was asking questions of my Religious Knowledge teacher like, 'Can God go against the laws of logic?'

"And I was suddenly captivated by the beauty of the night sky. In Hull you get these very clear northern skies, radiant, mysterious. I got a sense of something beyond us, something we could reach for. At the time there was every possibility we *could* reach for it, and even get it. Sputnik had just gone up, there were astronauts and cosmonauts in space, there was 'something out there.' Here was something deeply mysterious and yet deeply familiar, the night sky."

And could God go against the laws of logic?

"The RK teacher said no, of course not. Logic is logic. But my reasoning was that if God was truly omnipotent then he could do anything — even defy the laws of logic — something I was reminded of many years later when I started to learn about the strangenesses of quantum physics where a sub-atomic particle can seem to be defying the laws of logic. And then, though God was omnipotent but Jesus clearly was not, yet Jesus was God: given such paradoxes, surely it would be possible for an omniscient God to be in a place and *not* be in that place at the same time. My RK teacher, though he was keen to debunk Christian beliefs, thought this absurd. Much later I came across what Teilhard de Chardin said: 'God is a circle whose centre is everywhere and whose circumference is nowhere.'[3] Then, in my early teens, there were real stirrings of something beyond the given. Not just sensual; certainly that, but something spiritual too, that wasn't fully answered by Christianity. In a metaphorical sense, I suppose, the stars were calling me.

"Every Easter from about the age of twelve, I went to a Christian 'house party' — a kind of retreat — at Moreton Hall in Shropshire, and would spend the whole summer at a Christian camp in Anglesey, presided over by David Tryon, a man who was a great force in the Christian Youth movement at the time. The teen stage lends itself to an emotional link with the spiritual, doesn't it? Everything else seems contaminated in comparison. Jesus was a central figure in my life. We were encouraged to pray, to talk to Jesus, it was an almost continuous conversation."

Did he get replies to his prayers?

David thinks hard. "I got *guidance*. An acceptance. A glow in the centre of my life." Did he ask, for instance, what O level exams he should take? "No, it wasn't as specific as that. For me it doesn't work like that — like talking to an agony aunt, with clear sensible answers from above. It was more like my use of the *I Ching* later, not fortune telling or precise answers, but more an opening up to the possibility of guidance.

"At that time I didn't know what anxiety was. My mother wasn't anxious, I suppose because of the strength of her faith. 'Be not anxious for the morrow' seemed to me like good advice." If he'd failed the eleven-plus, would his parents have accepted it? "Yes. They were like that. There was no academic pressure."

So where did the next phase of questioning come? Was it when sex came in?

David glances at his notes, smiling. "My next line says 'Sexual Awakening.' But it started with something quite straightforwardly religious at these house parties in Shropshire. I was about sixteen. A few of us discussed in depth what the relationship of body and soul and spirit might be, and we came to a tentative conclusion it was a kind of human Trinity. We saw it in terms of coloured glass, one layer over another and modifying its colour — rather like the Hindu idea of auras, actually — and in a sense it showed us human beings becoming a manifestation of God.

"It seemed very clear to us, and we proudly explained our ideas to our elders. But our philosophizing was shot down as heresy. It was made clear that we should never try to formulate our own dogma, but should be guided in all things by the teachings of the church.

"That was fair enough. But for the first time I became aware of dogma, that there were things you were supposed to believe. There were Thought Police, and certain things that seemed rea-sonable to me were, in their view, sins. This place had been my home. But the questioning had originated from my heart, and I knew it did not quite belong here."

The persistence of the virus

Does he now, I wonder, see himself as a religious person?

"No, I don't. One way of looking at the position I'm in is that I caught a virus at a very early age, the virus of spirituality. My whole journey has been spent in searching for a cure, if you like. T.S. Eliot says ..." He gets up again to find the book. It's *Four Quartets,* and is another of the very few books he's kept beside him. "Our only health is the disease," he quotes from "East Coker": "To be restored, the sickness must grow worse." My sickness is spirituality, and often I wish I could lose it."

I argue with David here. Surely he must have accepted the virus into himself in some way? I've known people equally "injected at an early age," as he puts it, and the virus simply didn't take.

Up to a point he agrees. "Maureen is like that. She was brought up Protestant Irish and was even sent to a Catholic school, but apart from some residual guilt these questions don't bother her. Maybe I've been too intellectual about it, there's too much 'head' in there, and I've needed to get to a deeper level than the head. Reading the writings of Alan Watts led me to the Tao.[4] He talks about 'the watercourse way,' a way of living which simply finds its own natural level. I think Maureen's at that level, where she knows what she's happy with and doesn't struggle to articulate it. Yet I've been struggling all this time. My spiritual journey has been endless questions and not many answers. In fact I don't think there have been any answers at all."

I quote a Zen saying that I'm fond of: "The work is to go on doing the work."

"I like that," David replies. "The problem is, we're always trying to say what others have said much better before us. As Eliot says, there's no competition. But there's always the struggle. The struggle is the given. For those with the disease there's no choice.

"I have no feeling that it's better to have the disease than not. My parents and Auntie Marjory would think you're saved if you've got the disease and not if you haven't. But I have no feeling like that. Some people have the disease, others don't. That's just how it is."

Believe only ...

Back to the journey out of Eden. "When I found people telling me that what I felt to be true wasn't true," David goes on, "it was a pretty precarious time. The beginning of the end. But also the end of the beginning. I'd call the next stage 'Growing Away.' It was an intellectual rebellion: I'd try to persuade my head of something, and if I couldn't persuade my head then I'd give it up."

I've noticed that his intellectual processes seem very soul-related?

"They're very much connected to my life. At that time, for instance, to the question of whether I went to church. The main issue for me was to justify myself in opposition to fundamentalist Christianity. They knew what they believed, so I had to know what I believed, and it had to stand up.

"I discovered *The Christian Agnostic* by Leslie Weatherhead — actually it was on my mother's bookshelf (my mother mischievously called him Wesley Leatherhead) — and it really opened things up for me.[5] It made me see that it *was* important what one felt. The central idea in the book was this: 'Believe nothing because a so-called wise man said it. Believe nothing because a belief is generally held. Believe nothing because it is written in ancient books. Believe nothing because someone else believes it: believe only what you yourself judge to be true.'

"That was revolutionary for me at the time. But the people at church considered it terribly dangerous. They thought that you're adrift if you follow your own beliefs; you need to be led, to be guided. But what kind of leading, what kind of guidance? I saw that it needn't come from atrophied notions laid in stone."

So how did his questioning of his parents' beliefs come to the crunch?

David sits back in his chair and remembers. "A new minister came to the church and asked us to sign thirteen 'essential articles of faith.' I refused to sign. I said, 'It doesn't seem important to me'." Wasn't that even more shocking than lack of belief? "It was simply the case. I didn't need to believe all the things that those church-goers believed. I don't blame them. My place was not within that church."

Did it cause a terrible rift with his loving and much-loved parents?

"No. They were disappointed, naturally, but they thought it was just a phase I was going through, that I was under the influence of this friend or that. They never loaded me with guilt, and I'm very grateful for that. Their emphasis was more on forgiveness than on guilt.

"At those Christian house parties and summer camps as a teenager I was struck by what David Tryon said: 'Up to a certain age you can't really *think,* you can only rearrange your prejudices.' Despite his strong Christian stance he helped me to think things through more clearly. 'Imagine,' he'd say, 'trying to explain a tennis ball to someone who lived in a two-dimensional world. Concepts like the Trinity, they're mysteries. If we're to understand them we have to learn a greater than three-dimensional way of thinking.'

"Even as I moved away from Christian belief I still retained a respect for the church. James Joyce says in *Portrait of the Artist* that he doesn't want to take the church for granted, because so much has gone on in that space, its prayers have been so important that it would be a sort of sacrilege. I don't want to sneer, to trample on it. If I have to go on without that belief, if this is the journey I have to go on alone, then so be it."

Patterns of trinity

So off he went to Manchester University to study drama. Had he always wanted to be an actor?

"It was a teacher at my primary school who picked me out as someone who could act or even produce a play, and I took it on without question as something I was 'meant' to do. It was quite unexpected, yet it totally changed my life.

"As Christianity dwindled for me, acting became a passion, and so did other things. When I was fifteen or sixteen, sex, sexuality, became very important to me — as it does, I don't think that's anything out of the ordinary — though I did start taking a philosophic interest in it, too, and read lots of D.H. Lawrence and books on Tantric yoga and other sexual practices. When I was at university I had a girlfriend from Hull who was already at Manchester and almost immediately we started living together. Quite early on we went round trying out lots of places of worship. I wanted to ask questions of the people in those places. When Christ said, 'In my Father's house are many mansions,' does that imply a diversity of beliefs — that those of other faiths, those who are uncertain, even those with no belief may be accommodated under the one roof? The two-year-old inside me wanted to sing, 'One roof and only one, and not kept up by walls, We're all on the inside — or is that a load of balls?'

"And the saying, 'It is easier for a camel to go through the eye of a needle than for a rich man to enter the kingdom of heaven': is that a social gospel? For me it was, for many years. I saw my relationship with God, and with man, in that socialist way. So I was beginning to see the outline of a belief in a series of trinities: there was the original trinity of the Father, Son and Holy Ghost (Spirit); the trinity of the self we had struggled to define — Body, Soul and Spirit; then came the socialist one, God (Spirit), Self and Neighbour; and mirroring it, the sexual one, God (Spirit), Self and the Loved One. Put together these four triangles — if you can imagine it — and you have a four-sided pyramid of existence, with Spirit at its summit and around the four corners of its base Self/Body, Soul/Beloved, Self/Son, Father/Neighbour. And for me, at that time, the sexual trinity was central. It was beyond any other experience, this bonding in the act of sexual union, the sensual enjoyment of life. But what was a central truth for me was evidently not necessarily true for others.

"Pilate's question in John's gospel: 'What is truth?' It's the fundamental question, and you ask it when you've been through the process of accepting what the truth is and then realize that it isn't your truth. It's like the journey of Parsifal, which is a very important story for me. Parsifal sees the Grail but doesn't he know what it's about and leaves the castle oblivious. He's the Holy Fool, he could have extended compassion but instead he wanders around for years trying to find the Grail Castle once more. Even when he gets there, in Wagner's version, he doesn't recognize it. 'Have I found the place,' he says, 'or am I still in error?'"

I point out that the Latin derivation of "error" is from the word "to wander, to stray," and that to David seems exactly right. "You have an initial vision, then you lose it and wander through your life until maybe you reach ... As Eliot says:

> 'The end of all our exploring / Will be to arrive where we started / And know the place for the first time'."[6]

The paranormal and the normal

As a student in Manchester, did he still trail round places of worship? David laughs. "No. Sunday morning had other things to offer. Jesus was still an important figure for me, though. There was a kind of inhabitation in me. It wasn't the historical Jesus. The pictures we have in our heads are better than the ones we're given from the outside, and I had a picture of Jesus in my head, a sense of him. I don't think it was paranormal."

Has he ever had any sense of his mother or his father since they died? "Yes, but not in a spooky way. Though my parents were so good about my break from the church I was a bit callous towards them at the time, and my father felt a very real disappointment about what I did. After his death, just a day or two after, I was in the car, taking the death certificate ... It was almost as if he said to me, 'It's all right now.' The misunderstanding, the disappointment had gone. *Now that he knows everything ...* was how I felt it.

"I see that experience as explicable in terms that Hofstadter might use to describe the workings of the brain. We're each a universe unto ourselves, it's a monodrama going on here, everything that happens is us-centred. The feeling that things were all right with my father was because some sort of harmonization was going on within myself. But at the same time I do regard it as a spiritual experience.

"Then after my mother died I had the well-attested experience of having guides on my shoulders: my mother on one side, my father on the other. But that doesn't mean I believe in the afterlife.

"When I was about twenty-two, at the Bristol Old Vic Theatre School, I went to see a fortune-teller, a psychic. She did the Tarot for me, and she said, 'The person you're living with, she's not right for you and you'll be parting soon.' At the time I was married to my original girlfriend, and I thought, 'That can't be right.'

Yet within three years we split up. I don't claim anything for the Tarot reading itself, more for the effect it had on me: I saw it as having significance. Coincidences do this for us, don't they? They invest cause and effect with meaning."

The Tarot, the I Ching, the Tao

Now we're approaching the questions about David's more recent spiritual practices, and the meaning of them for him.

"One of my enduring beliefs is that we create our own beliefs. It's an idea Hermann Hesse explored — he was deeply influenced by the Hindu concept of *maya*. The universe is at play. Everything is illusion. We construct our own meaning. The playwright Arthur Schnitzler says a similar thing, something like 'Only those who look for meaning will find it. Security exists nowhere. We know nothing of ourselves. We always play. Wise the man who knows it'."

He's mentioned the I Ching. *How did he come to that?* "I was in a play by Julian Mitchell, *Half Life,* with John Gielgud. The company manager had the Richard Wilhelm edition of the *I Ching* with that preface by Jung. I'd been reading quite a lot of Jung and had just finished Hesse's *The Glass Bead Game,* which explores the curious nature of the *I Ching.* So I bought a copy and used it to ask questions: should I change my agent, what about this or that relationship? I asked what to do about a girlfriend, several times over a period of weeks, and each time it came up with exactly the same unmoving hexagram — Opposition. An amazing coincidence. It was saying 'No.'

"Like Parsifal, you only gradually learn the necessity of asking the right question. The important thing is not to be told the right answer — not at the beginning anyway — but to understand what the right question is. You approach the *I Ching* in a similar way. You can even ask the question, 'What is the right question to ask?'

"Using the *I Ching* seems to me rather like prayer. I take Jung's view of the *I Ching,* that the answer comes from inside yourself, that the falling of the coins connects with the here and now and represents your own answer to the question. It's a path to self-knowledge, and asking the right question takes you a good way along that path. Interpreting the answer is the second part of the journey and may take you into territory you've not yet explored.

"The *I Ching* has its origins in Taoism, something I became increasingly interested in, especially an ancient book known as Lao Tzu's *Tao Te Ching*. The *Tao* is devoid of God but deeply spiritual. I turn to Eliot's *Four Quartets* in the same way: they're unfathomable, endless in their wisdom.

"This seems a healthy development for someone with my religious background, a way of dealing with the disease, of finding patterns and guidance in my life. I also do T'ai Chi, which is a moving meditation. I learnt it through a group but I'm not very good at groups, I see them as places where I have to tailor parts of myself to fit in — a kind of death by amputation. So I do T'ai Chi by myself. The meditation is the important aspect. With T'ai Chi I can become part of the things around me. It helps me to get to where *things are as they are*. Where *it* happens. What is, is what is. But this simple fact eludes us. Ironically — especially for one who feels he's still on a journey — the truth, if only we could grasp it, is we don't have to go anywhere, we're here already, and our task is simply to know it."

Maureen calls us to the window to see the heron perched at the edge of the canal searching warily for fish. When we sit down again, David finishes.

"There was a void in me which Jesus left. But the void is all right. It's not blackness or emptiness, it's more like the void before things were, and it seems to me that in that place everything is all right. Along with the trudging, along with the endless seeking and searching, there's a kind of comforting murmur, like the distant toll of a bell — calling me home perhaps. Eliot puts it best, echoing the words of Julian of Norwich: 'And under the oppression of the silent fog the tolling bell ... All shall be well and all manner of thing shall be well'."[7]

Benjamin Zephaniah

I was the area champion at Bible knowledge, I could quote them any of the main bits of it, and I got highly praised, I was the church's star kid in the big conventions where the churches all got together. "Listen to this kid preach," they'd say. I was really loved, anything I wanted I had. But the moment I started asking questions, I was a devil.

I feel — not that I have a spirit, that I am a spirit. I'm a spirit connected to a body, not the other way round.

My God, Your God

Benjamin Zephaniah grew up in Birmingham in the 1960s; his father was from Barbados and his mother from Jamaica. He got very little education because he was dyslexic. He truanted, was deemed uncontrollable, "a born failure," and drifted into crime. After serving sentences in various different penal institutions he decided to break the pattern and go to London, where he started to perform his own "rap" poetry. In 1989 he was proposed as candidate for nomination as the Oxford Professor of Poetry, and ten years later was talked of as a potential Poet Laureate. He has published six books of poetry for children and adults, writes novels and plays, and often broadcasts.

Questions

We're sitting in an upstairs room in Benjamin Zephaniah's London stamping ground, West Ham, the setting for his novel *Face,*1 and I ask him: *as a child, did he have a picture of God?*

"I was a bit, what's the word, ambivalent about God. I tried to believe in the God my parents were telling me about. The world all round me was black, but this God dressed in white, with a beard, who looked like a white man, who stood up there watching that we did the right things. If he liked you He was good to you but if you crossed Him He was full of brimstone and fire.

"All round me there were adults who believed that. They seemed educated people, so I wanted to believe it too.

"The church was very fire and brimstone too. For a short time I went to a white church, it used to have a little Sunday school, and you sat down and answered questions about the Bible. It was very calm, very different from the black church. But when I asked them, 'What does God look like?' the answer came out just the same, 'He's a man and He's up there watching you ...'

"But I thought, 'This can't be right.'

"I never came across anyone agnostic. No one knew anything like, Hindu or whatever. When I first came to London I'd go to Hare Krishna, Mosque, anything, and I asked them what they believed. But when I was young there was nothing but this God. I was the area champion at Bible knowledge, I could quote them any of the main bits of it, and I got highly praised, I was the church's star kid in the big conventions where the churches all got together. 'Listen to this kid preach,' they'd say. I was really loved. Anything I wanted I had. But the moment I started asking questions, I was a devil."

And he wasn't saying it was rubbish, he was just asking questions?

"Yes! My questions were simple: 'Why there are only four gospels?' 'All the people around Jesus were women, so why didn't women write any of the gospels?'

"I was having a bad time at home. I was nine, ten, eleven, and my dad was beating my mum up and I'd stand in front of her to defend her, and that got on my dad's nerves. I'd go to church and hear all that about loving your neighbour and I'd come home and ask my dad why he was hitting my mum. The line was, 'God's the head of the church and Man is the head of the house, God punishes people if they get out of line so Man has to punish people like that'."

> She is flesh of me flesh
> I am bone of her bone
> So please stop kicking her
> Beg yu leave her alone,
> She is not fighting back
> Find de love dat yu lack
> Dat's me sista yu beating upstairs.[2]

Did he believe God and Man had that sort of authority?

"It was difficult *not* to believe it because everyone around me believed it."

The culture he grew up in was a very strong and united one. "All the food was Jamaican, all the music was Jamaican, all the people were Jamaican. My mother told me that someone from Jamaica was coming to visit, so I ran out into the street looking at the buses to see which one was coming from Jamaica.

"I asked my mum about where babies came from, and she was pregnant with twins so she told me about it, and she showed me a female dog that was having puppies. So I asked, if women create these living things and God is supposed to have created living things, and no one's seen God, we've never had an example of men creating living things, so why isn't God a woman? To me it was very simple."

Contradictions

Benjamin had a chequered education. When his mother got a job in a hospital in a poor white working-class area he found himself the only black boy in the school, and was stereotyped. "I injured my finger when the teacher forced me to play cricket. She said, 'Every dark person must be able to play cricket.' When Cassius Clay won a fight — that was before he was Muhammed Ali — the kids wanted to box me and I got a bloody nose and lips. The teacher just laughed and said, 'You've got the same colour blood'."

But when a white boy slammed a brick against his head — he still has the scar from it — his mother moved him to a cosmopolitan school where at last he could express the artistic side of himself.

Not in the written word, presumably?

"No, I made up poems. I've always done poetry, even before I knew what the word 'poetry' meant. I was a great rhymer. We had competitions where someone picked a word at random and we'd improvize a poem around that word, and I usually won."

What happened to his parents' marriage?

"I saw my mum get beaten, but fortunately I didn't see her beaten like other women I've seen, continually, but staying in there. She had a threshold she wouldn't go beyond. She'd leave, but then she'd go back. But eventually she left, and I went with her.

"The other kids stayed with my father. My father had something against me because I was always the brat who was in the way, I was the one who always defended her.

"They had this memorial occasion to celebrate his life, and me and my mum wouldn't go. The rest of the family all see him as this hero who held down a good job and brought up seven children on his own. Whereas my strongest memory is of this maniac."

How did he cope with this contradiction?

"There's something about me that can see their point of view. They saw that Mummy had taken off and didn't care. But they didn't see what I saw. They don't know that sometimes, when Daddy was supposed to be at work, actually he was beating up Mummy. He worked for the Post Office in different cities, so he could trace us, and when he found us he'd beat Mum up again. I can see what they're seeing, but they can't see what I'm seeing."

Is that what he means by being ambivalent? Is it that for him things are like the proverbial mountain, some of it's rocky and some of it's smooth, that's just the way mountains are?

"Yes. That's how I try to be with everything. With every issue I try and really understand the opposing point of view. In some ways I believe 'Thou shalt not kill.' But I can also believe that, if you're being killed, you have a right to defend yourself. There's the old biblical saying, 'There's a time to reap and a time to sow, a time to kill and a time to heal.' I can understand that.

"But in some ways I'm an extremist. Like, if I believe 'Thou shalt not kill' then that means animals as well." *He's vegetarian?* "Yes. And I believe 'Thou shalt not steal,' and that means females produce milk for their children and I shouldn't steal it from them." *So he's not only vegetarian but vegan?* "Yes."

"I believe we're all equal, and I have no place in my 'church' — I don't have a *church,* but I use that word — for discrimination against women. I like the Council for Racial Equality slogan, 'All different but all equal.' I listen to a lot of religious people and I think, 'You're like bigots, your view's the only right one and everyone else is going to hell.' I know Christian people who say, about a woman who's asking for an abortion after a rape, 'She shouldn't have put herself in a position to be raped, if she'd had the Lord Jesus Christ with her it wouldn't have happened.' They just don't know what real life is like."

His mother and his sister say, "Just believe, be good, go to church, don't worry about poor people or people caught up in wars." "My mum even says, 'Thank God for slavery because it brought us Christianity.' I say to her, 'You can have God without slavery!' She hates that."

Being a very political person, Benjamin is also a very political writer. "At one time I'd be performing one week at CND demonstrations, the next at animal rights or ANC demonstrations. It may sound like 'rent a militant' but I felt passionate about those things. If I get asked what a poet's role is in society, I say it's to be a newscaster when the news isn't picking up our stories, so we must tell them that news through our poetry. Here they ask you, 'Do you want to be a poet or a comedian or an actor?' But in the *griot** tradition you can be all these things."

> Dis poetry stays wid me when I run or walk
> An when I am talking to meself in poetry I talk,
> Dis poetry is wid me,
> Below an above,
> Dis poetry's from inside me
> It goes to yu
> WID LUV.[3]

In his poetry for children he tackles issues of war, racism, bullying, animal rights and environmental issues, and he thinks that's why they've been so successful. He sees it as a woman's right to choose if she needs an abortion, though abortion shouldn't be used as a method of contraception. We now have an interesting discussion about the many pros and cons of this fraught issue. Does he, I ask, have any concept of an unborn soul that might be waiting to come into the world? Any lives outside this one?

Benjamin thinks for a long time.

---

* African and Afro-Caribbean story-telling tradition.

"I think that there is Something Else. But I also think that we'll never know." We laugh. In fact our conversation is often punctuated by laughing. "I think we'll know when we get there. I imagine two people out there, and one of them's in the material world saying, 'Do you think there's a spiritual world after this one?' and the other's in the spiritual world saying, 'Do you think there's a material world after this one?'"

Failure ...

After hearing about his strong sense of right and wrong, I want to learn how he moved into and then out of crime.

"Well, I hated school. And school hated me. When I had the opportunity to truant, I did. Then they expelled me for spraying the toilets with graffiti. Yes, I was dyslexic, but if you're dyslexic it doesn't mean you've got a criminal mind. If you can't read then you want to get out, so you truant, or you're suspended, you mix with kids who've been suspended or excluded from school, then you need money so you can look cool ...

"There was something about me that always knew what I was capable of. If I came from a middle class home, where people read, I might have been encouraged. But I was discouraged.

"Again, I try and look at the way they were seeing it. What they saw was, black people were finding it difficult enough getting jobs in factories in them days. You became a car mechanic or a painter or decorator. Or you were like my dad and you worked your way up. It was difficult enough, if you were white, to be a writer. And here was me, I always knew I wanted to be a poet, and I couldn't read or write properly! I did all the things that black guys did, I was a great athlete, I was a great dancer, that was fun. Being good at church, being good spiritually.

"But I had to get a trade, and I wouldn't. I went to approved school, and then to Borstal." *His crimes?* "Thieving. And fighting.

"First I went in for a short time, the Short Sharp Shock, and I thought, 'When I come out I'm going to get my revenge.' So when I came out I beat up a policeman. And I went back inside for a longer stretch. Prison this time. Winson Green in Birmingham.

"And I took a look at what was going on and thought, 'I'm still going to beat up policemen, but I'm not going to do it physically.' I got political without understanding politics. I knew I had to be different but I didn't know how."

Did he get any spiritual guidance? Say, from the prison chaplain?

"I had an experience with a prison chaplain ... When you get to prison you queue up, and they ask 'What's your religion.' The guy before me said 'Rastafarian' but they wouldn't accept that. Somebody said to me, 'Say Roman Catholic, we meet at the Catholic church and we have a laugh.' So I did.

"After a day or two, this Roman Catholic priest walks into my cell. And he's like a wrestler. Massive. He looks at me and says, 'You're not a fucking Catholic. When did you fucking become Catholic? Go on, prove it!' He was in prison uniform, with just this little collar. 'Were your fucking parents Catholic?' I said, 'I just converted!' He said, 'I'll see you in church, you black bastard,' and he walked out and slammed the door." *I'm shocked, but he laughs at the memory.* "It completely blew me away."

... *And success*

How did he get out of the cycle of crime and imprisonment?

"I wanted to get out of the crowd I was in, so I left Birmingham and went to London. They said, 'Don't go there, the gangs are even worse in London,' but I went. There was a shop in East Stratford called Page One Books, and I told them I was a poet. I had a girlfriend who wrote my poems down for me and typed them, and I took them in there. My poems then were very angry. The National Front were on the streets then, the SUS laws were in force,* and the police were picking me up, locking me up and dropping me back on the street."

Handsworth, Brixton, St Pauls, Broadwater Farm,
Toxteth, Highfields, Bradford, Ladbroke Grove,
Somebody better mek a U-turn

---

* Laws under which people could be stopped and search on police suspicion. It was used almost exclusively against black people.

Before de fire start to burn.
De culprit is hidden
In a very nice house, in a very nice town ...
Somebody better check it out,
Somebody better get it right ...[4]

"This writer called Derek Smith, he said, 'Yes, we can do something with you,' and I did my first poetry reading in London. Someone booked me for North East London Polytechnic, and someone there did bookings for the alternative comedy circuit, Rik Mayall and Dawn French and so on. Next thing, we were on Channel 4.

"So it was a kind of sweet revenge: they'd warned me about gangs and crime in London and next thing was, they saw me on television.

"Now I do a lot of work in prisons. I've performed my poems in almost every prison in this country — though I've never been invited into Winson Green — and in other countries, in Colombia, on Death Row ... The last one I did was Rampton, the high-security psychiatric prison.

"One thing they always say is, they never feel I'm talking down to them. Sometimes I see my old mates in there. They're looking at me and seeing what they could be, and I'm looking at them and seeing what I could have been.

"There's some innocent people in there. And in the justice system there's no taking account of the individual. No judge ever asks, 'What's right for this person? How can we rehabilitate them, how can we put them back into society?'"

It seems to me that, if he ran society, he'd run it not by rules that must be applied, but by seeing the problems and talents of each individual.

"That's right. I want to ask kids what it is they want to do, what they think they can do. No one ever said to me, 'What do you want to do?' The conforming bit of me would have said 'I want to be a fireman' — but if they'd asked me 'What do you *really* want to do, I'd have said 'I want to be a poet.' I say to kids who are wasting themselves, they say they're nineteen and they've got a gun and if anyone messes with them and so on, and they can't read and write, I bring them into my studio and I say, 'I've done all that. It's up to you what you do, obviously, but if you want to be a writer, if you want to be a singer, you've got to learn to write. If you're going to be a singer, even if it's only to read your contract — you've got to be able to read to do that!'"

But this is about self-worth, surely. What was it in him that knew he was worth it? What gave him the confidence to say, 'I'm a poet,' and stand up there in performance and be one?

Silence, while the traffic roars outside.

"I have that part of me that wants — that wanted — to be part of the crowd, that wanted to conform. That wants to accept that there are people who are experts, they know about God, they know about space, they know about politics. And then I have this other self. That's the complete opposite. That questions. That doesn't believe anything they say — unless it strikes true with me. And I can use that self in poetry."

> Open up de border free up de land
> Open up de books in de Vatican
> Open up yu self to any possibility
> Open up yu heart and yu mentality,
> Open any door dat yu confront
> Let me put it straight, sincere and blunt
> narrow mindedness mus run an hide
> fe a shot of overstanding
> Open Wide.[5]

"It's not scientific, it's not logical, I can't prove it. That bit that's inside me says, 'God can be a woman. There's something after death' ...

"I've been fascinated by near-death experiences. I researched them for a while. I've never had one myself, but out of all the theories I've heard about life after death these are the most believable. There are similarities between them, right across the cultures. Their attitude to life changes after it. They don't fear death. They even drive differently — slightly crazily, as if it doesn't matter too much any more. They believe in a kind of afterlife, they believe in a God, but their God isn't the sort who watches you and makes sure you pray five times a day. It's the sort of experience that makes you open up like a flower. You've seen your pain go, your mortgage go ... They're afraid that if they talk too much about it people will go and try it out! A friend of mine who's a musician had a near-death experience and when he came back he said he'd heard the most perfect music.

"I think the important thing is to approach it so you can go through it with a clear conscience."

Resolutions

Does Benjamin connect this with his father? Now that his father's dead, does he feel there might be an afterlife for him where he might learn something?

"I don't know. I did what I needed to do while he was alive. A couple of years before he died I went to Barbados and made peace with him. I disagreed with my father most of my life. But when I went to Barbados to see him, I didn't analyse it. I just went and hung out with him for a couple of weeks, and it was the best time I'd ever had with him. We were just like two mates. Every so often he'd bring up the past and I'd go, 'Shut up, don't talk about my mum, I didn't come to hear that.' I didn't know he was going to die, but after I'd been he started to get ill, and some-one told me that in his last weeks he had a photograph of me and my mother and he'd stare at it constantly. I think that was his conscience.

"I can understand what it was like for him. He'd come over here in the fifties, he was in one of the early rush of people from the Caribbean, and he went to the GPO as a sweeper-upper and he worked his way up till he was boss of his department. He had this work ethic — which was good — but he took it to extremes. If you broke a cup he'd shout, 'That cup! I worked for that cup!' He'd put cardboard in our shoes. I had this funny walk so people couldn't see the cardboard in my shoes.

"I think to myself, if my dad heard me talking about him now he'd think, 'God, isn't he honest.' I'm not praising him or blam-ing him, I'm not overplaying it, I'm just saying it. If my dad was a ghost, a spirit or whatever, and if he'd seen me at the celebra-tion of his life, he'd have thought, 'What a hypocrite.' I know that he was a nice man in a suit during the day, and at night he had blood on his hands. That's just how it was."

A spiritual discipline

Benjamin's spiritual practice is doing T'ai Chi. "I do it every morning. Or if I miss the morning I'll do it in the evening. Fifteen minutes at least.

"The martial arts are associated with Buddhism and Zen, but you don't have to sign up for that. It's to do with breathing. You time your breath, and all the time you're doing the movements as well" (he demonstrates) "so you've got to be completely concentrated. You're slowing your heart rate down, and you're exercising your *Chi*. That's your energy, life force, vital energy. You're moving your energy around: now it's in your fingertip, into your other fingertip, into your feet ... It's like yoga, where they do postures. T'ai Chi is like moving yoga.

"My sister's a Jehovah's Witness and she says T'ai Chi is rubbish. I tell her about the meditation, when you sit still, breathe, try and empty your mind. 'Rubbish,' she says. 'Jesus Christ is in my mind twenty-four hours a day!'"

> Before Religion,
> before Politricks,
> Our names meant someting ...
> Rumour has it
> Jesus (Peace be upon him)
> Krishna (Peace be upon him)
> Mohammed (Peace be upon him)
> Harriet Tubman (Peace be upon her)
> Yim Wing Chun (Peace be upon her)
> Amina (Peace be upon her)
> All came
> Rumour has it
> Our destinies are all
> (Rumour has it)
> De same. [6]

Has he ever had a spiritual experience by taking drugs? "No. People say you can have one that way, but I don't really think you can. I've never taken drugs so I wouldn't know. I believe you should be very clear-headed if you're going to have a spiritual experience. To be fully awake, fully aware.

"Yogic deep breathing in meditation is the closest I've been to a spiritual experience. It's the only time I've felt ..." Words are nearly failing him. "... Not that I *have* a spirit, that I *am* a spirit. I'm a spirit connected to a body, not the other way round.

"I can understand, though I've never felt it myself, how people can leave their body and look back at it, or raise their bodies up, levitate ... I can understand it because I've had that intense feeling. You're sitting so still, and you're there but you don't feel your body. Then you can think 'I'm going to connect back to my body again.' The technique I use is from the Tibetan form of martial arts, it's called *Kateda,* and you keep your eyes open. So it's not about dreaming, it's about being fully awake, alert."

What does he feel now about the concept of God?

"One thing I'm sure about: there is a God. There's a power behind us all. It's daft to try and fit it into our little minds, our little shapes, cultures, races ... I've travelled in India, Africa, and you can say they believe crazy things. But who am I to say it's not true?

"Germaine Greer says her 'hobby is thinking.' I'm like that. As I question about religion, I believe more and more about God. But at the same time I can take on board the scientific facts about the world. I feel a kind of loneliness, because there are so many people I get on with intellectually, and we talk about all these questions, and at the end of the night I say 'God be with you' and they're horrified. Yet my spiritual friends often avoid grappling with the intellectual questions. I want both.

"I see no religion that can manage my spiritual thirst. Most religions are restrictive and in many ways oppressive.

"In the days of the Cold War I went to Russia. I was talking to a Russian woman and I asked her, 'Do you want to attack us?' 'No!' she said. 'All I want is education for my children, love from my husband, and God.' That's how it is. Priests and politicians think we need them to negotiate our relationship with God, but we don't. It may seem that we have a new or modern way of looking at spiritual matters, but in truth many of us are going back to the

old way, the original way. We're getting back to the roots and
going straight to God."

Does YOUR GOD love children
Does YOUR GOD love peace
Could YOUR GOD bring justice to de Middle East,
Does YOUR GOD love anyone whatever dere kind,
Is YOUR GOD dis brutal, or is YOUR GOD blind,
An is YOUR GOD willing to talk to a nation,
Or did YOUR GOD come here to wipe out creation.
My questions are childlike but I'm in confusion,
My question is,
Where is YOUR GOD?[7]

Facing suffering,
evil and loss

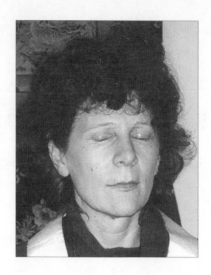

Dayachitta

I felt that the world was a malevolent place, where people could be murdered for having the wrong identity. I thought the world might be out to get me. My inward struggle has been against that, towards a sense of trust.

The Dharma was the only thing that made sense of what I was going through. The idea of impermanence, the fact that everything changes and dies. Yes, there's healing, but nothing can take you back to the place that you were before.

Against the odds, a new world out of the old

Dayachitta was born Marian Monas in 1953 in Melbourne, Australia, daughter of Dutch migrants. Her father was Jewish, her mother Protestant; her mother's family sheltered her father from the Gestapo. After the break-up of her parents' marriage and a financially impoverished childhood in Tasmania, she dropped out of higher education and came to the UK. She developed skin cancer in her twenties, and gradually discovered that the way of Buddhism was right for her. Now living in a small house in Cambridge which she shares with other women associated with the Friends of the Western Buddhist Order, she teaches Buddhism and leads retreats, and works part-time at the Cambridge Buddhist Centre and part-time as an acupuncturist.

Dayachitta has told me that she lives in a small Buddhist community, but her directions are surprising: "It's a little end-of-terrace house next to the airport." *She shares it with two other women members of the Friends of the Western Buddhist Order. From the outside it looks little different from its neighbours, and even inside there's no sense of asceticism around. We drink excellent coffee, and Dayachitta says it's handy to have Sainsbury's round the corner.* "The money we put into the pot's enough to buy whatever we want. I find the sort of poverty mentality that says 'You shouldn't, you oughtn't' really depressing."

'*I don't believe in God or marriage*'

She tells me that, as Marian Monas, she wasn't looking for a religious faith when she came across Buddhism. Far from it: she had always been hostile to religion. At the age of four she had witnessed her mother throwing her wedding ring in the corner crying, "I don't believe in God or marriage," and that always resonated with her. Now she was on the far side of the world from her origins, she'd left behind a turbulent family, a sexual relationship had turned empty, and she'd developed malignant melanoma. A colleague belonged to the Friends of the Western Buddhist Order (FWBO); she was sceptical, but questioned him about it. He took her scepticism on, and the more she learned the more relevant it seemed.

She still doesn't believe in God or marriage. But the practice of Buddhism stands up to her inner standard of truth. "My life seems to be a reflection of themes that run through the second half of our century: war, displacement, family breakdown, the Holocaust. But I feel fortunate that I've had lots of joyful times, and I've been enriched by my experiences not diminished by them."

When I ask her about the beliefs commonly accepted as Buddhist, like reincarnation, she shakes her head. "People often think that reincarnation is being reborn exactly the same as they are now. I can't relate to the continuation of myself exactly as I am now, unchanging. Perhaps it's more that what goes on is a continuously changing current of energy. The idea of reincarnation in Buddhism is too complex and subtle to be understood in a literal fixed sense."

What attracted her to Buddhism in the first place, and one of the things which still holds her, is the fact that you're not expected to follow without thought, or blindly, but to test everything out in the light of your experience. It's not about God, or believing. It's a way to live skilfully.

"For me Buddhism is a coherent philosophy, bigger than me but not God based. It gives me a view of life that isn't based on blame or punishment, but which still faces the issues of life such as suffering and impermanence. It helps me to develop more patience and kindness, and more understanding of the imperfections of other people."

From the Holocaust and the Resistance

Marian's father was an Amsterdamer. His family descended from an eminent Portuguese-Dutch-Jewish family that included Menasseh ben Israel, who was painted by Rembrandt and Flink. When her father was in his early twenties he'd been to music college and was playing the violin in the Concertgebouw. Her mother's parents were very different: they were country people, good-living Protestants in the town of Oldemarkt, in the north of Holland, where her grandfather was Burgomaster for a while.

"They ran a stationery shop from their front room. A salesman came in and said, 'How many envelopes do you want, and pens, and will you hide a Jew, and what colour would the pens be?' That way, if my grandparents said, 'What? Hide a Jew? Unthinkable!' the man from the Underground could pretend he'd said nothing about Jews. For a time my grandparents hid the whole of my father's family.

"Then they moved on. My father somehow got picked up and he was sent off to a concentration camp on Dutch soil. Paradoxically, he was saved from death by being ill: he contracted hepatitis. At this point the Nazis put out the fiction that the Jews weren't going to their death, but to labour camps ..."

Arbeit Macht Frei? *

"Exactly. So if they were ill they were sent to hospital.

"My father was in a hospital where the nurses were sympathetic to the Underground. The man in the next bed died, and they swapped the papers and smuggled him out. Eventually he found his way to my mother's family house." *What happened to the rest of the family?* "The immediate family all survived, though some of his uncles and cousins and his elderly grandmother were killed in concentration camps.

"My mother's parents knew the Gestapo would probably come looking for my father, so they hid him in a small wooden compartment. Two feet wide, four feet high, three feet deep, this little false wall with two leather straps to hold it shut ..." *Dayachitta describes it so vividly that I ask if she's seen it.* "Yes. When I was twenty-two I turned up on my father's doorstep back in Holland.

---

* "Work Makes You Free" — the slogan above the gates of Auschwitz.

That was the first time I'd seen him since I was four, and together we went to my mother's parents' house and I met them for the first time. They'd kept that little compartment exactly the same."

So what happened when the Gestapo raided the house? "They'd wake up children and asked them questions — who was living in the house, what did they look like, and so on — and my grandparents were sheltering a two-year-old Jewish boy as well. The Gestapo went to wake him up, but my grandmother was having none of it. 'Don't you dare wake him!' she'd say. 'My cousin's little boy' — this black-haired toddler in a blonde family — 'I've only just got him off to sleep!'"

And the daughter of the family fell in love with this man on the run? "He was handsome, charismatic, and a violinist. She was a teenager and very pretty. It must have been a hothouse sort of environment, very intense and dangerous and romantic. They married soon after the war, and my two older brothers were born in Holland. However, they wanted to get as far away from Europe as possible, so they decided to emigrate to Australia.

"That seemed to spell freedom. And it was freedom, if you came from the UK. But it wasn't freedom for non-Brits. They were sent straight to a migrant camp. It was a bit like a work-house, and you could only get out if you were sponsored by an employer. But how could you get contacts of that sort if you didn't know anyone?" *This bit of history was new to me, and shocking.* "Yes, it's a part of Australian history that's been kept well hidden, though it's coming out now in films like *The Silver City,* which I saw in Australia in the eighties." *After a war like her father's, to be shoved in a labour camp must have been a desperate experience?* "It wasn't only the work he had to do. There were Nazis among the migrants too. Everyone was dumped in together."

For two years, and fearful for the fate of his violinist hands, her father scraped rust off gas pipes. Then he forged a letter from a fictional employer in Queensland, and got out. He went off south to Melbourne, where someone offered him a garden shed to live in, and he joined an orchestra of the Australian Broadcasting Corporation. Her mother and brothers joined him, and Marian was born.

Three years later her mother was pregnant again, but the mar-

riage was failing. "By this time we'd moved to Tasmania, where my father had got a job with the orchestra in Hobart. He was having an affair with a woman in the orchestra. My mother had known about the affair but she'd thought it was all over ... My parents decided to part, and that was when my mother declared she didn't believe in God or marriage."

A childhood of poverty

The family were left destitute. Marian's mother had left school at thirteen in Holland in the 1930s, and as an intelligent girl she had watched her brother going off to higher education and getting a good job. "My father left Australia, and there were no Social Services at that time. We were already living in a council house, but otherwise my mother had to scrape together what she could. She was lucky in being offered a job in the local kindergarten, work she'd done as a teenager before the war, but my sister was only six weeks old and we were still so poor that one Christmas a prison warder came round with a bag full of presents the prisoners had made in the local jail. Beautifully crafted wooden toys. I've always had a soft spot for prisoners since then! But it was very difficult for my mother.

"She played the church organ to earn a bit of money and she left me at the Sunday School to be minded. I hated it. They must have found me a bit difficult. They said I'd get a free illustrated copy of the Bible if I learnt all the books of the Bible in order, but I wouldn't go in for that sort of bribery. I also had the cheek to ask if the Nazis were Christians. They couldn't answer me, and I was asked to leave. My mother tried to get me to join the Brownies but I refused to go. A uniform, and brown shirts! I can't at that age have known about the Nazi association, but I didn't want to wear a uniform, I didn't want to be regimented, I didn't want to be told what to do."

Hardship and struggle were taking their toll. Her mother was overworked and exhausted, and the dynamics between the children were often competitive and unchecked.

Was there a spiritual dimension to her life at this point? "Not really. Very anti-religious. Any inspiration I got was from music. My brothers played trumpet and violin, my sister sang, I played

the violin, and my mother joined a record club. I remember the
first recording was Tchaikovsky's *Nutcracker Suite*. The landscape, too: Tasmania's so beautiful, and we had the freedom of
the bush and the creeks.

"But God? No. Only fools believed in God. I thought He was
just a way of getting you to toe the line. I still believe that organized religion is often corrupted by authoritarianism: 'You're miserable sinners' and all that. So I wasn't having any of it. With all
this going on I think I must have been quite disturbed as a child,
over-responsible, too self-sufficient."

*Her self-esteem was low, both because of her father's absence
and because of the stress and poverty. I ask what made her feel
she'd got the right to ask these penetrating questions and to reject
this notion of religion.* "Well, I've never felt that I needed permission to ask questions! I wanted to get at the truth. It's been a
thread throughout my life: I've refused to have the wool pulled
over my eyes. My two older brothers and sister were also rebels
at heart, probably more than me. And the Aussie character is one
which rejects authority.

"But I think the most important person was my mother. She's
an extremely honest and ethical woman, as well as being very
intelligent. To have brought up four children with minimal support in a country where she had no relatives, having to learn the
language and to forge a career for herself with no education, is an
amazing feat. She ended up training student teachers and was
awarded an honorary teaching degree for her work at the local
kindergarten. She kept the family together, she encouraged us to
think for ourselves and not rely on material values, she was generous with her time and resources. Without the stability she created I'm sure I wouldn't have had the confidence to follow my
heart after I left home.

"But from Nazism I absorbed a fear that is another main thread
in my life. I felt that the world was a malevolent place, where people could be murdered for having the wrong identity. I thought the
world might be out to get me. My inward struggle has been
against that, towards a sense of trust."

Facing malevolence

Her mother was determined that all her children should be prop-
erly educated. Marian won the school physics prize and got a
scholarship to the University of Tasmania in Hobart to study
maths, physics, chemistry and psychology. But at this point the
stresses caught up with her, and she quit. She went to live with her
boyfriend in Sydney and, like a lot of young Australians in the sev-
enties, they decided to visit Europe.

"From that point my life started to get wider and better. For one
thing I'd made some friends. We went overland by bus — Aard-
vaark Expeditions was the outfit! — but my boyfriend wanted me
to stay by him and not mix with anyone else. I didn't want only
to talk to him because I really enjoyed meeting other people on
my travels. In spite of my low opinion of myself — I can't think
why it was so low, I look at photos of myself and I was quite okay
really — I realized how important friendship is. I'd had a best
friend at High School, she was very precious to me and still is.
But I started meeting all sorts of people, and it really opened
things up."

When they arrived in England she did some training in com-
puting and got various jobs in that line. Then she decided to go to
Holland and meet her father.

"After nineteen years! I thought he might not want to see me so
I decided not to give him any choice. I knew where he lived, in
Enschede, and so I got on my bike and caught the boat and the
train and rang him from Enschede station. 'Hi, this is Marian,
your daughter.' 'Oooh!' he said. 'Whereabouts are you?'
'Enschede station,' I said. I thought he'd have a heart attack, but
he came to meet me. And it was lucky timing, because six weeks
later he was going back to Australia so I'd have missed him.

"But it was pretty strange for both of us. I don't think, in retro-
spect, that I was emotionally prepared for it.

"We went to see my mother's parents. He hadn't been in touch
with them since returning to Holland because they felt badly towards him for leaving my mother. Here was a granddaughter they'd
never met. Here was me staring at the compartment where they'd
hidden him all those years ago. It was too much for us all, really.

"Because my parents had such a difficult time, at some point

I'd formed the idea that everything that happened to me was less important than what happened to them and their parents. When I went back to Sydney a few years ago I visited a museum dedicated to Holocaust survivors, and I understood more deeply where this view of mine about the world being malevolent had come from. It's obvious now, but visiting the museum and talking more to my parents helped me to realize that it wasn't my fault, all that suffering. Like many people who've been touched by their parents' suffering I'd thought as a child that I'd got to make it all right somehow, but I couldn't and felt guilty.

"It also puts it into perspective to go to a place like Enschede, so near to the border. The people on the other side of the border may be your friends, you probably all speak the same dialect, yet suddenly they want to kill you for what you are or what you do. With these visits to the museum and to my parents I finally realized I couldn't do anything about that suffering. I'm beginning to see it archetypally as well as personally: the unenlightened mind at work, the pull towards hatred and ignorance."

Experiencing cancer, experiencing Buddhism

Marian's boss at work in London was a member of the Friends of the Western Buddhist Order. He was attractive and intelligent, and she started to go out with him and challenge him about his Buddhism. He talked about it readily and she was interested enough to go along with him to meditation classes. "I responded, and it felt good. I loved the meditation, and I started living in one of the FWBO women's communities.

"Then when I was twenty-six I got cancer: malignant melanoma. My GP sent me to the Royal Marsden and I thought they'd say, 'We need to do more tests.' But they said, 'Come back tomorrow, we've got to operate.' If I'd left it any longer the cancer would have spread into the lymphatic system and I might have died. As it was I had to have six or seven operations over the next ten years to make sure that I was free of it.

"That first day I felt so alone. I was fairly new to Britain, I'd got no one to go to. I remember walking past this park and longing just to sit down and lean up against a tree. But it was locked. A private park, so British, so alien. Bizarre!

"I was pursuing Buddhism in my own rebellious way. I went on a retreat and I asked so many awkward questions that the leader said, 'Look, the man who founded the FWBO lives just up the road, why don't you go and ask *him.*' So I did, I made an appointment and went to see Sangharakshita, and we talked for about two and a half hours, a great philosophical discussion about the nature of reality and so on. I thought, I can't dismiss this. I felt utterly expanded, as if I was at the edge of something that was so much bigger than me, something huge. It was fantastic."

Her boyfriend was finding it difficult helping her to deal with the cancer, as were most of the women in the community. "The Order was very new and idealistic. There was also a split between the men and the women, and there was a bit of a downer on people who had sexual relationships. They didn't know how to deal with me, they were young and healthy, they couldn't help me face a life-threatening illness. Probably I was hard to help too, being in such a panic about it. It must have been difficult for people to get close and give me the support I needed." *How did she cope?* "I went many times to see Sangharakshita. We talked and talked, and he suggested meditations to help me through the illness and the treatment."

Living with the possibility of death changed her. "There was a lot of fear. It brought back all my feeling that life was malevolent, life was against me. 'Here it is again,' I thought, 'I've got to fight it again.' The Dharma was the only thing that made sense of what I was going through.* The idea of impermanence, the fact that everything changes and dies. Yes, there's healing, but nothing can take you back to the place that you were before.

"The other thing I became interested in was acupuncture. I had some acupuncture to help me get over the effect of the anaesthetics and operations, and it worked. I decided to come out of computing and train as an acupuncturist, and eventually I started my own practice.

"I was told at that time that I shouldn't have children because it would make the cancer come back. That was a very strange thing, the concepts of life and death coming together so closely." Had she wanted children? "Not at that time, but years later, in my longest relationship, we planned to have kids. So I went back to the Royal

---

* The sum of Buddhist teaching.

Marsden for advice. 'Oh!' they said. 'Did they tell you not to have children then? That wouldn't be our advice now.' We tried to conceive but nothing happened. It put a great strain on the relationship.

"At first the relationship was great, it was the first taste I'd had of some sort of happy normality and stability living with a partner. But it became difficult. Here was me, not having babies but going off all the time to retreats and getting ordained as a Buddhist. The urge to be ordained seemed very much connected with the urge to have a child, they were both very life-affirming."

At this point I need some clarification. Ordination, in the Christian way, means being set apart as a priest. "No, Buddhist ordination into the Western Buddhist Order doesn't have to mean that. It means a commitment to the 'three jewels,' as we call them: the Buddha, the ideal of human enlightenment; the Dharma, the teachings which aid our spiritual growth; and the Sangha, the community of people practising the teachings.

"My partner wasn't religious at all. He was a scientist and a musician. We were going on in our different ways, I coped by compartmentalizing things, and he didn't tell me he was unhappy. But I went for a few weeks to Australia because my mother had a heart attack-stroke, and he met me at the airport when I came back and said, 'I want to end the relationship and I don't want to talk about it.'

"After ten years! It was incredibly shocking. Devastating. He'd got nobody else. For him it was just over.

"Looking back, I think he found it difficult that I was so absorbed in something so outside of him. He was unable to talk about how he was feeling about what I was doing.

"Things then got really bad. I was homeless and had to stay in many different places. It was difficult to keep my work together. I became depressed, and I had some therapy with another Buddhist who'd trained in psychosynthesis.

"At last I began to look at some of the Jewish stuff. I read about the Second Generation phenomenon* and I could see the wider context of some of the things I'd been feeling. I began to understand my father more, and forgive him for leaving us. I could get my life more into focus."

* An association of children of Holocaust survivors.

Community and relationship

One important issue in her Buddhist life has been the question of individualism and conformity. So we return to the practical and emotional questions around community.

Dayachitta* had been living alone for a couple of years when one day a friend came round and put a cup down in the wrong place. "I caught myself thinking, 'She shouldn't put that there!' and I realized I was getting set in my ways. I needed to live with people again. But I'd tried living with sexual partners and it hadn't been right for me. I'd tried living in large communities and that wasn't right for me either. So what about a smaller community?"

She moved to Cambridge, which was near enough to London to keep her acupuncture practice there going part-time but also establish a practice nearby, and established this mini-community. Each of the three community members puts £15 in the pot for food, they each cook an evening meal once a week, and they each have a particular household job. "We have a community night once a week. That's when we get together, whether to talk or to meditate together or to go to the movies."

Is it anything like the communities she used to live in? "In some ways. But there are no fixed rules for a Buddhist community. Each one makes its own rules and boundaries.

"The women who live here work for Windhorse Trading, a Buddhist Right Livelihood business that has its headquarters in Cambridge. It runs on co-operative lines, 'each gives what they can, each gets what they need'."

But that's Marxism!

"Yes, and it's a Buddhist tradition as well, from way back in time. At Windhorse the managing director, if he's single, might earn less than a warehouse worker with a big family. Recently I've decided to give up some of my acupuncture and work half-time at the Cambridge Buddhist Centre. That's me the individualist setting some of my non-essential needs aside for the sake of the community."

Do they have conflicts in the house? "Sure. But you've got to

---

* She was given this name on becoming ordained.

keep talking about it. The Buddhist thing is to try and reach con-
sensus. That doesn't mean you all have to agree, but if you mildly
disagree you might go along with a decision for the sake of the
greater good."

Questions of morality and causation

*I want to ask Dayachitta more about the relevance of the Buddhist
teachings to her life. Did she, for instance, feel that the cancer
had been given her as a result of her actions in a past life?*

"No. Some of the people I knew offered me the idea of karma
in that sense, but it didn't feel right to me. Everything I'd come
across so far in the Dharma had felt good, expansive, but this attitude wasn't. It felt dreadful, punishing. So I started reading
around it — I've got this rational side, this scientific side that
insists on looking into things — and I found that in Buddhist
thinking there are five aspects of conditionality, the five Niyamas.
Karma, the result of your own actions, is only one of them. There
are others, like the tree that falls on you or the microbes that
attack you and so on. What happens to you could be the result of
any of those things. If I'd stuck with the concept of karma alone
as it was given me, I'd never have stayed with Buddhism."[1]

So there is free will? "Certainly. But it's not total free will.
There'll be things that are beyond my control. The sun might suddenly explode and I'd have no control over that, obviously. But
the area of free will that I do have is where spiritual progress can
be made."

*I'm struck by the way she tests everything, not only against her
own standard of truth but against her own experience and needs.
She is in a relationship, but he doesn't live with her. She doesn't
want to live with him?* "No. Again, I've tried that several times but
these days I prefer to live separately from my partner." But they
are in a real sense partners? "I think so. We have a lots in common, with our mutual passion for the Buddhist life, and we're
also committed to a monogamous relationship. It's very important
to me, because of my various experiences, to decide that I won't
sleep with anyone else. Obviously I can't be sure my partner
won't go off with anyone else, but he knows that I would like the
same commitment from him and he has agreed, for the time being

anyway! The Buddhist commitment is to kindness, contentment and skilfulness in sexual relationships, not to a rigid set of rules."

But does she take advice from more experienced Buddhists, from leaders, or gurus? "Sangharakshita is my spiritual teacher. Almost everything he's said to me in the past has made sense to me. So if he says something that doesn't make sense, I'll give it more weight, more time, before I turn it down. But still I may turn it down if, after trying it out and trying to understand it and discussing it with others, I just can't see the sense of it. At the same time I'll remain open to it, because I could still be wrong."

Within the movement, she's not rejected for being arrogant?

"Hopefully not! If the movement ever gets like that, not being open to disagreement, I'll be off. It works both ways: I have to accept when I'm in the wrong, when people come to me and say, 'Come on, you're not being kind to these people or whatever, you've got to sort it out with them.'

"In the end people must be free to make up their own minds. Sangharakshita encourages peer discussion, he's not a guru in the sense that he expects everyone to do exactly as he says or to adore him blindly. He's getting older now, he's in his seventies and he's withdrawing, letting go."

Gifts and visions

We return to the question of trust. That seems to lie at the heart of Dayachitta's journey, at the heart of her recovery from feeling that the world is malevolent. "I can believe now in people's basic good will, and if they go wrong, in their ability to salvage the situation. An important element in Buddhism is, if you possibly can, not to blame people. Maybe they were wrong, or I was wrong, but we were doing our best."

So life can be trusted?

"There are different sorts of trust. There's naive trust: James Hillman* writes wonderfully about that, about betrayal, the sense you have of being betrayed when you've trusted too naively. One way through that is what we do in puja.† In a section focusing on

---

* The originator of post-Jungian "archetypal psychology."

† Puja: a devotional ritual.

confession, you acknowledge that you and others get things wrong, and you or someone else got clobbered by that, so you forgive yourself for your ignorance or unskilful actions, and you forgive the other person too. It takes away the blame. It's a middle way between naiveté and cynicism. Hillman says you need to have experienced betrayal to understand that. You have to come out of the Garden of Eden."

There's a transformative quality about Dayachitta's story, and about her demeanour in telling it. I ask her if she still sometimes gets angry. She laughs. "Oh yes!" But she hasn't allowed her anger to run her life. She refuses to be a victim, to become part of the hierarchy of virtue and blame. Again and again she says, "It was bad at times, yes. But — excepting Nazis and others like them — I think they were doing the best they could at the time. Buddhism says that human beings behave largely out of greed, hatred and ignorance, and if they don't behave this way it's a sign of spiritual progress.

"In the end you've got to tread your own path. No one can do it for you. But I've learned that there is something bigger and better than me out there. Some people may call it God, but that doesn't mean much to me. Maybe it's the power of other people's practice. One thing that has helped me to move away from my individualistic self-determining position is my meditation practice.

"I once had a kind of vision in meditation, when I was sitting in front of my shrine and suddenly it was as if the walls dissolved, and it was as big as the Festival Hall, and in it were all the bodhisattva-type figures,* and people like myself walking around, and I wandered in and I could sit at anyone's feet. It was this whole new world open to the archetypes, offering me wisdom, and I could take it when I was ready for it."

It's a wonderfully generous vision, and the feeling of generosity continues as Dayachitta shows me the works of art hanging on the walls. "Many of them were given me by people as payment for acupuncture treatment. Look: this one's a mermaid, and here's an angel. I'm really into angels, things with wings. This one here, it's very archetypal, very visionary ..." *So gradually I take my leave, taking with me a vibrant vision and a hard-won sense of trust.*

---

* *Bodhisattva,* an archetypal enlightened being who is motivated by altruism.

Adam Curle

Surely it's his duty as a citizen, never mind as a spiritually minded human being, to tell killers and terrorists that what they're doing is wrong? "I try and see beyond the uniformed or scowling or aggressive individual who's standing in front of me. I try to see the person in their true, full spiritual nature, and realize that what they're doing is unworthy of that nature."

"I can't believe in a personal God. That implies a dichotomy, an opposition, a separation. To me the universe and everything in it is a vast system of interlocking sub-systems. It includes us all, right down to the smallest sub-atomic particle."

From the Somme to the Hydra

Adam Curle has held chairs in psychology, education and development studies at the universities of Exeter, Harvard, and Ghana, and from 1973–78 he was the first Professor of Peace Studies at the University of Bradford. He has worked as a mediator and promoter of peace in India and Pakistan, Nigeria/Biafra, South Africa, Zimbabwe, Northern Ireland and Sri Lanka, and is now helping to set up peace groups and trauma counselling facilities in Bosnia and Croatia. He is active in the Religious Society of Friends (Quakers) and reveres the teaching of the Dalai Lama of Tibet.

I know that Adam Curle has been a mediator in most of the major wars of the second half of the twentieth century, and there's an element of relief as I come in to his south London house. It's not hung with posters declaring that war is wrong, or decorated with photos of Adam shaking hands with dignitaries from around the world. I sink on to a comfy sofa and am plied with Anne's coffee and home-made cakes.

The details of Adam's work as a mediator and a theoretician of conflict resolution are well documented.[1] What he has to say about the origins of violence and the subtle ways in which we might realize (in the sense of "make real") our spiritual nature are striking and important, and I will return to them. But what kept cycling and recycling round my mind after my interview with Adam were certain moments of revelation which have come to him, vividly but not as visions, clearly but not as voices, quietly prompting a change of direction or a further opening of his heart. I was also left with an undeniable sense, paradoxically entwined with these promptings towards change, that his life is a coherent whole, like a complex fabric being unfolded with steady purpose. The moments of spiritual prompting and clarity also hang in tension, especially in the early years, with times of anxiety, unhappiness and confusion.

Adam begins right at the beginning: 4 July, 1916. The pivotal point of the Great War. Four days after the British infantry went over the top and lost 20,000 dead on the first day of the battle of the Somme, Cordelia Curle gave birth to a son, Adam, in a hospital behind the lines.

Why there? "She loved France and wanted to be there." *How was she able to travel at such a time?* "Oh, you could travel." *Where was his father?* "He didn't want anything to do with it. As soon he heard she was pregnant he vanished off to Africa on some journalistic job and came back a few years later." *But why did this remarkable woman go to the Somme at the time of the massacre to give birth, on her own, to her only child?* "Her three brothers were fighting in this terrible war. She wanted to be close to the scene of the action."

Three years later, in 1919, his mother took her toddler back to the battle-fields. She walked him up and down the trenches and what remained of the over-turned metalwork and gouged-out landscapes of war, for him to learn what war was and find it unthinkable that such events should ever occur again.

Spirit and body

One of Adam's first moments of insight came during his time in North Africa in the year before war broke out. He had gone to New College, Oxford, to study History, where his uncle, the historian H.A.L. Fisher, was warden. (Other branches of the family lead off to names like Virginia Woolf and Ralph Vaughan Williams; he spent many holidays with the Vaughan Williamses as a child.)

"I found my tutors boring — they were called Legg and Ogg, and inevitably we nicknamed them Logg and Egg — and a Civil Service career was mapped out for me and that looked like a continuation of boredom. I discovered there was the new discipline called Anthropology, and decided to cross over."

He was invited to Egypt to accompany the man who later became Professor of Anthropology at Oxford, and was able to roam freely in the desert among nomads and dervishes. "They called them 'primitive peoples' in those days," notes Adam wryly. "They understood far more about how to run a good society than we do. They respected people who were generous or pious, or who remembered the people's history or told a good story. No one bothered if they were rich or poor.

"It was one dervish who gave me an insight that I've never lost. He asked me if I'd like to have immunity from snake bites. I said yes, and took part in a ceremony. He went into a trance, put one snake round my neck and gave me the head to hold. Then he made another snake bite my ear. Then, while reciting Sufic charms, he smeared the blood from my ear over my forehead and ankle."

But wasn't he afraid of being bitten and poisoned?

"No. I'd already had a glimpse of this man's power. I'd seen him pick up a scorpion, which then whipped round its tail and stung him on the wrist. Immediately he cursed it and threw it to the ground, and as soon as it hit the ground it was dead, and ants came and carried it away."

And the insight?

"That there are forces in the world that we may not understand, but we must still respect them."

Another example of an inexplicable physical phenomenon came many years later in connection with one of the most important individuals in Adam's life, the Dalai Lama of Tibet. He had already met the Dalai Lama several times and realized the importance of his teachings,[2] and on this occasion he was talking to one of the Dalai Lama's officials in preparation for a Tibetan Buddhist initiation the next day.

"While we were talking I felt ill, and began to get vomiting and diarrhoea. It was so violent that I knew there was no way I could attend the empowerment ceremony the next day. But next morning I woke up and I was perfectly well."

What had happened?

"I was told that when the Dalai Lama is nearby, powerful spiritual forces are swirling around that can produce physical reactions of this sort. They cleanse the body in order to make you receptive to the empowerment."

The necessity of alertness

South Africa, 1961. Adam had begun to get to know some members of the African Resistance Movement. As an academic he was able to travel freely, and he had agreed to act as courier for sensitive information and documents. Then he was invited, with his wife Anne, their baby daughter Deborah and his elderly mother Cordelia (known affectionately as Cork), to stay in South Africa for some time with one of his friends.

"There came one of those incidents that unfortunately seem to typify this century," said Adam. "The sharp rap on the door in the middle of the night, the brutal hand on the shoulder: 'Get a move on, you. He's waiting'."

It was the South African Secret Police. One of his poems describes one of them like this:

... gross with authority,
a mauling beast with male suspects,
capable of strangling an obstinate
prisoner in the cells bare handed,
yet somehow shifty, ill at ease with women ...[3]

They took him in for interrogation and for a month they questioned him about his contacts in the ARM. They didn't keep him overnight, but came day by day to fetch him: "in fact Cork had no idea what was going on, she thought I was ill and was going off to hospital each day." *He was actually ill for some days, with kidney stones, and had to go into hospital. The Secret Police arrived at his bedside to carry on their interrogation.* "But Anne fought them off. She was like a lioness. She chased them away."

But the illness and the pain were minor elements compared with the effort of concentration. "It was so exhausting. I was terrified I'd forget which lies I'd told and they'd trip me into revealing the names and whereabouts of my friends."

Did he feel the presence of some power greater than his own? Of God?

"No. Just this intense concentration on being alert. I knew I had to keep up a front of complete innocence. I told the most involved

tales ..." *Such as?* "Oh, they'd say, 'You know Bill Jones?' 'Yes,'
I'd say, 'he's a good friend of mine.' 'What's he like?' 'Oh, bit of
a left-winger, is Bill.' And I'd tell them all sorts of things: true
things, about what I knew of this Bill Jones. Then they'd lean forward and demand, 'Right! Where is he now?' 'Oh, I'm dreadfully
sorry (I'd say), he passed away about five years ago.' They were
furious — 'We asked you about Bill *Jones*!' 'But I *told* you about
Bill Jones! I'm sorry it wasn't the Bill Jones you were thinking
of. I'm trying to be as helpful as I can ...'

"Oddly enough," Adam says, "the best preparation for these
ordeals — though not one I'd recommend to anyone — was my
school at Charterhouse.* I hated it there. I was utterly miserable.
At Charterhouse I learnt what it was to be a victim, to be ignorant
and powerless." *Did he just accept it?* "Yes. I accepted the whole
system because I'd no inkling of what I could do to resist it. Or
even handle it better."

Movement towards the mystical

*Anyone who was adult in the 1960s will remember with horror the
Nigerian war against secessionist Biafra. The term "Biafra
baby" was used for a decade or more to denote an image of utter
starvation and desolation.*

Into this war Adam Curle went, with two other Quaker peace
workers. He had joined a multi-racial meeting of Quakers in
Ghana in 1959 and been involved in medical, educational and
feeding schemes there. Now he was to mediate between Lieu-
tenant-General Gowon, head of the mainly Northern Nigerian
government, and the leaders of the largely Igbo rebels in Biafra.

Wasn't he afraid? "Yes. But I find that if I try to accept that my
life isn't important, that's the key to staying alert. It means that
I'm not swayed by the human instinct for self-preservation, so I
can concentrate on the task in hand."

Their first task was to go and see General Gowon. "He was
courteous, and told us the government position. When we said we
were going to fly to Biafra to see the rebel leaders he said, 'I
wouldn't advise it. Your plane will be regarded as an illegal rebel

---

* A major English "public" i.e. independent school.

plane and our forces will be under orders to shoot it down.' We said we were willing to take that risk.

"When we got to Biafra we talked with the rebel leaders. They were courteous too, and told us their position. Then back, again by the most devious route, to Gowon. He was glad to see us and impressed that he'd heard nothing at all on Biafran radio about our visit. So he was convinced that we were simply working for the sake of peace and not for personal advantage. Most vitally, he could see we understood how necessary confidentiality is when you're negotiating for peace. So back and forth we went, telling each other the truth of the other side's position as accurately as we could."

But how could each side appreciate the other's position when they were killing them in such numbers? "I'll give you an example. On one of our visits to Biafra they took us to a market place where a single cluster bomb had killed one hundred and twenty-eight women and their children. When I next saw General Gowon I told him how tragic I thought this was. 'Well,' he said, 'maybe it will convince them that rebellion doesn't pay.' 'And so?' I asked. 'So they will lay down their arms.' 'But,' I said, 'the Biafran leaders aren't doing that. They're giving out propaganda saying, It's genocide, those people want to wipe us out as a nation.' 'But that's not true!' said Gowon. 'No,' I said, 'but tragedies like that market place bombing make them *think* it's true. It makes them think that if the only alternative is to be butchered in their beds, they may as well go on fighting for victory.' And he understood."

When, quite suddenly, the war ended, Adam was absolutely sure there'd be massacres. "The Commonwealth Secretary General asked me to go back to see what I could do, because I knew the leadership on both sides and might possibly be able to do something to prevent a bloodbath. I went full of dread. What could I do — stand like a traffic cop between two advancing armies and try to stop them?

"But it was wonderful. There weren't massacres. They treated each other like brothers. Nigerian soldiers drove wounded Biafrans to the nearest medical centre. Food was given out — even the Nigerians' own rations — and money, too. There were no rapes. The rebel leaders weren't imprisoned. One friend of

mine was reinstated on his old salary. There was a passionate
desire to rebuild the country."

But how did this happen?

"Well, no one can be sure. It seemed like a miracle. But some
people told us that those efforts we made to explain one side to
the other did actually change perceptions: it helped them to see
the other side as real people. General Gowon was a generous man
at heart. We had helped him to see through the haze of violence
that's bred in time of war and allowed some of his generosity to
filter down to his commanders in the field."

*This experience gave him, through the sense of joyous relief, a
knowledge that he needed to move from a Quaker activist way of
life to something more mystical. How did that knowledge come?*

"I heard an inner voice saying, 'Now is the time to look to your
inner life.' So I began very consciously to search. First Anne and
I explored Subud.* Then I discovered spiritual riches in Gurdjieff
and Ouspensky that I'd first come across as a young man.†

Then eventually I came to the teachings and the personality of
the Dalai Lama."

Interconnectedness

*One of the ironies of Adam's life is that though he has been a life-
long peacemaker, he also served in the armed forces in World War
II. It was a time in his life when he felt spiritually and emotionally
"on ice," and because of his qualifications he was invited to go
into Military Intelligence. His mother, who had been so determined her son would turn against war, saw no contradiction in this
either. They both knew the terrible consequences of Fascism, and
they both understood that life cannot always take a straight path.*

*Adam's first professional job was to do research with prisoners
of war in 1945. In the course of this work he saw the psychological damage caused, not only by the violence of war, but also by*

* A movement founded by an Indonesian student of Sufism. Its spiritual practice
allows the power of God to express itself through unrestrained physical activity.

† Gurdjieff was a Greco-Armenian mystic and philosopher who held that human life
was similar to sleep, but with work this state of sleep could be transcended and vital-
ity and awareness acquired. Ouspensky introduced Gurdjieff's teachings to a Western audience.

the humiliation and guilt that was caused by capture and the pro-
longed violence of imprisonment. "Today they'd call it Post Traumatic Stress Disorder. In another sense it's a grave example of the
sort of 'soul wound' we all have. In small doses this soul wound
stops us making real relationships, and in extreme cases makes us
terribly cruel.

"It reminded me of what I'd felt when I first took up anthropology and went to live for some time among the Lapps. We were
going up into the hills to herd reindeer, and all the time I felt
acutely miserable and uncomfortable. Everything the Lapps did
rubbed me up the wrong way. But then one morning it all cleared.
I could see that their ways were perfectly all right for them, just
as mine were for me. Though when I got home my old way of life
irritated me in exactly the same way! And that too passed in a
short while."

From this he learnt lessons about how alienation from familiar
things and people can make you judgmental, fearful and then vio-
lent. "Our century has been so full of these dislocations. It makes
us forget that we're all part of one another."

Adam wasn't born with a sense of inter-connectedness; it grew
in him over long years, and has come to him especially vividly at
certain periods of his life. One such period was in the 1960s when
he was professor of Education and Development at the University
of Harvard in Cambridge, Massachusetts.

"People tend to deride the sixties now, with its flower power
and its drugs. But for me it was a time of great openness, of readi-
ness to make leaps of understanding. In America we were all facing the gigantic tragedy of the Vietnam War, with hundreds of
thousands of Americans and Vietnamese dying for no good reason. I was challenged by my students. They told me I came from
the most privileged of positions: secure, rich, white, male. I
looked at myself, my family with its connections, my lack of
appreciation of everything that women did for me and for society,
the unearned advantage my race gave me. I realized that all the
time I'd been trying to be part of the solution, actually I was part
of the problem. I hated racism and sexism, of course, but I'd been
superior, sexist, racist, too. As a father and as a teacher I'd
imposed my whims and predilections on children and young
people who couldn't do anything but agree with me. I saw that

'development,' which for a long time had been my academic line, was often the source of conflicts rather than the healer of them. I'd played my own part in creating violent situations."

Was this a painful realization?

"It was liberating. It helped me see that everyone is linked, spiritually: that when you do harm to others you do harm to yourself as well."

Adam talks a good deal about the "Three Poisons" of Tibetan philosophy: ignorance, greed and hatred. "We're ignorant of our true spiritual nature, and this cuts us off from other people. Then we feel unsatisfied, so we get greedy, we rely on possessions or youth or good health to make us feel good. Then we feel desperate because other people have these things when we don't, and because the things we're relying on all fade.

"The Dalai Lama opened the doors of reality for me. He has also given me very wise advice, for instance when I was starting to work in the Sri Lankan conflict. I think he's one of the few people, like Jesus and Gandhi, who truly manifest non-violence in their very being."

The story of how he met the Dalai Lama is both funny and instructive. "I was chairing a discussion group at a conference on education, and he was a member. Scary circumstances — how does one 'chair' the Dalai Lama? I'd told the others they must keep their contributions short, but they prima-donna'd like anything, they just bashed on and on. The Dalai Lama was charming and modest and listened intently. On and on they went, like waterfalls. What should I do? If I didn't shut them up the Dalai Lama would be late for his next appointment, if I did shut them up it would cause a row ..."

I leaned forward for the dramatic end to this tale: how did he solve this dilemma?

But typically Adam defused my excitement. "Somehow I found a Buddhist middle way, and it was all right."

Many elements

There have been many ingredients in the development of Adam's spiritual philosophy. As well as Subud and the work of Gurdjieff and Ouspensky, he has gained insights through psychologists such as Freud, Melanie Klein, Erik Erikson, Jung, and especially through Erich Fromm. His Quaker life brought him into practical peacemaking; he has written a poem about the Quaker belief in "the essential goodness of / Our being, exploring its deeps / Together in worship."[4]

An image dear to Adam's heart is that of Indra's net.* "The legend of Indra's heaven is that it contains an endless net, and at each intersection of this net there's a bead representing a life. Each bead reflects every other, and each one is reflected by every other. I think it's a wonderful way of describing the way everything we do has consequences, even what we eat, what we buy, whether we smile or frown, or how we behave even casually and to strangers."

"I've also learnt from people who aren't religious at all. I once met a young Westerner who, in Calcutta at the time of the Watergate scandal, was in a crowded taxi and suddenly felt a tremendous sense of identification first with his fellow passengers, then with everyone else in the world, including Richard Nixon. 'I couldn't be hostile to Nixon,' he said, 'because in a sense I *was* Nixon'."

Adam meditates regularly. I ask him, "What are you doing when you meditate?"

His answer isn't a straightforward account of method: "First I steady my breathing, then I count to ten, then I bring into mind people who are in trouble," that sort of thing. He's silent for a while before replying. "I'm trying to see who I am." Silence again. "I'm trying to watch what I'm doing."

He quotes a story from St Francis of Assisi: "He was travelling with his donkey, and got into discussion with another traveller about concentration and prayer. The other man maintained that it was easy. 'I think it's hard,' said Saint Francis. 'If you can say the Lord's prayer through to the end with complete attention, I'll give

---

* Indra is one of the principle Hindu Vedic gods.

you my donkey.' The other man laughed and said, 'The donkey's
as good as mine.' He began: 'Our Father, who art in Heaven,' and
so on, until he came to: 'Thy will be done on earth as it is in
Heaven — and will you give me the saddle as well?'"

Adam's is an intensely practical mysticism. "When the
Tibetans meditate," he says, "the aim is to get rid of the things that
isolate us into individuality, and restore a kind of communal spiritual communication. That's what I'm doing."

Again and again the concept comes up in talking with Adam:
alertness, watchfulness, awareness. He quotes Jesus in the Gar-
den of Gethsemane: "I say unto you, watch." He goes on: "And
take the word 'Buddha.' It comes from the root BUDH, which
implies being watchful, aware. Shankara talks about the 'negli-
gence in recollection' that distracts us from awareness of our
divine nature.* We so easily become half-asleep machines. We
get trapped in illusion, the illusion of separation."

God Questions, or just Questions?

Towards the end of our long talk Adam and I look back and see
that the word "God" has hardly cropped up once. Despite the fact
that the spiritual path underlies the whole of his life, Adam hardly
speaks the language of religion at all. "No, I can't believe in a
personal God. That implies a dichotomy, an opposition, a separation. To me the universe and everything in it is a vast system of
interlocking sub-systems. It includes us all, right down to the
smallest sub-atomic particle. Maybe there is some sort of original
motive force — the Dalai Lama thinks there is — but I haven't
got a name for it. Though I do have an increasing sense of universal holiness."

The paradox of that last comment is that the great questions for
Adam at the moment are about violence, its roots and its cure.
"There seems to be an exponential increase in violence just now,
and it often seems to be without purpose. It's fuelled by rampant
nationalism, or by ethnic awareness in for instance Africa, and by
social dislocation, what sociologists call 'anomie,' here in the
affluent West."

* Shankara (?700–?750) was the most renowned exponent of the Vedanta school of
philosophy.

This preoccupation contradicts, or balances, or lives in tension with, his temperamental optimism. It's counteracted by the awesome courage of friends like Katarina Kruhonja of the Centre for Peace, Non-Violence and Human Rights in Osijek, Croatia, and his peace-working friends in Moscow and Chechnya. He's especially involved at the moment with the establishment of peace groups and trauma counselling schemes in Croatia and Bosnia.

His latest book shows how the "hydra" of inter-communal violence is institutionalized in our economic and hierarchical systems, and that if we are to tame it we must understand that we are the hydra.[5]

I ask him: if you think of enabling everyone, from politicians and powerful business leaders down to ordinary people, to understand this, isn't the task so massive that it would dismay anyone, however peace-oriented and naturally optimistic they might be?

Adam agrees: the immensity of the task is dismaying. But he has practical suggestions for a programme of education to counteract the current false assessment of our needs, and ways to weaken the hydra's hold over our minds. "At the Osijek peace centre a group of workers seem to have moved into a consciousness of each other that I call 'extended mind.' They're conscious not only of each other but of the people around them whose wellbeing is the purpose of their work. It's as if there's a process of feeling and thinking that's not confined to a single body but is in some sense shared. I'm exploring this concept of extended mind. It seems to mean that we can both influence others and be influenced ourselves. Of course this extended mind can be associated with mass violence and cruelty, but it can also lead to large-scale action for peace and justice. At Osijek there's an infectious courage, wisdom and altruism, a sympathetic sensitivity that raises ordinary mind-consciousness to a different level."

I'm struck by the absence of a restless search for capital-M Meaning in Adam's account of his life. The spiritual message is couched in active terms.

"There are lots of ways to be peaceful that can simply be learned. You can learn how to listen, how to avoid ways of speaking that are covertly aggressive — so common in the way we live now — and how to state a case, and to negotiate. Then there are the subtler things, like whether or not you're respectful, whether you have real concern or compassion."

And whether or not you're religious?

"I don't think that matters. It's just about being realistic. If you think human beings are worthy of respect and compassion, then these are the best ways of bringing about what you want to achieve. You need training, and you need systems of support, you need ways of boosting people's courage and enthusiasm."

But what about condemning evil? Surely it's his duty as a citizen, never mind as a spiritually minded human being, to tell killers and terrorists that what they're doing is wrong?

"I can't do that," says Adam. "How could I have preached pacifism to the oppressed blacks of South Africa, for instance? I do tell them, though, that personally I don't believe in violence, that I don't think it's either effective or moral.

"The other thing I do is try and see beyond the uniformed or scowling or aggressive individual who's standing in front of me. I try to see the person in their true, full spiritual nature, and realise that what they're doing is unworthy of that nature."

When it comes to epithets like "courage" and "modesty," it seems to me almost pointless to apply them in Adam's case. It takes super-human courage to do many of the things that Adam has done, and super-human modesty not to dine out on it. Yet the matter-of-factness with which he recounts these episodes points not to faith in the common sense of that term — a conviction that things will turn out, by God's will, for the best — but to acceptance: that things are as they are, and will be as they will be. The task is to concentrate on becoming clear of ego and delusion and on behaving with love and compassion to those around you, simply because that's the wisest thing to do in the circumstances.

I finish by asking Adam two things about his astonishing acceptance of people and events, regardless of their threat to his life and safety. The first is human and worldly. "How does Anne see your peacemaking activities? Isn't she frightened? Doesn't she ask you to stop, for her sake?"

"No," replied Adam. "She accepts entirely what I do. It's wonderful." *The truth of this reply is borne out by the relaxed atmosphere of the time I've spent with Anne and Adam before and after the interview: the meal-times studded with laughter and gossip,*

*the walk round the south London garden which they tend together.
There's no sense of other-worldliness or sanctity here.*

*Which leads me to my other question. "Do you think that
you're an 'old soul' in reincarnation terms? That maybe you've
had many lifetimes before this one, to teach you this way of
being?"*

Again, silence; then a broad grin.

"I don't know. I just don't know. Maybe not. Maybe. Who
knows."

Here is the end of his poem called "Action:"

The real effects of our actions remain hidden.
So why do anything?
There's no option: even to do nothing is to act ...
We must have faith that if we purify our hearts,
making our motives more compassionate,
what we do will strengthen, unimaginably,
the great forces that can save humanity.[6]

Naomi Gryn

"Sometimes God lets us down, too." Oh? Isn't God by definition the One that doesn't let you down? "There are hurricanes, famines, diseases, accidents. Shit happens. What's best for the individual isn't always in the best interests of the collective. We're tied into a constantly evolving ecosystem with God at the helm. Sometimes God acts like a parent, sometimes like a partner, and just like any relationship, sometimes God lets us down."

"It's about how you treat your own pain, and how you treat other people. My people have been treated like vermin, so I don't treat other people like vermin. And unless you integrate the most painful parts of your history it's going to come up again in all sorts of unexpected ways and you're not in a position to control it. I have to be able to understand what's gone on."

A true maverick

Naomi Gryn is a film-maker and writer. She was born on New Year's Eve 1960 in New York, the second daughter of Rabbi Hugo Gryn, who was later rabbi of the West London Synagogue and a much-loved broadcaster. Several of her films and radio programmes have touched on the Holocaust and other Jewish themes. Resident in central London but a frequent visitor to Israel, she loves the Jewish practices that pervade her daily life but allows her spirit to be moved by a wider faith than that devotion implies.

Naomi Gryn and I have only just started talking and already there are half a dozen of her precious photos lying in a pile beside us. Two are icons of her life: one, the front page of an Israeli newspaper dated 26 January, 1994 showing the car in which she was a passenger crushed to less than a metre high under the weight of an overturned articulated lorry; the other, a head-and-shoulders shot of herself and her father wearing dark indistinguishable clothes so that they look like one body with two heads. She tells me, "It was a tight bond. We were very close indeed."

Of the accident in Jerusalem, from which she still gets posttraumatic flashbacks, she says, "It gave me my own experience of survival. My father was a Holocaust survivor, but my knowledge of that was second hand. Now I know what it is to survive a brush with death and experience it as a re-birth."

Naomi's flat is on the fourth floor of a housing co-operative off Marylebone Road in central London: study, bedroom, sitting area and kitchen crammed into one room, hung and draped and scattered with artefacts and photos and mementos from friends and family all over the world. She grinds coffee beans, adds cardamom before putting the coffee maker on the gas stove and sits cross-legged on a cushion, gesturing with long arms and articulate fingers and leaping up every so often for another book or document or picture that will throw light on what she's saying. Once she stops in mid-sentence: "There's the heron!" and we run to the window and gaze at the roof opposite, astonished at the appearance of this huge grey bird in the city centre, and its alertness to specks of moving orange in the garden pond far below.

Father, daughter

Chronology gets little chance in the order of Naomi's account of her thirty-eight years of spiritual enquiry. Yes, her birth was induced four days early in the final hours of 1960 because a $600 dollar tax rebate was being offered by the American government for babies born in that year. Her father ("the most charming and charismatic soul, loved and cherished by everyone who met him") became Rabbi of the West London Synagogue when she was three years old and the area around Baker Street has been her home ever since. She talks with her Lebanese and Iranian neighbours every day because she's known them all her life. On our way to lunch she argues with the Balkan Romany girl who's begging in the street — "No, I won't give you money, but I will give you food" — and tells me the central Romany myth, that the "little Egyptians" (hence Gypsies), when they were in the desert with Moses, refused to give up worshipping the golden calf and so were condemned by God to wander, not forty years like the Jews, but forever.

Naomi begins the story of her life with her father. When and how did he die? "August 1996. He was sixty-six. We got two months' warning. He had three brain tumours, one in the brain stem, diagnosed the day after he officiated at my brother's wedding. The whole family was gathered and my father walked in and said, 'Kids, I've got some bad news.' They didn't try operating, they gave him steroids and radiotherapy, but within two months he developed pneumonia and was then put on a ventilator. That's one of the cruellest things, they give you a paralysing drug to stop you coughing up the pipe shoved into your lungs. So he looked unconscious. But I saw a drop of water on his face and I said, 'He's crying,' and they said 'It's not possible, he's unconscious.' But he was. He was trapped in some degree of consciousness.

"Now this will show you how bonded we were. His shoulders shook, he was agitated, and I put my hand on his forehead to calm him. They whacked up the drugs, and I passed out. *Me, I* passed out! I came round and thought, 'This is really weird.' So I tried it again. And it happened again."

This is where she shows me the picture of the two of them in their "tight bond." And a photo of her brother's son, "the first baby born after my father's death, Isaac Hugo Leonard Gryn, and of course we're all finding it remarkable that aged five months he loves looking at books, and he listens very nicely to Jewish music ... As if this fabulous wise spirit has been travelling down through the centuries ..."

"My father was Super-Dad. He took responsibility for millions, as teacher and guide. However much they asked of him, he always found more to give. I think possibly the most damaging thing he ever did to me was never to let me down! I grew up with this quite unrealistic expectation of people's ethical stamina.

"I was reading something quite recently by James Hillman on betrayal, about the story of Abraham and Isaac, how the father has to let the son down or else the son can't maturate, can't stand on his own feet.[1] And maybe this is why God lets bad things happen to people. I have a veritable catalogue of nightmarish betrayals of trust. I was molested by a doctor when I was a child, I was raped twice, once at sixteen, once at seventeen (I suppose you'd call it date rape), I was in this terrible accident which was the result of poor driving, betrayed by lawyers, insurers and medical professionals ... And there's the usual list of employers, employees, lovers, teachers, friends. Of course I've done my fair share of betraying too. It's as if I've got to learn this very important lesson: that inherent in any relationship of trust is the possibility of betrayal and failure. We all live in fear of rejection and abandonment, but they are realities, we've got to live with them. And sometimes God lets us down, too." *Oh? Isn't God by definition the One that* doesn't *let you down?* "There are hurricanes, famines, diseases, accidents. Shit happens. What's best for the individual isn't always in the best interests of the collective. We're tied into a constantly evolving ecosystem with God at the helm. Sometimes God acts like a parent, sometimes like a partner, and just like any relationship, sometimes God lets us down." *Shit indeed. Naomi goes on,* "The best title I ever heard for a book was: 'A flea's eye view of the dog show.' Sadly the writer died before he finished it."

Discovering the Holocaust

Hugo Gryn used the occasion of each of his four children's bar *and* bat *mitzvah to take them, alone, to Israel.* When it was Naomi's turn in 1974 they travelled to the north, to the south, they met the Prime Minister Golda Meir, and then they visited Yad Vashem, the museum and monument to the victims of the Holocaust. When they passed the small-scale model of Birkenau, her father pointed to one of the barracks and said to her,* "That's where I spent some weeks with my father when I was your age."

Over the years she pieced together his story. "But of course there were things I couldn't ask him." *In fact after his death she realized how much she had backed off asking him, as indeed he backed off asking her about her accident, her own experience of near-death and survival.*

What about her father and Auschwitz? She responds with some weariness, but then starts to articulate it as if counting through until the recitation is complete. "He and his family lived in the Carpathian mountains, a small town called Berehovo. They rounded up the whole Jewish population of the area in 1944. About half of the population of 25,000. Vast resources went into it, even at this stage in the war. A relentless death machine. Processing 10,000 Jews through the gas chambers every day. They were taken to Auschwitz under the pretence they were being resettled in the east to do agriculture. As they were disembarking from the cattle wagons after their three-day journey, this man looking like a lunatic in a striped uniform came by, saying in Yiddish, 'You're eighteen and you have a trade, you're eighteen and you have a trade, you're eighteen and ...' So when my father, who was thirteen, got to the head of the selection line, he said he was nineteen and was a *Tischler und Zimmermann,* carpenter and joiner. And his father brought down *his* age by twenty years and they pretended to be cousins. His eleven-year-old brother also

* Celebrations to mark the child's entry into adulthood: *bar* for a boy, *bat* for a girl.

tried to say he was eighteen, but they sent him straight to the gas chambers, and my father's mother ran after him but was dragged back and watched helplessly as her baby went to his death. So ... My father stayed together with his father, and they were sent in a transport of slave labourers to Lieberose, where they were supposed to be building a resort town for Nazi officers in Ullersdorf, then on a gruesome death march to Sachsenhausen, the kind of journey where 3,000 set off and 800 arrived. From there on to Mauthausen in Austria, then on another death march to Gunskirchen ... And there they were liberated by the Americans on 4 May, 1945.

"He and his father had been together all that time, and they all were starving, and they all had dysentery and typhus, and a few days later his father died."

How did he survive? "He would always say it was just luck, his brother was a much nicer person than he was, the other people who didn't make it were much better people, it was nothing but pure chance.

"And then, like so many others who survived, he was motivated to justify his survival. Plus —" *at this point Naomi's reportage eases up, because this is anecdote rather than enforced narration* — "now I learnt this only after he died: I was in Israel hiding from well-wishers when I heard that a friend, Yossi Czucker, was in town, who'd also been with my father throughout their time in the camps. Yossi was an epileptic, and he'd had a fit on one of the marches, and my father put down his own blanket and carried Yossi for the rest of the day. Which was an amazing thing to do, given the shortage of calories and so on, but anyone who fell by the wayside was shot.

"What Yossi said to me was this: 'You know, it was unheard of for a father and son to survive together in the camps.' Suddenly I understood the profundity of his observation: that my father, uniquely, had had the love and protection of his father throughout their ordeal.

"In fact my father said that his worst moment was when he was caught with a spanner he had stolen, and he was given twenty-five beatings by their captors, and how awful it was for his father to be forced to watch the spectacle. His father must have given him some of his rations and taken care of him in all sorts of ways.

"After all this, he held very little bitterness. Why, I don't know."

This is Hugo's story, not Naomi's, but she accepts that it has made an enormous impact on her own life "I made a film called *Chasing Shadows* about my father going back to his home town, Berehovo, after forty-five years. It was my way of entering directly into my father's memory. But people zeroed in on me as if they were hoping for some kind of perpetuation. What was it like, they asked, to be a victim of the Nazis? And I got very depressed, because it didn't feel like my story. I was asked to record my story for the National Sound Archives when I was thirty-one years old and hadn't had a life yet!

"It's as if some people think that the Holocaust is not a universal story, as if it lies only on the descendants of those people who were directly affected by it. Because people want ... Yes, to *contain* it. People sometimes ask me, 'Why are you always harping on about the Holocaust?' But my father only spoke of it very reluctantly. We were expressly not told about it for many years as kids. I speak of it myself very seldom in public. I'm very nervous of risking the tag of 'victim,' and even worse the tag of 'child of victim.' What a double muting you can give to someone! Just stick a Naomi cardboard cut-out on the table and let that do the job, then everyone else is free to project their own fantasies. My question is this: what possessed White Christian Man to carry on like this, enslaving millions in their empires, wiping out native Americans, Australian aborigines, burning women at the stake? The Jews were just next in line. This is not the Jews' story, it's a universal story."

And how can we go forward from it? How does she go forward from it?

"It's something about how you treat your own pain, and how you treat other people. My own answer to the question, 'How do you go forward from a position where your family were herded into ovens like vermin?' is that you don't treat anyone as vermin."

Like that Balkan girl who was begging, I remark. Naomi had acknowledged the girl's humanity by talking with her, person to person.

She nods. "But it's more than that. Unless you integrate the most painful parts of your history, then it's going to come up again in all sorts of unexpected ways, and you're not in a position to control it. I have to be able to understand what's gone on, in myself and in Judaism.

"But I also have to understand Christianity. How did such hatred emerge? There's the question raised by James Hillman of whether the 'child' religion can mature unless it kills off both its 'parents'."

What does that mean, in this context?

"If you think of Christianity as having been fathered by Jesus and mothered by Jewish culture, then with its central story, the crucifixion, it succeeds in killing one parent and with the Holocaust it almost succeeds in 'killing off' the other parent as well. If Christianity wants to evolve into something more civilized and decent — and I say this as someone who has as one of her 'rabbis' a Methodist minister in Manchester called Kathleen, and I like to think that I'm her 'rabbi' too — then it has to look into its complicity in all manner of dreadful things, including the Holocaust."

Crushed, uncrushed

We breathe deeply to absorb something of the enormity of these questions. Then we move on to her accident in 1994.

How did it happen? "I was working on a documentary series in Israel about the peace process. The night before, my father had called me to say that he'd been diagnosed with prostate cancer, and I was devastated. The next day I had to go with my director and researcher to Jericho, and from there we were to go north to interview Jewish settlers in the Golan. As we were driving round a bend in the road, a huge semi-trailer heading south overturned and its cargo — thirty tons of Jaffa oranges — landed on my head.

"Miraculously, I didn't break anything apart from two back teeth, but I looked like I'd been in a major boxing match and lost. Injuries to my head, back, neck and face left me in agonizing pain for many, many months. Bruising to soft tissue in my brain gave me a throbbing headache that lasted for four years. I couldn't read, write or think coherently and for a while I spoke with a curious stutter.

"At the beginning, I was much more concerned about my father and his cancer. But I knew I was very sick, and that it was more than just a head injury. I called a trusted doctor friend for help. He figured I was suffering from post-traumatic stress disorder and got me to see a wonderful Scottish Jungian psychotherapist called Derry MacDiarmid. I knew it was right to go to a non-Jewish psychotherapist so that I could unload a lot of Jewish stuff, as well as issues about my father and the trauma itself, and I've been going ever since. He guides me through all my complicated paradoxes, helps me to sort my city-rat self from daughter-of-saint self."

In what way did the accident give her an experience parallel to her father's? "I was cast into the role of victim, and I found losing my independence very humiliating. It made me understand what it was like to be reviled for being weak and vulnerable." *She experienced that as a result of being accidentally injured?* "Oh yes. Again and again. Once the clerk in the post office forgot to say good morning to me, and such was my self-loathing and lack of self-worth that I wanted to commit suicide for the rest of the day. I was disfigured and lost all my self-confidence. It was very scary to be around me for a couple of years because my behaviour was so unpredictable. I was an emotional disaster. I dissociated frequently and became very phobic in crowds or noisy places. The insurance company sent private detectives to interview doctors and friends to find out what psychological defects I might have had prior to the accident, how I couldn't possibly have been earning £40,000 a year — a woman! I thought of myself as something of a warrior, I'd proved myself in the television community and triumphed over a catalogue of tragedies and disasters. But what the insurance company hooked onto in the end was that my father was a Holocaust survivor. Every single medical report started with this. Not 'This is Naomi Gryn who was born in New York and was enjoying a happy and successful career until the subject road accident' but 'This is the daughter of a famous Holocaust survivor.' The final psychiatric report concluded that I had been fifty per cent damaged by my father's Holocaust experiences.

"But I refuse to accept victim status. I'm glad I didn't report my rapes. I wouldn't want to be dragged through the courts, an object of pity and sympathy.

"There's something animal in the way we react to trauma. Have you read Peter Levine on healing?[2] Where is it? ... Here.

> 'People who have worked through traumatic reactions fre-
> quently tell me that there is both an animalistic and a spiri-
> tual dimension to their lives afterwards. They are more
> spontaneous and less inhibited in the expression of healthy
> assertion and joy. They more readily identify themselves
> with the experience of being an animal. At the same time,
> they perceive themselves as having become more human.
> When trauma is transformed, one of the gifts of healing is
> a childlike awe and reverence for life'."

*With her accident and her father's death, she was four years in
the wilderness. But an encounter in an actual desert place of
retreat made her come back.* "Another English woman, on hearing my name was Naomi, asked if I was Naomi Gryn. My heart
sank: 'Here we go again, she's going to overwhelm me with sympathy.' Instead it turned out that she was the cousin of a dear
friend, and that her aunt had just died in terrible circumstances.
This was a kind of signal to me, that I couldn't run away, I was
involved. I had to ring my friend to see if she was all right. I had
to go back.

"I find that I get involved in other people's vulnerability. For
instance, when I saw the dreadful poverty and degradation of the
Palestinian refugee camps in Gaza, I related it to the photographs
of Jews in the Warsaw ghetto during the last war. I want to build
bridges across this divide, to look at the culture of the 'enemy'
people and understand what makes them smile and what gives
them pain. So, with Yasmin Alibhai-Brown, I set up Daughters of
Abraham, which is a forum for Jewish and Muslim women. And
not surprisingly we're discovering what a lot we've got in common, and what a lot we've got to learn. Maybe together we can
forge a voice that's loud enough to make a contribution towards
ending the violence between our warring communities."

Jewishness as family and tribe

"My father's mission," Naomi says, "was to try and find ways to make his cherished Jewish heritage relevant to the modern world. Mine is to find my own spiritual path in a Jewish way.

"Growing up I had three wardrobes: my school wardrobe, my Synagogue wardrobe, and one that was 'me.' At school, Queen's College in Harley Street, as the representative Jewish girl I would be called into the head's study at the beginning of every school year and asked the dates of Jewish holidays, and I was very careful to give only the dates that Reform Jews observe, rather hoping that the Orthodox Jewish girls might get into trouble because they always had to take two days for each of our one."

Really? Fomenting conflict at that age?

"Oh yes. Day One at that school, my now longest-enduring friend, Caroline, jumped me from the wall bars of the gym, and we had a total dog-and-cat fight on the floor of the gym because she was Orthodox and I was Reform. We had to. Animal to animal. We literally fought it out and concluded that we were equal. Again, it's our animal nature. We've got that as well as a spiritual nature. We must hold on to that truth.

"I was a spiritual child, I suppose, and a great show-off. At the age of ten I was leading the children's services at my father's synagogue. I gave my first sermon at fifteen on the subject of Messianism. If you'd asked me what I wanted to be when I grew up I'd have said, 'The first woman rabbi.' But then someone pipped me to the post and I lost interest."

She studied what, where? "Philosophy of Science at LSE (London School of Economics). I had a wonderful time there. A nonstop party. My posse, if you like, was the LSE unofficial fifth football team, the Cosmos. Academically, the philosophy lecturers spent three years trying to bash God out of me. I knew that they were simply looking in the wrong place: they were hanging on to a very childish notion of an entirely trustworthy father-like figure who sits up in the heavens and smiles benignly. I countered it privately, not loudly, but I could counter it because every Friday I'd see my father in his position of spiritual authority, whether in the synagogue or at the head of our dining table, and he had this very fleshed-out God, with emotions like compassion and anger and humour and justice and imagination. That was my God, that was my world. And he instilled in me a great love of Jewish ideas and values.

"I relearnt my Jewishness as an adult, though, with a friend Geraldine who converted. For five years I tried to answer all her questions and doubts. Finally I went with her and her children to Cardiff, then the only place where non-orthodox women could have their *mikveh,* the ritual bath before conversion. I saw the Jewish faith through the eyes of someone coming new to it, and again a few years later when my brother's wife, Jane, became Jewish."

The workings of God

"My father's dying, for me, seemed just like giving birth but with an inversion of all the emotions. A child delivering her father to death. And it was my deepest insight into the workings of God.

"On the first Saturday afterwards, it was Shabbat, and I didn't know what to do with myself. I certainly didn't want to go to synagogue, with everyone staring at me. I went to Victoria and caught the train to Brighton. I stood on the beach, staring out to sea, and I said the morning prayers. Then I walked around, and I saw in the eyes of the people around me not the fear and hatred I'd seen after my accident, but pure love. I had this very clear thought, and it's still with me now, about God: that He's a cosmic stage manager, who causes our paths to cross, and gives us all these opportunities. We are His partners in the ever-unfolding story of creation and we can embrace these opportunities or not, that's our free will."

"Stage manager": doesn't that seem manipulative?

"Well, when I want to describe the ways of God I use a vocabulary that's familiar to me. Stage manager, script writer, storyteller, these are the sort of terms I use every day when I'm filming, so I think of God in those terms too."

Could she try and find words for God?

"My grasp on God is constantly shifting, and always full of contradictions. Sometimes it's a distinctly male energy, which combines with a feminine energy that's more physical, mirrored in every act of creation. But at other times I think of God as being the whole show, God as eternity and infinity and everything in it, all the colours in the rainbow and the spectrum too. Like a beam of white light refracted through a glass prism.

"I had a discussion with my father about this a couple of months before he died. It was one of those incredible God-given moments. I had been unexpectedly struck with a post-traumatic stress disorder flip-out, and my parents were just about to leave for a health farm, and they asked if I wanted to come too. So I had these precious four days with my father, not realizing that within a month he would be diagnosed as terminally ill. He and I went for a walk in the forest, and I was saying, 'Dad, how can anyone deny the power of God when they see how these ferns unfurl every spring just as they've done for millions of years?' He laughed and said, 'Naomi, I'm getting worried about you, you're sounding rather pantheistic!' and I realized that we had very different ideas about God, that his was a purely intellectual energy whereas my God goes belly-dancing.

"Then a deer ran across our path, and my father's Hebrew name 'Zvi' means 'deer,' and it was so beautiful the way we and it gazed at each other. A moment of recognition. Dad and I decided that this marked the end of our walk and headed back. In hindsight, it was as if he was being called back to the place where everything comes from. The next day, over a lettuce-leaf lunch, for no apparent reason I asked my parents what they'd each like as their epitaph, and my father chose the words from Micah: 'Do justice, love mercy, and walk humbly with your God'."

And what would she choose for her own epitaph? "Oh, 'A true maverick.' I live in dread that someone will write, 'She was a dutiful daughter'!"

Spirituality and integrity

"I love those moments when we glimpse infinity, the thrill of revelation. I was staying on a Greek island, maybe ten years ago, it was a beautiful sunny day, I was on a ferry and there was a red rock rising from the blue ocean, and I understood with a clarity I could never hope for, 'I *am* the rock!' Like the deer and the ferns, that's also our relationship with God. We are all part of the totality."

Does her faith also include forgiveness?

"Yes. If someone says they're sorry. But you can only be sorry on one's own behalf. You can't ask for, or give out, blanket absolutions. Saying sorry is what Jews do during the ten days of penitence between Rosh Hashanah and Yom Kippur. And forgiveness in our day can be done in conjunction with psychotherapy. I think that psychotherapists are latter-day priests. They are there to help us come to terms with our pain and resolve feelings like anger and guilt.

"I understand so clearly the text 'Vengeance is mine, saith the Lord, I will repay.' It's never my responsibility to take revenge. It is always done on my behalf, if it's warranted. What's necessary for me is to shake off the binds of regret or anger. You say that's a Buddhist principle as well? Even though anger is very necessary and appropriate in small doses, it's destructive if you hang on to it. It implodes. I had eczema for many years, and I think it was unexpressed anger, but in the months following my father's death I was so unabashedly angry that the eczema vanished."

After her father's death, a healer she consulted described how she had previously accessed God through her father. "At first I felt disenfranchised and entirely disaffiliated from the Jewish world. The funeral was a pompous, stately affair, not at all what my father would have wanted for himself — he was always a modest, humble man. In a letter that was leaked to the press, the Chief Rabbi of England declared my father to be a destroyer of the Jewish faith, and a national scandal ensued. Meanwhile in Israel I saw Orthodox Jews throwing dirty nappies at non-Orthodox women who had supposedly dressed inappropriately and passing laws against non-Orthodox conversions to Judaism. I felt marginalized by the Israeli legal profession as the daughter of a Holocaust survivor, and in England my whole family were roasting under the glare of public attention which always makes me horribly uncomfortable.

"So from that point of total cut-off I've had to find a way back. It starts with how I relate to God. I realized how many occasions I'd been given to be close to my father before his death, and with what kindness God had stolen my father back from me. Maybe He was bored with His available after-dinner conversation and asked Himself, 'Who can I bring up here to entertain me? Ah! I'll have Hugo Gryn!' But then He realized, 'That's the worst possible thing I could do to Naomi.' So —" and here she ticks off on her fingers again — "He very kindly sent this truck to fall on my head, just the accident that I needed, so I could find just the right psychiatrist to see me through, get the right insight into trauma and loss, so that I might survive the death of my father and find my way back. It was also just big enough to stop me in my tracks, rethink my manic lifestyle so that now I can re-emerge as a creature with much more space for tranquillity and reflection."

Is that all God's work? Does she not believe in chance at all?

"Not really. Sometimes when I'm feeling unsure of things I visit an astrologer or draw Tarot cards. Cosmic career guidance is how I think of all that. I find all sorts of implausible symbolism for things that happen. It's the poetry that saves daily life from tedium. The man I've just been going out with, for instance: the photos he took of me came out blurred, the fish we were rearing together all died, so did the plant he bought me, all signs and wonders that it wouldn't work out!

"To be honest I'd rather not know what the tide is bringing. I prefer to let it all gradually unfold and not grip too tightly onto dreams and ambitions. To quote Rabbi Nachman of Bratslav, the important thing is not to be afraid. My favourite line in Jewish liturgy is from the song we always end the Shabbat morning service with, the *Adon Olam: 'Adonai li v'lo ira* — in my God I will not fear.' Basically it's God who's in charge of my life. Stage manager, carer, God of the whole world, of all things. Do you know the story *Footprints in the Sand*? I don't know who wrote it. It's about a dream where there are two sets footprints in the sand, and the writer knows that it's God walking with him. But at the worst times in life there's only one set, and when he asks God why He left his side, the Lord replies, 'My child, in your time of trial I was carrying you.'

"I find the rhythm of my life through the Jewish calendar. That's partly why I love being in Israel so much, and also because there I'm not the daughter of Rabbi Hugo Gryn, I'm just Naomi the film-maker from London. I love how on Friday everyone, religious or not, rushes home to get ready for Shabbat and how before the Passover the whole country is gripped by a frenzy of spring-cleaning. Though I certainly wouldn't want to raise children as Jewish in a world where you have to bow down to the will of the rabbis. I'd find it suffocating if I had to live in an entirely Jewish environment. Judaism has oppressed women terribly. I'd like to storm all the synagogues in England and hold up the Torah scroll and shout, 'Come on, people, this is yours! Take it!'

"My Jewishness is family. It's a tribal thing. My spirituality is my own, and it's influenced by lots of other cultures. Sometimes the Jewishness and the spirituality connect, sometimes they don't. There's this still small voice, the intuition and the inspiration that transforms our lives from the mundane into the mystical and magical. But there's also the discipline, the moments of prayer when we reaffirm our willingness to offer our services to man's eternal partnership in the work of creation, asking for the necessary tools, the strength to carry out our tasks, to fulfil our calling.

"What I hope is that by steadfastly living my own style, declaring myself one hundred per cent authentically Jewish, just like anyone else Jewish — born or become — I can encourage other people, especially women, to be confident that whether or not they keep every minute observance, they too are legitimate Jews. Do it with pride! And if you don't like it, don't do it! And in my deepening awareness of Muslim culture, I see clear reflections of my own. I can understand how, just as Islam offers a language to access spirituality, so Judaism offers the same to me.

"My spirituality must be consistent with the rest of my life. The most important value for me is integrity. I'm willing to compromise a lot for that. That applies to my work too. I'm interested in seeking the truth of the situation."

We're getting towards the end of our time together, and we've been laughing about relationships, men, fate and so on. But Naomi suddenly turns serious and says, "There's something else I want to tell you about. Years before my accident, a friend of mine was murdered. A beautiful and gutsy young Israeli woman, Sharon Chazan, who I'd worked with on a film about Shabbat. Killed by a seemingly innocent old Jewish man in the East End of London who was obsessed with her. How could I work that dreadful murder out of my system?

"Some years later I tried to fictionalize her story. I wanted to follow what happened after she died. It was told in the first person and I had to envisage my own death. How did I do it? On page two I had a truck turn over on me. I had pre-empted what was to happen to me by two years.

"Maybe we write our own stories. So we have to be careful, and we have to take responsibility. I've known great terror and sorrow, but I now think that this was some sort of test to challenge my courage and determination. Just as I inherited my father's story of survival, his legacy includes also the memory of the courage and determination that he used to rebuild his life.

"To me he imparted this very important message: life is meaningless without hope. My own journey has been littered with disasters and I've had to learn how to reconcile myself with a great deal of sorrow and loss, but part of that process has allowed me to develop a rock-solid faith in my own worth and in the indomitability of the human spirit. Not to mention my child-like trust in tomorrow.

> Search me, God, and know my heart,
> test me, and know my thoughts.
> See if the path to despair is within me,
> and lead me in the path of eternity. (Psalm 139)"

Marian Partington

On one retreat I decided that I should try to forgive the Wests, and the first thing I felt when I got home was murderous rage. If you're going to forgive, I think you've got to get to the depth of the enormity that you're trying to forgive. Forgiveness, in this case, began with me experiencing murderous rage.

I think grace is something that's with us all the time. So the question is, why do some people lose touch with it, like the Wests did? And how can we create the conditions for it to flourish?

"A precious treasure
very difficult to find"

*Marian Partington is in her early fifties. She grew up in
Gloucestershire and studied English in Manchester and London. In December 1973 her younger sister Lucy disappeared.
In the next twenty years Marian brought up two children,
became a homeopath, and settled in Wales with Nick Salt, son
of the broadcaster Olive Shapley, with whom she had a third
child. In 1994 Lucy Partington's body was among those
found buried at Fred and Rosemary West's home in Gloucester.* Marian's way through was to try and find words for her
experience of Lucy's life and death, which culminated in her
article* "Salvaging the Sacred" *for* The Guardian *in May
1966. From 1997–99 she was funded by the Joseph Rowntree
Charitable Trust to continue her quest to find peace without
denying human atrocity.*

Marian begins, "What I want to say isn't complete. Maybe it's
undefinable." *We're sitting in her garden hut which doubles as a
study and meditation space. Outside, Tibetan prayer flags wave
on a line and a little farther away, nearer to the old Welsh farmhouse where Marian lives with her family, the day's washing is
blowing in the wind. The hut is lined with her children's paintings, her books, and artefacts from Nepal where Marian visited
her daughter, Marigold. Near the word processor hangs the photo
of Marian and Lucy, taken at Fountains Abbey in the Yorkshire
Dales, which accompanied her May 1966 essay in* The Guardian
Weekend.

* The Wests lived at 25 Cromwell Sreet, Gloucester. Frederick West committed suicide while on remand. Rosemary West's trial and conviction took place in the autumn
of 1995.

She has been writing recently about the different kinds of silence. "There's the silence of denial, suppression, editing out: pretending the difficult pain of life isn't there. Then there's the rich silence that I'm exploring in Ch'an Buddhist meditation and in Quaker worship, a silence that shines and reminds me of my essential purity. But in order to find this place I've had to face and accept what I call my 'rotting pile of mistakes.' That's repentance: taking responsibility and letting go."

I ask if she give me an example of what she means by "the silence of denial." "Yes, I can. In fact it was a real spiritual crisis for me. I was in a retreat, in this group of spiritual people, and I was trying to explain the path I've tried to follow since finding out what happened to Lucy. A woman interrupted me and said, 'Have you quite finished yet?' and 'I think this is leading us down a wrong path.' It seemed as though what I was saying, or something about what I was, threatened her existence in some way.

"I was profoundly upset. It seemed almost violent. At the same time I knew it was the end of the day and we were all tired, and that what I was saying wasn't appropriate for those people at that time.

"But this is something very basic in my life, the need to be heard, for my spiritual search not to be suppressed. When I wrote *The Guardian* article and there was such an amazing response ..." (she received three hundred letters) "... it seemed a confirmation of my urge to speak. It seemed that not only were they my words, but they were a gift that needed to be shared."

Sisters

Marian and Lucy and their two brothers were great-grandchildren on their mother's side of missionaries to China. "My grandmother rebelled fiercely against it, almost physically. Hearing hymns sung and bells rung made her feel ill. My mother inherited that feeling; in fact when a vicar came to the door after we found out what happened to Lucy she found it impossible to ask him in. So I grew up feeling aware of a kind of prejudice against spiritual things, a kind of fear of it.

"But my father had a sort of faith that waxed and waned, and at one point we went to Sunday School. I remember being the

Archangel Gabriel in the Nativity Play, and I had these wings of pink and white crêpe paper, and the vicar flew me out from behind the stage to my place in front of the shepherds. What I had to say — 'Tidings of great joy' — that word *tidings* has such resonance. I feel it's part of my work now, to find the 'tidings of joy' in the face of human atrocity."

Her father's on-and-off faith meant that Marian and her older brother weren't christened, but Lucy and their younger brother were. "Being the older sister I was very bossy, and I realized that she'd got a godmother and I didn't. Her godparents gave her a little book of prayers, and for some reason I felt it was my responsibility to make her say her prayers at night.

"But in some ways Lucy seemed to be aloof from me. My image of her is of Lucy reading. And that meant she was unavailable. To me that was a really irritating stance, her being cut off and superior."

Eventually, she says, they had the intelligence and sense of irony actually to define it: that Lucy was "classical" and "disciplined" while Marian was "romantic" and "undisciplined." When did they find those definitions? "I'm not sure ... There's so much I can't remember ... One of the joys of the response to the essay was other people who knew Lucy getting in touch and sharing their memories with me. One of them reminded me that she and Lucy came to see me in the lodgings in Bristol where I was re-sitting my A levels, and I had a painting on the wall with a verse from Yevtushenko. This friend told me that Lucy's favourite poem was one of Yevtushenko's about hanging poems in trees. In it he says, 'Don't worry, I can write as many poems as there are trees.' I think he's saying that writing is an act of faith, you mustn't wait till something's perfect, you must trust that if this poem isn't right then other poems will come. Lucy was waiting for everything to be right. She wouldn't go in for the sixties, sex and drugs and rock 'n' roll. She scorned all that, preferring to be protected by the academic tradition. She seemed to feel a mixture of disapproval and admiration for me. Yet a poem about trust was her favourite."

It was in those lodgings, in a tiny attic room above a rather grand private school in Bristol, that Marian, desperate to know what she was supposed to be doing with her life, went to bed for a week with flu. "And suddenly the words came to me: 'It doesn't matter what you do, it's how you do it that matters'."

Did God say those words?

"No, I've never had an outside God like that. It was the illness ..." Like Hildegard of Bingen, I suggest, who suppressed her individual spirituality until illness weakened her. "Yes, and Julian of Norwich* too."

Did she take the words seriously?

"Very. I looked at the inheritance I'd been given, the concentration on academic success, the cycle of abuse and grief. The grandfather on my father's side was a professor of chemistry and he valued academia above everything, including relationships, and his wife committed suicide. My father became manic depressive, and I think it goes back to this unresolved grief in his life. There's so much suppressed grief. I've realized how important it is to get in touch with these feelings, to express them and not to deny them."

The spirituality of the body

I ask Marian to expand on her childhood awareness of the spiritual. "It came to me through nature. We grew up in a village, in an old cider mill. My parents split up when I was twelve and I found refuge in being alone in nature. I could explore the old woods, all the wildness, and there was always something reassuring and uplifting and sensuous. I could always feel more at home in my body in the country. Myself, in nature. Being outside felt the right place to be.

"Though there was also a sense of threat because of being female. What we called 'the village yobbos' used to sit on the Coronation Seat and jeer when middle-class girls like me rode past on my pony, and they'd yell, 'Therre goes farrrting berrrm!' Once a whole gang of them ran after me — I remember I fancied one of them — shouting 'Therrre goes farrrting berrrm! Let's shag 'errr!' I ran and ran, it felt as if I was running for my life." *She shows me something she's written about the cruelty of village life.* "Fred West was also brought up in a Gloucestershire

---

* Anchoress and mystic who lived 1342–*c*.1416, author of *Revelations of Divine Love,* a document of religious experience.

village. I don't find it difficult to imagine the brutality of his childhood."

How did she recapture the sense of herself as spiritual in nature in her adult life? "When I was in London I earned my living doing life modelling, mainly for the Jewish painter Leon Kossoff who was a kind of father figure for me. That was like my introduction to meditation. While I was lying naked, with someone painting me, I learned to relax and express my being through my body. I learnt that Being was connected to Spirituality and could also be connected to Sexuality, and that being comfortable with myself would allow this union of the physical and the spiritual. There was something about trust, too. Things were very confusing at the time. I thought I was 'living in the present' and 'connecting' through so-called sexual liberation and smoking dope, but that was an illusion, or delusion.

"When life got very difficult — Lucy had disappeared, I'd had my first child and the relationship with the father was a real problem — I started learning T'ai Chi, which is like a slow moving meditation. All the postures are related to what happens in nature. It came from a Chinese sage watching a crane fighting with a snake, seeing how these two energies are related, using the energy of your opponent and sending it back. On a spiritual level it's about connecting with the energy around you. It's not aggressive: if something's attacking you, you yield to that energy and send back your strength. So what they're attacking you with becomes your strength, rather than knocking you over. It's about being flexible, truly living in the moment.

"It's another example of truth, the Quaker principle of truth that I believe in. I think you always sense if there's something wrong in a situation. If it's not talked about it gains extra power. It's important not to hide things. When we found out what happened to Lucy, there it was in a graphic physical way: she was buried under concrete, unable to speak her truth."

So back to the spiritual group to whom Marian was unable to speak her truth. "I felt gagged. Yet I know there's a problem with my story. What happened to Lucy was so horrible that I have to be very careful about whether and when that subject comes up. Because it's so difficult and painful, because it's so full of all the things that people want to edit out — the violence, the sexual abuse, the cruelty, it's like a microcosm of, say, the Holocaust — there's the urge to deny it in some way. Like they assume that everyone who was in there, in 25 Cromwell Street, had already been brutalized. Part of my need to tell people about Lucy's life and aspirations — her focus on truth and beauty, her passionate search for meaning in life through art, literature and religion — is to show that wasn't the case."

Disappearance

I ask her to describe what happened when Lucy disappeared. "I'd been at Manchester University studying English Literature, but I dropped out after a year and re-took the rest of my degree in London. So we were both in our final year together, even though Lucy was four years younger than me. I was in London, she was in Exeter. We'd spent time together in the summer before that — yes, that's when the photo was taken at Fountains Abbey. By that time Lucy had become involved in Roman Catholicism. I had noticed that the Catholicism brought about a change in her ..." *What kind of change?* "I can only describe it as a sort of softening. She wasn't needing to keep me at arm's length. Whatever I represented to her wasn't so threatening any more.

"We were all at home together for the Christmas holidays. It was 27 December, and we all went out for the evening to different places. Lucy went to visit her friend Helen. Helen was disabled and they used to play the recorder together. Lucy took some of her Christmas presents to show her: there was a little glass Victorian night-light that I'd given her, and a book, a medieval dream vision called 'Pearl,' which is a father's grief about losing his child. I've been discovering the importance of dreams in my own experience, as a way of trusting myself, trusting that I have resources within me that can show me the way forward. Metaphors and visions and dreams develop a language to express an area of consciousness that's not easily expressed in our culture.

"Well, my brother had given Lucy a lift to Helen's and we'd all offered to give her a lift back, but she said no, she'd get the bus. My boyfriend Patrick and I were staying over with our friends, and the first thing I remember when we got back was my mum rushing out of our front door saying, 'Lucy didn't come back last night and we don't know where she is.' There was this terrible panic. I don't remember a lot of it. At first the police didn't take it seriously, but when they saw all the books in her bedroom they realized she wasn't the sort to go off with her boyfriend and not let anyone know. So the next day they started to do road checks and drag the lake."

What was Marian herself feeling like at this time? "I've been trying to find the words for that. Part of my spiritual way forward is to find the words. Once you find the words something changes. Like the Jews once they'd found the word 'Holocaust': once you've named something it helps the process, you're not quite the victim of it, you've got a perspective. Yet on the Ch'an Buddhist retreats I've realized that I can sometimes use words to protect myself from the true emotions.*

"Lucy disappearing. Think of losing something, anything. You're permanently scanning to know where this thing has gone. If it's a book, or a purse ... But if it's a *person*! Until you find it the loss is acute. We couldn't find her. She just vanished. You're dragging this hole around with you. At the same time I wanted just to forget about it. But whenever I tried to forget it something caught up with me again. It was a bit like the irritation of the younger sister dogging your footsteps, only it's the absence of the younger sister.

"And not only Lucy had gone, but the firm structure of her classical, Catholic self had gone too. That was like a pillar that also suddenly vanished. So, in a strange way, maybe my romantic undisciplined bit went even wilder.

"Another thing I've learnt recently was that one reaction to grief and loss is an increased need for sexual contact. Patrick went back to America — he was dodging the draft and there was an amnesty — and I fell instantly for someone else. Then Patrick came back, and ... It was as if I didn't have a sense of morality any more, as if there was some terrible self-destructive process going on. I seemed to want to wreck my whole life. I got pregnant and didn't know whose baby it was and had an abortion.

"But I did do my exams and I did get my degree. A short while

---

* Chinese Zen, a way of life that encourages clarity of mind, compassion and wisdom through meditation.

ago I discovered my father didn't even know I'd got my degree. When Lucy disappeared, my parents in a sense both disappeared too. However much or little they'd been there before, they couldn't be there at all for me then. The grief was disabling.

"I get help from the Quaker way of sitting in the light, seeing what images and words come up, waiting to see what feels uncomfortable, not trying to solve it intellectually but letting it come. That's what I do with my writing. I meditate, and I see what's asking to be looked at and explored. You stay in touch with whatever it is, you don't suppress it. And that includes the grief. That's the only whole way forward, and you don't know where it's going, so it's quite scary. It's the only way that has the sense of truth, the sense of reality about it for me. Olive said in a letter to Nick and her other children about their father's early death: 'The bad unwelcome thing must be taken in to the centre of your being and accepted; ... it must be looked at and looked at again. That is the only way to live'."[1]

Marian and I both need a break at this point, so we go for a short walk up the wooded valley. When we're seated comfortably again, she tells me more of what she has learnt from Buddhism. "The Buddhist way of learning from the mistakes you make seems more constructive than the Christian way of offering absolution. I've been tempted by the notion of absolution, but I've been more helped by the Buddhist retreats. There was one retreat I went to in 1997 when I had a terrible experience of panic and grief and suffering. But I came through to a profound moment when I sat on the scaly branch of a Scots pine tree that had been torn away from the trunk by the wind. When I accepted the altered rhythm of the tree without the balance of the severed limb, I accepted the depth of my own wound. My sister has been torn out of our lives. We're living with the raw stump that is left behind."

Didn't anyone, in that time of anguish following Lucy's disappearance, help her to interpret it as a reaction to grief? "No. No one. Except Nigel, the father of my two older children, because he was disturbed himself. He was the only one who could speak about pain, and that was the pain of his own nervous breakdown. He'd taken himself out of the Maudesley Hospital, got himself off medication and walked the Pennine Way. No one knew how to deal with me. I thought I could get over it by smoking lots of dope. But that was the way of denial."

Marian had two children, Luke and Marigold, went to live in Wales, and Nick came into their lives when Marigold was eighteen months old. "I'd resisted having children. All that was partly my own confusion, but also it was fear of bringing children into this world. But the whole business of being pregnant and giving birth were so powerful. As soon as I got pregnant with Luke I gave up dope. We were living in Student Community Housing, a creative but chaotic legal squat, and I had a home birth by the Leboyer method. This allowed me to give birth without medical interference and stay in touch with my body. During my pregnancy I heard about homeopathy: there was a homeopath living nearby who wanted to treat a pregnant woman.* I'm sure this helped me to move out of the self-destructive mode I'd become stuck in. Eventually I trained as a homeopath myself and I've been practising since 1983, when Jack was born. It fits in with the rest of my experience in that it brings hope of change at a deeper level than the physical."

Just after Marigold was born they lived in a council flat in London. "We were very poor, but I took pleasure in the limits of it. At one point the Social Services nearly put us on some list of families who were 'at risk,' simply because I was a single parent with two children.

"Then I moved to Wales, and we were living high up in the hills. Once we were snowed in and it seemed that I had nothing. But I had the sense of being held. I had an absolute trust that this was the place to be. The farmer came and sawed up wood for us. I knew that if I stopped looking at myself as other people would see me and trusted in my environment, the beauty of it, what I needed would be there. I found a packet of marshmallows left over from bonfire night and it was like finding gold.

"But the terrible irony is," Marian goes on, "at that very same time as I was considered potentially 'at risk' in London, up in Gloucester Fred and Rose West were known to the police and

* Homeopathy is a system of medical diagnosis and treatment pioneered by Samuel Hahnemann (1755–1843), based on the principle that "like cures like" and the patient is treated rather than the disease.

the Social Services and were torturing and murdering their victims and burying them in concrete, and no one did anything
about it."

Discovering the truth

Just over twenty years after Lucy's disappearance — almost as
long as her life — Fred West told the investigation team in
Gloucester that there were more bodies in the basement on 25
Cromwell Street, and one of them was Lucy's. By this time Mar-
ian and Nick Salt were long-time partners, and their son Jack was
twelve years old. Maybe the worst part of that "purgatorial"
time, Marian says, was when the newspapers published Fred
West's fantasies about Lucy, making out that she wanted more
than he did and he was "doing her a favour."

We're looking at Marian's writing about reclaiming Lucy's life
and dignity, and she points out that the title of her Guardian *arti-*
cle – "Salvaging the Sacred" — was very specific: she was sal-
vaging whatever could possibly be sacred from the wreck of this
atrocity. "Words must be found," she wrote.

> "There must be something for all of us to learn from this
> profoundly shocking profanity before it gets buried under
> the concrete of fear, prejudice or, even worse, indifference
> ... It is about poetry and transformation. It is about living
> with the reality of violence, rape, torture and murder. It is
> not always rational. I have followed my heart."

Two years after the trial there was a proposal for a film about
the Wests' murders. I ask Marian how she felt about that. "I campaigned against it. I had no choice. Lucy's name and Lucy's life
have a meaning to us, we remember her warmth, wit, intelligence
and sense of humour. We'd found ways and rituals to reclaim her
from the Wests and the media and lay her to rest. And then, not
only did we have to live with the terrible reality of Lucy's death
but we had to live with the fact that other people were ruthlessly
trying to make money out of it."[2]

Lucy reduced from a vibrant human being to a mere victim of
the Wests? "Yes. I felt triumphant when I was able to place the

black-and-white cropped image of Lucy's face that was used by
the police and the media during the West trial back into its original family context: a coloured snapshot of us two sisters on a day
out with our father at a beautiful place." *We look at a poem of
Lucy's:*

> Things are as big as you make them —
> I can fill a whole body,
> a whole day of life
> with worry
> about a few words
> on one scrap of paper,
> yet, the same evening,
> looking up,
> can frame my fingers
> to fit the sky
> in my cupped hands.

"Four months after her disappearance," Marian wrote, "I had a
dream. Lucy came back to me and I asked her where she had
been. She said, 'I've been sitting in a water meadow, and *if you sit
very still you can hear the sun move.*' This image filled me with a
profound feeling of peace, the kind that 'passeth understanding,'
and I woke up with that feeling."

"Those words and that image have never left me," she says
now. "It felt like a real communication, and also it felt that
whether she was dead or alive, if she was in that state she was all
right."

Knowing the whole self

"What happened to Lucy has brought me up against the absolute
need to find some method of reaching inner peace. I don't want
to pass on any residue of this horror to my children, so I have to
find a way to deal with it myself."

*But she hasn't protected her children from it, has she? Her
daughter Marigold has spoken and written about it.*

"It's been a matter of discerning what to share and what not to
share," says Marian. "Clearly I couldn't protect them completely.

Once, when I was campaigning against the film, I remember Luke saying, 'I wish we didn't have to hear any more about the Wests.' I took notice of that. The main thing was, I wanted to find a place where I could experience my rage and grief so that it didn't come through, via my physical way of being, indirectly to them.

"I think the ritual of re-burying Lucy's remains was terribly important for them." *This is the process she described in* The Guardian: *bones, gifts, poems, a rosary, a crucifix, a piece of enamel work and a drawing of a Celtic knot made by Marian's children, a jar of honey, a piece of weaving, two of Lucy's toys and her snuggler blanket, all laid in Lucy's coffin and buried in quiet ceremony in consecrated ground.* "That came from a dream as well. In the dream I asked the pathologist what was left of Lucy, and he said 'Look in that pink sack over there.' Inside the sack there was a sort of skeleton kit, and each bone had a number on it, and the kit assembled itself into a whole skeleton. I had this urge to embrace the skeleton, and I did, and it became Lucy, and I remembered what she felt like to hug. I knew I had to reclaim and cherish what was left of Lucy's physical body.

"The phrase 'Be still and know that I am God' is important to me. Not that I like the word 'God.' But knowing God, then knowing myself, knowing that I have the capacity to murder, knowing that Rosemary West has the capacity to love ..."

She's fumbling for words here, and I need to recap. "The 'being still and knowing' leads to a self-knowledge that acknowledges the capacity for murder, which in turn leads to the acknowledgement that a murderer also has the capacity to love? How is that?"

Marian says, "I'll take you back to a Ch'an Buddhist retreat I went on just after I'd had that dream about Lucy's bones. What happens after trauma is that logic doesn't work. You have to follow your heart. This was a liberation for me, it left me open to my heart. I was in that state of mind when I went on this retreat.

"I'd followed the dream, and I'd been to Cardiff to rescue Lucy's remains. I phoned up John, who runs the Retreat Centre, and said, 'Maybe it's not appropriate for me to come because I'm carrying all this,' but he said, 'It's absolutely appropriate, and if you're open to it I think you'll help everyone.'

"On a Ch'an retreat, at first your mind drives you crazy, you don't want to be stuck there, a victim of your thoughts and your anxieties and your ego, but you don't know how to get out of it. But I find that after about four days it gives me the space to experience who I am in more depth.

"At one point on the retreat I suddenly realized that I was doing exactly what Lucy said to me in that first dream twenty-odd years ago, which was, I was sitting very still, and I was getting close to hearing the sun move. I was living in the present. It seemed as though every time I breathed in, I was moving out, and every time I breathed out I was taking in. It was an exchange with the universe. My whole sense of 'who I was' wasn't just limited to me and things around me, I was connected to everything. At that moment I realized that's what Lucy is as well — connected to everything. We were both part of everything."

And this connection isn't just with the good, the light, the wholesome?

"No, it's not about judgment at all. It's not about separation, about the discriminating mind. That keeps you apart from things. It's about reaching an alignment when your ego is less prominent and you're able to experience a sense of spaciousness, of deep inner peace, where you're able to be very relaxed and live in the moment. I found a part of myself that I've suppressed over the years of being a parent, a wildness that I'd kept down because it wasn't something I thought was acceptable, wasn't what people expected me to be. But I found it again."

The question of forgiveness

I *nudge her now to return to what she said about her own capacity to murder and Rosemary West's capacity to love.*

Marian breathes deeply. "I have experienced murderous rage. On one retreat I decided that I should try to forgive the Wests, and the first thing I felt when I got home was murderous rage. If you're going to forgive, I think you've got to get to the depth of the enormity that you're trying to forgive. Forgiveness, in this case, began with me experiencing murderous rage. I knew at that moment that I had the capacity to kill, which I chose not to carry out.

"For eighteen months now I've been trying to understand how

the Wests became how they were, and I feel that at the root of it lies a feeling of impotence and rage, which must come from their childhood. They both experienced brutalization and sexual abuse. Rosemary West seemed to want to make her victims feel what she had felt.

"Experiencing the grief deeply has also been vital. When my grief finally came up on retreat, I stayed with the group and let myself make whatever noise I needed. The amount of liquid that poured out of my eyes and nose and dripping off my chin, what kind of a bowl did I need to catch it! The grief was coming up physically, and it needed to come. It was hot too, as if I was being purged with fire and water. I thought of the phrase 'the vale of tears,' it was like a lake full of tears, and I was in it on my own, and full of self-pity and isolation. Then the image changed, and the lake was full of people, and it was the millions of people who have known this grief of losing someone they loved through violent death. At that moment I reached a deep state of peace, an experience of being human. I knew that everything was impermanent, and none of us is unconnected or separate. That is a silent place, like a Quaker meeting at its best, which embraces everything and allows for true compassion.

"So I can't just write Rosemary West off as evil or different. A woman who has an abortion destroys the potential for human life. And because I am human and because she is human, the way I choose to express my life is a potential in her, and the way she chose to express her life is a potential within me." *Is that a moral statement? Could she call it her creed?* "No, but it's something that I know, that I have experienced in the vastness and spaciousness of the moment, with whatever is contained in it."

As we've talked the dog and several cats have been going in and out, and now Marian needs to go back to the house to feed them. She also needs to listen for the phone: their son Jack is today making his first solo train journey and they're waiting to hear whether he has arrived safely. As we cross the grass the evening light is soft over the valley and we briefly share thoughts on Rosemary West in such different circumstances in prison.

Finally, as we go through the door, we touch on the concept of grace. "I have experienced moments of grace, when I've felt strengthened and upheld. Certainly it happened when I went to wrap Lucy's bones. It was empowering. It helped me to approach the situation without fear. The imagining of it was terrible, but the reality of it was actually healing. That was grace. I think grace is something that's with us all the time. So the question is, why do some people lose touch with it, like the Wests did? And how can we create the conditions for it to flourish? What I'm learning to do is to 'cherish beings of bad nature,' like in the Dalai Lama's poem:

> 'I will learn to cherish beings of bad nature / And those pressed by strong sins and suffering / As if I had found a precious / Treasure very difficult to find'."

Relating
to spiritual community

June Raymond

*I saw there was a mystery here that I somehow understood.
I stopped pitying the nuns. But I became terribly afraid,
and knew I couldn't handle it. So I asked God to handle it
for me. There was a note, a kind of voice that grew more
insistent, until I thought, "This must be a real vocation."*

*I envisaged myself as living in a cottage in Wales, but when
I invoked it the place was in shadow. Then I visualized the
centre of Liverpool, where the convent is, and it was bathed
in light.*

At the still point of the turning world[1]

June Raymond, born in 1943, took a degree in English and became a teacher. She had also considered marriage but realized that her true calling was to be a nun. She entered the Congregation of Notre Dame and continued teaching while a nun until her health broke down. She discovered the Creation Spirituality of Matthew Fox and asked for a discernment process after which, while still under vows, she lived for two years on the island of Erraid, off Mull in Scotland. She returned to the Congregation and now lives in a flat attached to the convent in Liverpool, where she does earth-centred meditations and offers healing through Bach flower remedies and through listening.

June Raymond's voice on the phone is gentle and refined, but when she gives me her address I recognize it immediately: it's in the heart of Liverpool, where two universities and two cathedrals lie cheek by jowl with a mixture of local and in-coming populations that's vibrant, chaotic and often rowdy with police sirens. June takes me in to the quiet sitting room of her flat, in a corner of which lie boxes of healing remedies.

The vision

She gives me the key experience straightaway. Early on in life as a nun she had an experience of the infinite love of God. It wasn't a visual experience: it didn't come through her senses, her humanity. It had nothing of the ecstatic about it. It was direct knowledge, transmitted from spirit to spirit. "We had a thing called 'examen,' and we had a little book in which we had to tick off all our faults. One day I went into chapel at midday and I thought, 'This is silly. God can't possibly be interested in all this.' But then I thought, 'I'll just give God a chance today. I'll let my mind go blank and see what comes.'

"And it happened. It was different from any other experience I've ever had. Everything else comes through my humanity. Even if it's very intuitive, it comes through my senses, my bodyliness. This was a direct knowing. There was no possibility of doubt or ambiguity. I saw that I was loved, and that all the love I'd ever had in my life was like a breath compared with the ocean. The experience didn't come with an image like that: I had to keep making up images to find ways of holding on to it. It was a completely personal love. If everybody else in the world answered God's infinite love, and I didn't, that hole — the hole of my denial of the love — would be as big as the universe. The love was free, but it was compelling. Being there for it, responding to it, being part of it, was the only thing that mattered."

She knew that the mere memory of this experience would be the most certain thing in her life. "I also saw that we have to exist eternally. If love exists only for a time, it isn't love. And I knew that what I had seen was just a thread of the whole."

Did she tell anyone about it? "Not for a long long time. I couldn't have coped with anyone besmirching it. I remember telling one person who said, 'Yes, it has all the signs of authenticity.' But I knew, 'No no no, you've got it absolutely wrong. You measure the authenticity by *this,* not the other way round!'"

Ironically she didn't at first realize who it was that could love her like this. Then she thought, "Silly, it has to be God." *But it didn't seem to be the God who she'd been worshipping so far. Which person of the Trinity was it?* "But that wasn't a valid question, because there wasn't room in the whole of the Cosmos for more love than that. This love, this extraordinary intimate love, this knowing Presence, lies behind all religions and everything in the Cosmos. From then on, even when I got lost, I knew this was absolute reality and was wholly, utterly dependable. Because of it, I've always said *yes* to love in my life."

Childhood

"I was a very philosophical child," says June. "I asked lots and lots of questions, and I found that the grown-ups couldn't answer my questions. I saw that it wasn't that they *wouldn't* answer them but that they *couldn't*. So I knew I had to work things out for myself, and if it took forever, well, it took forever."

June's account of her life begins with her actual birth. "I have an identical twin sister. Many years ago I did a re-birthing, and it was very exciting, there was a sense of something really marvellous happening, of being surrounded by the love of people around me. But there was something in the way, stopping me being born. Later I told my twin about it, and she roared with laughter because she'd had a similar experience but felt that she was kicked out of the way! And, by about twenty minutes, I was born first."

As a child, did she think of herself as being philosophical or spiritual? "No. I thought of myself as being over-sensitive. My brother used to rag me, and I'd rise every time and blow up into a tantrum."

And no one understood her? No one could answer her questions? "The adults couldn't answer me. But in a sense I always had somebody who understood the way I thought, because of being an identical twin. That was a great advantage. But it also made it very hard to find, later on in life, that I was experiencing and knowing things that are almost unknown 'out there.' I think that seventy-five per cent of my life was actually hidden until I went to live on Erraid. Only then was I among people who talked the same language, the language of mysticism. The mystic is not honoured in our society. That has made things very hard for me, very hard indeed, because the foundress of Notre Dame was a mystic."

June's mother was an Anglican. She would read Six O'Clock Saints *to the children at bedtime. When June asked her, "Why do those people say the rosary and go to Mass, and we don't have rosaries and go to church services?" her mother answered simply, "Because we're Church of England and they're Catholics." June asked, "Which came first?" "The Catholics," replied her mother, and June took note of that. Her father didn't go to church:*

he was a humble man, and he felt that other people understood the spiritual things that were hidden from him. Made deaf by wounds in World War One, he was interested in the healings at Lourdes. He said, "I'll get to heaven because all of you will be praying for me."

From the age of about eight June sensed that God was infinite love. "I heard a sermon about St Paul's list of the fruits of the spirit — love, joy, peace, longsuffering, gentleness and so on[2] — and I wondered why these things weren't just a reality, instead of a kind of historical statement.

"I was also quite psychic. From my babyhood up to when I was about ten — I can date the first time, because it was when my younger sister was born and I was fourteen months old — my nights were punctuated by nightmares. Years later I read *Schindler's Ark,* about how the Jewish children of the ghettos hid in terror from the Gestapo, and I went cold because I knew, 'That was me! That was the terror I felt in my nightmares!' Some of the fear and horror of Nazism and the Holocaust had come through the atmosphere, and I had absorbed it. I think I was not the only child who felt it. But I was almost neurotically sensitive, so I may have been more consciously aware."

For a short spell she and her sister were sent to a boarding school of evangelical bent, and sermons would exhort the girls to give their lives to God. Here was another example of adults not understanding. "I can't 'give my life to God'," June would think, "because God has always *had* my life." She prayed a lot, not only to God but also to her guardian angel, which seemed easier. Her angel protected her against terror.

A psychic friend of her mother's predicted that she would become a nun, but June couldn't bear the thought of not being married, of being confined, separated from the natural world. She still held in her heart Teresa of Avila from the Six O'Clock Saints, *who didn't found a congregation but came to an existing one and transformed it.* "That seemed a wonderful thing: to be a transforming influence. I realized I needn't lose my 'peace of soul' if I wasn't perfect. I couldn't be perfect anyway: I was slightly dyslexic and a late developer, and I never got my homework in on time. I didn't want to be a martyr, and I wasn't very keen on virginity either. But I did want to be a saint."

The journey to Notre Dame

The reaction against adult misunderstanding came up again when she was a student at the Froebel College in Roehampton. She and a few others found the lectures petty and boring so they went to pubs and drank lager and came back to mock the system. When the Principal summoned her and said, "Miss Raymond, would you like to leave?" she refused.

A couple of years earlier she had met, at a crammer in Oxford, some American students who were atheists. That was a tremendous shock. "I suddenly thought, maybe I too don't 'believe in God.' I could see the trees and flowers, and they were just trees and flowers. Perhaps I only believed because I'd been brought up to believe? It was terrifying! How was I to deal with it? I thought, 'I can do one of two things. Either I can give up, and have no hope at all. Or I can say, I can't even hope now — but I *can* hope that from somewhere, out of the Cosmos, some hope will come'."

To hope for hope! Gradually it came together again. She couldn't lose God. Another student, an evangelical who thought that Catholics were anti-Christ, spurred the rebel in her into investigating Catholicism. "The Catholics had answers to questions like, 'Why did Jesus Christ die on the cross for our sins?' In a Catholic church I had a tangible sense of the holy. I could see people actually *praying.* I knew intuitively I should go for this: that if I did, things would all go right, and if I didn't things would go wrong and it would just come up again and again till I accepted it." *So, while still at Froebel College, she became a Catholic.*

But it's a long journey from becoming a Catholic to entering a religious order. How, I ask her, did that come about?

"In my first job, two teachers were nuns of the Congregation of Notre Dame, and I pitied them. I couldn't bear the thought of not getting married. I was going out with a Rhodesian airman who was at Cranwell College, and we were thinking about spending our lives together. My family were comfortably off, I had a whole range of choices in my life, and those poor teacher nuns had none."

But her boyfriend (who returns to the story later) wasn't interested in literature or the things of the spirit, and having comfortable relaxing times with her family didn't seem sufficient either.

"Years before, I'd written an essay on T.S. Eliot's *Four Quartets* — you know, 'the still point of the turning world'? — and got a good mark. I saw there was a mystery here that I somehow understood. I stopped pitying the nuns. But I became terribly afraid, and knew I couldn't handle it. So I asked God to handle it for me.

"There was a note, a kind of voice that grew more insistent, until I thought, 'This must be a real vocation.' My boyfriend went back to Rhodesia and I didn't go with him, and I offered myself as a postulant to Notre Dame."

Notre Dame was strict in its regime, with a lot of silence and a highly structured day. Its founder, Sister Julie, was a Frenchwoman who escaped the terror that followed the French Revolution hidden in a haycart and experienced a miraculous healing from paralysis. It has been a highly successful teaching order, with many schools and teacher training colleges. For instance, the first Catholic Teacher Training College in Britain, Mount Pleasant, stood where the Liverpool John Moores University now stands. The Congregation is smaller now: in June's convent in central Liverpool there are just six sisters and her.

Sister Julie of Notre Dame became one of the guiding spirits of June's life. Thérèse of Lisieux was another, and later, Julian of Norwich, who also had a vision of the extraordinary dimension of God's love. The simplicity and trust of these women guided her through being a postulant, a novice and finally a fully committed nun. "It was hard and lonely. Curiously enough I loved it. Thérèse of Lisieux was my novice mistress in a way. She was neurotic, like me, but she had the confidence to say 'If I were to live my life over again, I would change nothing.' Ah! I thought: this woman, so deprived and highly strung and sick, who died of TB at the age of twenty-four, speaks my language." *Had Thérèse ever appeared to her?* "Yes. It was an awareness, rather than an appearance. I was praying, and I said to Thérèse, 'You must be so bored with me, the way my struggles go on and on and on.' 'No, indeed,' said Thérèse, 'I'm really rather thrilled with you.' I even experienced her presence much later, at Findhorn."*

But did she feel it was cruel to leave her parents and her twin

---

* The spiritual centre founded by Eileen and Peter Caddy and Dorothy Maclean near Forres, Inverness, Scotland.

sister? "I didn't feel I had an option. There has always been a streak in me that has to be my own person. My mother asked me to delay it a year, but I knew there was no question. Eventually my mother and my sister knitted a shawl for me, for my trousseau."

June's sister comes up often in the story: she has two sons who sometimes find it hard to distinguish between their mother and their aunt. So June has a substitute family who are as close as could be without being her own.

Knowledge of wholeness

June accepted the discipline of being a nun, but she always rebelled against the concepts of sin and guilt. "I've never wanted to sin, and I cannot believe that God wants me to sin. How can we repent, 'turn around,' when we already belong to God? Thérèse of Lisieux helped me with that one. She taught me that the religious life is not about being virtuous. You have to go through your inner work, and that work is surrender, trust and love. It's not difficult, but it is painful."

Many years after she was professed, a glimpse of Jung's vision through Irene Claremont de Castillejo's Knowing Woman *returned June to her knowledge that everything is a whole.*[3] "If everything is connected, I thought, there must be a dimension where this connection happens. The spirit of the Church was being diminished by the separation of the material from the spiritual, and this separation was institutionalized by patriarchy. Maleness and authority aren't harmful in themselves, but they are harmful if they downgrade the female, the feminine intuitive face of God."

Knowing that the material and spiritual worlds are whole, but living and working in a Church that didn't honour this, June was split into two selves. One was sustained by Sister Julie's founding conviction that God is good: "Qu'il est bon, le bon Dieu!" while the other tried to follow the patriarchal way of outward virtue. "When I was a postulant we were given instructions: 'When you wake in the morning, think this. Then think that.' That meant, 'Never be spontaneous. Do it by trying, by effort. Never let the spirit shine through.' I needed to be in tune with my own truth and follow it."

The obedient, people-pleasing nun in her did everything possible to reconcile these two opposites. In her thirties she went to Oxford to take a degree in English, where she lived in another Notre Dame house and had to fight for her freedom to study properly rather than look after visitors and the other nuns. Here she heard about Matthew Fox, about original blessing in place of original sin. It was a challenging encounter with the real world, and she said yes to it.[4]

Might that yes have made her abandon her vocation with Notre Dame? "Well, at one point of inner conflict I scribbled in my notebook, 'Dying will be easy after this.' But Sister Julie's vision required me to stay with it. I learnt not to be afraid of love, whatever form it came in."

After her degree she taught English in Leeds and in Norfolk. But the rigour of the life didn't suit her. If she had a cold she'd be ill for three weeks, and she always had a problem with her back. "Here's a paradox. The Catholic way is to ignore the body, in fact for most of my life I hardly knew what my body was or how it could speak to me. Yet it did speak to me, undeniably, through my back."

Time and again, when she tried to walk away from her central vision her back gave way. Once, standing exhausted on a railway station, she asked God, "Tell me, God, do I always *have* to be ill?" The answer came, "Well, maybe you do. But not everybody has the experience of My presence that you do."

Prayer and discernment

June describes prayer, talking to God, and meditation, waiting on God, almost casually as an integral part of her life. It was while she was ill in Leeds — resented by the other nuns, who had to wait on her hand and foot — that some airmen in Zimbabwe (formerly Rhodesia) were accused of sabotage, put in solitary confinement and then tried for their lives. One of them was Phil, June's early boyfriend. She felt consciously in touch with him in prison. She wrote letters on his behalf, she rang up Amnesty International, she got people to pray for them. "I could feel what an appalling psychological state he was in and I knew I could comfort him. I got his lawyer's address from Amnesty and wrote, saying I was now a nun and was praying for him. His wife wrote back saying Phil and the others all had profound religious experiences in solitary confinement; each had gone back to the faith of their youth. Phil was about to be confirmed in the Church of England — 'And that's a turn-up for the books!'"

One evening while teaching in Norwich, at a parents' meeting, she stood up to go home and found that she couldn't walk. She couldn't go any further. She had stopped fitting into the mould — "not that I excelled at the mould! I wasn't an inner-city, muscular nun at all. And there was something about me that threatened people. They weren't comfortable with me unless they were comfortable with themselves. I realized that you can't please people, and that was good for me." *She was offered counselling but refused it.* "I was neurotic, yes, but not cracked. And there had to be dialogue with the Congregation."

She asked for a discernment process. This was a formal procedure, during which two Sisters asked what had led her to this point of conflict and decision. For the first time June felt heard. Before this, when she asked for instance to eat wholemeal bread as part of her witness to the wholeness of creation, she was considered faddy. When she heard missionaries come back from Africa saying that the African communities were crippled by Western debt, she realized that "we are not part of the solution, we are part of the problem." *But that was thought eccentric and irrelevant.*

Now the Sisters asked what were the destructive elements for her in her vocation, and what was life-enhancing. At last the part of her that connected with Matthew Fox's "creation spirituality" and Fritjof Capra's The Turning Point,[5] the part that knew intuitively that everything was one, could be recognized by her fellow nuns. She was given leave to go first to Hengrave Hall, the ecumenical community in Suffolk, where she felt affirmed in her search for holism, self-sufficiency and justice for the poor.

Then, miraculously, she heard about Findhorn. "Findhorn, I thought? Me, a Catholic nun? I can't go worshipping the earth! But someone told me, 'There's a important place for building bridges between Christianity and the traditional, earthy ways of the spirit. It's Findhorn-based, an island off the coast of Mull in

Scotland, called Erraid.' I knew I was to be one to build those bridges."

It was the day of St Julie's feast when June heard about Erraid, and she was sure that Julie the foundress of Notre Dame was sending her there. She had to apply and go through a process of "attunement," a key concept for Findhorn people. "They needed someone who was spiritually in tune and who was not going to dump all their Christian stuff about sin and guilt on them. It was such an extraordinary thing, a nun going to this pagan island! But I knew it was right, and they accepted me."

The island of Erraid

Erraid has a little row of lighthouse cottages. Ten adults and a small child lived there during June's time: a varied, deeply spiritual group of people who took responsibility for their lives and their own spiritual growth. A ferry-full of guests and supplies came from Fionnphort each week. "They were fussed about social justice, about where their coffee came from! Two years on Erraid taught me more about wholeness than twenty years of reading books had done."

Wasn't it a shock, going from convent life to herding sheep and milking cows in all weathers on a Scottish island? "I loved it. I was a bit worried at first about missing the sacraments. But gradually I became aware of all food as sacrament, all creation as revelation. We all meditated. My way of meditating had been Zen, because I'd found the Catholic Ignatian meditation too cumbersome for me and I needed something simpler. On Erraid I grew more open to whatever meditations might come to me."

Her back gave way again, but this time she worked with it and accepted healing of different kinds. "I understood from them that I was trying to live only from the right side of my brain. The whole patriarchal thing hadn't allowed my creativity and my feminine side to exist. I'd known this already, but only with my head. Now I learnt it in my body. I became more in tune with the spiritual dimension of the material world.

"Yet in a way I *had* known it with my body. When I was about fifteen or sixteen I used to shut my eyes and get beautiful pictures, one after another. I wasn't consciously imagining things; they seemed to come from some other, subconscious place. I began to feel I was in another place, walking in this beautiful garden. I could smell the roses and the warm air. Then the vision changed, and I was in a tremendously long elegant gallery. Then the next thing was really horrid. I was in a courtyard with high blackened brick walls, everything very damp, the ground covered with dead damp leaves, trees dripping. There was a house with a green door and a very nasty feeling, and because I was inquisitive I had to open the door. Part of me said, 'You must find out what's in there, you might see more visions,' but the other part knew that it was more than my life was worth to go in there, it would be too dangerous. All the time I knew I was only playing with pictures. Yet the pictures were vitally important.

"Thirty years later I learned on Erraid that there is nothing out there that is truly frightening. All the terrifying things are inside, and if you look at the frightening things inside you won't be afraid of what's outside. When I came back from Erraid I knew that I'd checked out all my dark places inside. So I went back through those pictures, and I went in through that green door, down down through the darkness, and there were frightening things, but nothing that was a real threat to me. I went on for a very long way. Then I stopped at the moment of my conception. At that moment I was aware that some of the energy was the shadow that I'd picked up at the moment of conception."

Could she explain "the shadow at the moment of conception?"

"As I've said, I don't believe in 'original sin.' It seems to me that our journey is about transformation. But babies are very open, and all the time they absorb shadow stuff from around them. A lot of what people call 'original sin' is like the straw which it is our life's task to spin into gold."

So we're given a mixed bundle, and our task is to change the negative into the positive?

"Not quite. It's more that the material world is always coming to consciousness, and our part in the creative process is to bring what we do and what we are into 'God consciousness.'

"That's the reason why I now use the Bach flower remedies. I choose the remedies for a person by dowsing, by getting in touch with their body energies with this ..." *She shows me a small crystal on a thread.* "They work through the resonances of each remedy with a specific emotion. They see the negative, the shadow, as the flip side of your giftedness. Once, when I was feeling resentful, I went and stood in the arch of a willow tree, the remedy for resentment, and instead of making me suddenly all unresentful and joyful, it put me in touch with my sorrow. Once I was back in touch with it, I realized that when it's in tune with my true self my sorrow is a beautiful thing, part of my gift-edness."

Angels and goddesses

We return to her time on Erraid. "It's one of the most beautiful places on earth. I'd go over to the sanctuary and looked over the sea to Mull. From my meditations I learnt about the chakras, and that our bodies are all the time picking up dimensions of creation. I learnt too about angels: for instance, the angel of Erraid who's a face of God that's specific to looking after Erraid.

"One day I got in touch with an individual angel. The sage was perfect for picking, and it was a glorious day, and I came along with my scissors to harvest it, but suddenly I thought, 'Wait a moment! What does it feel like to have all your leaves cut off?' So I said, 'If there is such a thing as the spirit of sage, tell me what you feel about having all your leaves cut off?' And I got a power-ful awareness of what I can only call the essence of sage, this powerful plant with its almost magical healing properties. It said, 'It has taken a lot of time, and a lot of patience, to produce this beautiful thing. If you don't pick now, it will all be wasted.' And that was part of my original vision: that everything is pure gift, it's pure love, it's pure miracle."

There is another angel story. Saturday, the weekly guests were due, and she was cooking fishcakes for lunch. But there simply wasn't time to make more than thirty fishcakes. "I went to the out-side loo to attune with the kitchen angel, and I said, 'I really do need a miracle now. It's physically impossible to make enough fishcakes in time. What are you going to do about it?' The kitchen angel laughed at me, and the air was full of a myriad angels, all laughing at the idea that there was any problem at all. So I went cheerily back, and went on making the impossible fishcakes, and the telephone rang, and it was the Findhorn bus. They'd missed the ferry and would be late. The guests told me afterwards they'd never eaten better fishcakes. Angelic fishcakes!"

June did go eventually to Findhorn. There she experienced "really pagan stuff": powerful rituals allowing women to exercise their own priesthood. She learnt awareness of fertility and sexuality, ritual encounters with evil, and an initiation into the Mystery religions that took her to meet her guide.

"I was a bit nervous about this initiation. But when I met my guide it was so unmistakably the risen Christ that I thought, 'I don't need to worry.' So later when I was taken to meet the 'Goddess,' I wasn't worried. The Goddess, in human form, embraced me, and I knew she was saying, 'I'm so glad to meet you. I've been waiting for you'."

Findhorn reclaimed the aspects of spirituality that Christianity had excommunicated. "Among women, I learned to exercise my own priesthood. Christianity had condemned everything pagan, everything womanly, everything sexual. I was experiencing being, not a 'woman priest,' but a priestess!"

But she doesn't blame the Catholic church. "It's like driving a car half way up a mountain. You don't kick the car for not taking you all the way to the top, you thank it for bringing you thus far. Catholicism had taken me to the point where I discovered Creation Spirituality. I could walk on from there."

Finding a voice

Returning from Erraid was terribly hard. Simply coming back from that cleanness into the polluted world gave her two weeks of migraine. But members of Notre Dame accompanied her, and she was given a gentle re-entry.

Her vision of wholeness wasn't easy to carry through in practice. People didn't understand that wholeness was not mere theory but must be carried through in every aspect of life. She lived in a sort of limbo for two years in the provincial house of the Congregation in Woolton, Liverpool, full of anguished awareness of being over fifty years old, with so much to give and no way to give it. She could opt for nothing that wasn't Creation Spirituality.

She became very assertive and stopped apologizing for her needs. Then she was ill, and went back to Erraid for three weeks. "I spent the first week in bed most of the time. But for the other two weeks I was alive. It re-centred me in my own strength."

Then she went on to Findhorn, where she did a workshop with Dorothy Maclean. Inspired by Dorothy she decided to try and connect with the spirit of Liverpool. "I had envisaged myself as living in a cottage in Wales. But when I invoked the spirit of my dream cottage on a hillside in Wales, the sky was overcast and the place was in shadow. Then I visualized the centre of Liverpool and it was bathed in light. I asked the angel of Liverpool to bless the place I'd be working in, and I came back."

Now she lives in the basement of the Liverpool convent, separate from the other nuns. The Congregation of Notre Dame is in the process of spiritual renewal and June sees herself as a part of that, often in the eye of its storm. Her daily work is in healing with Bach Flower Remedies, in counselling and spiritual direction. She leads a weekly meditation group in her basement and runs a programme of workshops on holism and spiritual community. She sometimes travels and gives talks and workshops, and she acts as contact person for the Association for Creation Spirituality in Liverpool. She feels part of the earth becoming spiritually alive.

The theme of June's life, in a word, is transformation. "The task of our lives is to transform the material into the spiritual. 'Sin' is a part of this process. Sin is, in Julian of Norwich's word, 'behovable.' It's necessary, mistakes are necessary. It plunges us into that shadow without which there can be no transformation. The transforming power is love. There is no anger in God. Pain is part of the process. The suffering that comes through our own fault, as well as the suffering that comes to us from life, is an instrument, almost a 'reward' from God. The transformation goes on whether or not in our human terms we 'get it right.' Life goes beyond guilt and virtue. It's about joy.

"I learnt through Julian of Norwich, and I learnt on Erraid, that every negative — every sin, every night, every winter, every death — is part of an organic process which is life-giving. It's not something that went wrong. Negative and positive are both part of transformation, of creation."

The Day I Find A Voice

One day I'll find a voice,
and every branching tree
from darkest root to topmost bud
will hear the sound and will cry out with me.
Showers of rain will weep my grief,
the four winds shout aloud my joy.
Each chattering stream will chant and laugh with me,
the smallest opening flowers will celebrate,
and earth on tiptoe with delight
herself shall sing my song
upon that day,
the day I find my voice.

Brian Thorne

"Good Friday 1946. I was nine ... I'm not entirely sure what was going on inside me, but what I do know is that I was completely overwhelmed, and I ran home. I just ran. Went up to my bedroom, and sobbed and sobbed and sobbed. I don't know for how long. All I know is that from that day onwards I knew that I was infinitely loved."

What about his on-going relationship with the Church of England? He is a very prominent lay Anglican. Have there been any problems with the clergy? "Many profound friendships, but also some problems. There are some in the Anglican church whose theology I find extremely distasteful. At times I need to retreat for the sake of my own healing."

A secular priest?

Brian Thorne was born in 1937, the only child of a butcher's assistant in Bristol. From 1974 until his semi-retirement in 1997 he was Director of Counselling at the University of East Anglia in Norwich, where he continues as director of the Centre for Counselling Studies. He co-founded the Norwich Centre, committed to the person-centred approach to therapy of Carl Rogers, and has written much on this theme including a study of Rogers' life and work.[1] He also holds appointments in Paris and Vienna. A member of the Church of England, he has offered mediation and group facilitation to the church in conflict situations. He is currently Lay Chairman of the Bishop's Council in the Diocese of Norwich.

I meet Brian in the Norwich Centre and he warns me at the beginning of our talk that he might not be very lively because he has just suffered the death of his step-mother Daisy. His grief for her is great, because not only did she marry his father four years before his death, she was midwife at Brian's birth, cared for him for the first six months of his life and was present throughout his childhood. It is part of an extraordinary story.

"In some strange way that I've not always been conscious of, there has been a sense of danger around in my life. My mother had rheumatic fever as a young woman, and it left her heart so badly impaired that she was told she should never have children." *So he was born against the odds? She was willing to face the danger?* "Yes. And so was my father. I imagine it wasn't an altogether joyous time for me in the womb, and I decided to get out early, by about a month. My mother had had an appallingly difficult labour and went into what we would now call a post-natal depression. I was not only premature but very sickly.

"But though there was a lot of danger around — something of a leitmotif in my life — there was also the necessary help there." *His step-mother?* "Daisy was my mother's best friend. She also delivered me, she gave me maternal care during my mother's illness, and she became my godmother. It must have been a strange experience for my father. He was a very quiet man, a man of tremendous fidelity, equilibrious, always responsive in a generous way to those who came into the butcher's shop. Someone approached me after my father's funeral and said, 'You do know, don't you, that your father kept many of us going during the war?' He was such a symbol of strength and serenity, she said, he always smiled, and some people would go into the shop simply to exchange the time of day with him." *I suggest that there is something almost angelic in that, and Brian agrees.* "He played with me, cricket and table football. He was deeply involved in dealing with me in those early years."

Preserved from danger

The theme of being at risk and yet being cared for was strongly reflected in Brian's childhood experiences during the war. Does he interpret this theme in terms of God? "I do. I feel I have been preserved, I presume because it is important that I continue to exist. I have had a sense of vocation, at times very clear, at other times not so clear: I have been preserved in order to respond to my calling. It's only in the last twenty-odd years that I have reflected on these things and begun to make some sense of them.

"The first time that the Luftwaffe bombed Bristol was a Sunday night, and my mother and father and I were visiting my father's mother on the other side of Bristol. I was only three years old, but I'm sure the memory is mine, not a story told to me. Just as we were preparing to leave, the siren went and we had to go down and cower in her cellar. There was an incredible crash from above, and I remember my grandmother — an alarming woman, of whom I was frightened — shouting 'What's that?' and going upstairs and coming back down with an enormous piece of shrapnel that had come through the glass roof of the kitchen. It was almost beautiful, a big silver creation. Anyone in the way of it would have surely been killed. The all-clear didn't go for hours, till about 2 o'clock in the morning. Then we walked home through a city ablaze. I remember feeling more and more tired, and my father had to carry me. Because we were all so tired we decided to go to my mother's parents' house, which was about a mile nearer. I remember that Holy Nativity Church, Knowle — a church that for me was to become very important — was in flames. And I also remember, as we climbed the hill, how difficult it was to walk because the sweet shop at the top had been bombed, and all the stickiness was trickling down the hill, so it was like walking through glue. Then we turned the corner into the street where my grandparents lived and found, not a house, but a hole. The remains of a piano was hanging from the wall."

His grandparents were killed? "No. But I remember my mother screaming and fainting, and the neighbours running out and plying her with brandy and saying, 'It's all right, they went to the air-raid shelter,' which had only been completed the week before. Terrible danger, so close. But it was all right."

Did the rest of the family have a sense of being saved by God? "I don't recollect any expression of that feeling. But I feel sure that would have been the interpretation of my uncle, my mother's brother, who was also in the air-raid shelter. He was a church organist and a devout Christian."

I point out that he had mentioned "war-time experiences," in the plural. "Oh yes. There was another. It was in 1942 or 1943. My mother and I were out shopping and we were waiting for the bus. The bus came, and we had that tiresome experience of climbing on the bus and then being shoved off again because it was too full. As soon as the bus crawled away the siren went, and five minutes later that bus suffered a direct hit."

That's very scary. Has he ever suffered from what they call "survivor's guilt"? "No. But I have felt survivor's *responsibility*." *Quite a weight to bear?* "Yes. And sometimes I feel I've been deluded." Felt that it might just be chance? "Well, I try to think that. But it doesn't last more than five minutes. Which is tiresome, because I don't want to be that important."

Does he ever think, "You're an arrogant bastard"?

"Yes. Am I just a pontificator, am I suffering from a *folie de grandeur*? When I was about sixteen I went to see a Franciscan friar who was visiting my school, and I remember saying to him — as passionate adolescents are wont to do — 'I think I'm meant to serve God but I don't quite know how,' and him saying, 'Well you'd better go back and get on with your French prose, hadn't you'." Brian laughs. "And later in the same conversation he said, 'The trouble with you, I suspect, is not that you're arrogant, but that you're fearful you'll be seen as arrogant.' Very perceptive, and also very helpful."

There are other war stories, too. He was evacuated out of Bristol to two different places in the countryside, and on each occasion Bristol was completely air-raid-free; then, on, the evening he was brought back, all hell was let loose. So his parents gave up and kept him at home.

The pivotal experience of God

But he wasn't Mummy's little boy. His mother was naturally protective of him, but he resisted this. "I told her after she had collected me from school on my first day that she must never come to meet me again. She was terribly distressed. I was upset that she was upset, but at the same time I knew that I mustn't give way. Later I did relent on one issue: I consented to go to Clifton College on a scholarship rather than go with my mates to the state grammar school, because my saying No was causing her so much pain. It was good for my education, I think, that I did.

"My other memory of infants school is of the siren going and me sitting in the air-raid shelter telling stories to entertain the other children. I also invented a quite complicated language so that I could have secret conversations with a six-year-old girl called Pauline who I'd fallen heavily for. I wasn't lonely, though I did feel different from other children." *Why was that?* "I think partly because of the difference in intelligence, but partly because of what I now know is an empathic capacity, an ability to know what is going on in other people's minds. That was a source of great joy, but also of great pain. I picked up all sorts of things that I couldn't at the time understand."

Brian's mother was a fine singer, and with her brother also being an organist the house was full of music. He tells movingly of the last time his mother sang in public, and then says: "Now. That brings us up to what happened to me in 1946. It was the pivotal experience of my life. I've written about it, and I'll recount it again to try and give it some sort of shape.

"I'd started going to church. My mother went occasionally, my father not at all. An old lady who lived in the road asked if I'd like to go to church with her, a high Anglican church, the daughter church of the Holy Nativity. My parents agreed, and off I went. And I was hooked." *Was this G-O-D, or the music, or the drama, or what?* Brian ponders. "It was the immediate recognition," he says carefully, "that I'd stumbled into something that was of supreme importance." *And how old was he?* "I was seven or eight.

"I don't remember being 'close to God' as such. What I do remember is that in that church I could be really alive." *In what way?* "So many of my senses were being satisfied: the music, the beautiful flowers, the well-ordered liturgy, the colours, the vestments, the singing. And what's more, these young priests — there were four curates — preached sermons that I could *understand*!

"Then came the event. Good Friday 1946. I was nine. I was playing cricket in the park — I remember it was full of air-raid shelters with their roofs blown off — when suddenly, round a bend in the road came a religious procession, a Procession of Witness, from my church. Incense, the choir, the congregation behind ... I'm not entirely sure what was going on inside me, but what I do know is that I was completely overwhelmed, and I ran home. I just ran. Went up to my bedroom, and sobbed and sobbed and sobbed. I don't know for how long. All I know is that from that day onwards I knew that I was infinitely loved.

"I knew it almost in the articulated way that I'm now talking about it. If God was like this (for now I was articulating it as a 'God thing') then it was all right to be playing cricket on Good Friday. 'No matter what people tell you, you're all right. Don't ever forget that'."

How did those words come? Did they come this way (I put my hands inwards) or that way (outwards)?

"I'm not sure. The psychotherapist in me would like to say they came this way" (inwards) "but I don't think they did, I think they

came that way" (outwards). "Whatever was happening came from
An Other. Completely. No question."

Did he tell anyone? "No. Not until years and years later. But it
changed my life."

Commitment to the church, openness to the other

"My commitment to the church became absolute. My parents
must have thought it was a bit odd, but they didn't stop me. The
church was wonderful. By the time I was ten I became a friend of
Father Gerard Irvine, who was the first of many significant priests
in my life. He was eccentric, a brilliant young man, a poet, with
a lot of friends in high places. Through him I met John Betjeman
and Stevie Smith. He took a great fancy to me." *Of course these
days, I point out, we would ask "What sort of a fancy was that?"*
"Indeed. But Father Irvine was devoted to the notion of celibacy.
He related to me as an adult, which was what I needed. He took
me to the theatre, he came to the school and took part in the
Fathers' Race — 'I'm Father to everyone!' he said. My parents
loved him, he was so outrageous and so loving. The other priests,
including the vicar, were also very good to me."

*At the age of eleven, off went Brian the butcher's assistant's
boy to Bristol's premier academic "public" school, Clifton.* "It
was very lonely. Fortunately I've always been good at languages,
so I very quickly changed my accent from Bristolian to BBC.

"I also stayed very close to God. One thing I was quite sure of
was that whatever other changes were taking place in my life, my
devotion to God and to Holy Nativity Church were not going to
change."

*That was extraordinarily purposeful for a boy of eleven, wasn't
it?* "I wasn't conscious of that at the time. I just felt there were
things I had to do, even though I might want to do them and *not*
want to do them, both at the same time. I also found out what
'false religion' was. They had it at school. I had the real thing at
Holy Nativity.

"Then there was another priest, Stuart Tayler, who became an
enormous friend to me and to my family. When I was seventeen
Stuart took me for the first of many times as his travelling companion to Greece and Italy, and opened up their treasures to me.

My organist uncle who died young had left me some money which he stipulated could only be spent on foreign travel; he'd never been out of Britain and could have had no idea that I would study foreign languages. But it meant that I could go abroad and do a sort of Grand Tour."

At this point I ask Brian whether entry into a monastic community was ever a possibility for him. He hesitates before replying. "No. I don't think it was. But yes, there has always been in me a tension between being in the world and wanting to be apart from the world. There's a resentment sometimes that the 'apartness' gets a very small portion of my time. The yearning for it is now coming back quite strongly."

Did he ever want to go into the priesthood?

"Yes, but that was scotched very easily. I decided that I'd wear a priest's 'dog collar' when I was travelling from Bristol Temple Meads to Paddington, and just see what happened. I had a compartment to myself the whole way." *So the love of God was not to be transmitted that way?* "No. But at the same time, here were these phenomenal priests who were transmitting the love of God to me.

"I must mention my National Service.* That was terribly important. My basic training taught me not to be a physical coward. Then I went to Cyprus as an infantry officer. In the Officers' Mess were some of my mates from Clifton, and in the ranks were some of my mates from primary school." *Was that a problem?* "I didn't find it a problem. But there were some really significant events here."

We're back to the danger theme again. "The first was when we were driving along and out comes a terrorist and throws a bomb in front of the jeep. I shout 'Drive on!' and we go over the top of it — and it doesn't explode.

"The other one, we're driving down in a three-ton truck from the Troodos Mountains, the whole platoon in the back, and the driver turns to me and says, 'Sir, the brakes have gone.' That driver managed somehow to get this three-tonner off the road and save our lives, running up a hill instead of over the edge." *I know the Troodos Mountains and their gorges. I can imagine it.*

---

* British military service, which was abolished in 1963.

*I ask Brian if he had conversations with God at this time, par-
ticularly about the morality of the army's role.* "I had terrible
problems with my conscience over the British role in Cyprus. Particularly when I was guarding women in prison, young women
who had been distributing anti-British propaganda. I would get
the platoon out of the way and simply talk to them. And the compassion that *they* showed *me* was extraordinary.

"What was strengthened in me in Cyprus was my openness to
different cultures and belief systems. I ended up writing to
Archbishop Makarios after he became the first president of
independent Cyprus, wishing him well from someone who had
fought against 'his' men. He replied to my letter, and from then
on I got a Christmas card from him almost every year until he
died."

This openness to the 'enemy' wasn't wholly new. "At Clifton I'd
decided to study German — not a popular decision, one of my
uncles who'd been in the army didn't speak to me for two years
— and I'd been on an exchange to Hamburg and met a family
where the father had fought and been killed on the Russian front.
I felt very strongly about what had happened to them in the war.
It was in the German language, when I was staying with that family in Hamburg, that I managed for the first time to say things
from the heart. Clifton College had taught me how to say things
from my head, but German taught me how to speak from my
heart. I felt love for the younger son — I'm sure there was a
homosexual tinge to that — and for the mother, for the whole
family. I was able to tell them in their own language, and it was
accepted. I was aware that this was also a profound spiritual experience."

A psychotherapy of love

After National Service he went to Cambridge. "It had become
quite clear to me that I was to study and then teach modern languages, so that I could enable people to be more open to different
influences and cultures. That decision had been taken many years
before, actually, in a church in Italy.

"Then I went to Bristol University to do my teaching certificate. There my tutor was an extraordinary woman called Eliza-

beth Richardson, who pioneered the introduction of psychother-apeutic insights into the classroom. Throughout my year in Bris-tol I was a member of a 'sensitivity training group,' an outrageous thing to be doing right at the beginning of the sixties."

So how did his teaching career change into a career in psy-chotherapy? "My first school was Eastbourne College, which was changing from a traditional public school to one which was much more open to new and liberal influences. Boarding schools are filled with children with appalling stories to tell, and boys soon began to confide in me. I became a sort of amateur counsellor. The Head agreed, astonishingly, that I should follow some train-ing at the Tavistock Institute of Human Relations, and in 1964 he actually agreed to my facilitating a sensitivity training group of sixth-formers where we explored what was going on for them, both personally and inter-personally." *Subversive!* "Yes. But sup-ported by the Head.

"So then I had to decide which direction my career was going in. My decision-making was brought to a crunch when I was helping a boy who, looking back, must have been incipiently psy-chotic. Some of the staff were feeling I was getting too close to this boy, and in desperation I decided to ring up Finchden Manor, a therapeutic community in Kent for boys who had been written off by other people that was run by a remarkable man called George Lyward.[2] He answered the phone, and he invited me to come over, and George Lyward thereafter became one of the great influences in my psychotherapeutic career. He told me, 'You *are* this young man's therapist. Why don't you just get *on* with it?' So I did.

"George had the almost unique ability to relate to each person, with love, as they actually were. He was the only person I've ever known who could harness his anger creatively and lovingly. He was prepared to take enormous risks. I only learnt after his death that every time he did it he was afraid he was going to get it wrong. That taught me that to be a good therapist you don't always have to be secure. You work not from your strength but from your vulnerability."

Within the year he had married Christine, a house matron at Eastbourne College, and decided to retrain as a psychotherapist.

Almost fortuitously he trained in the client-centred approach of Carl Rogers (as opposed to other approaches, such as psychodynamic or Gestalt) with which he was entirely at home. "It has tremendous trust in the human organism as essentially forward-moving, so long as an environment of facilitative conditions can be created. And those facilitative conditions are, first, empathy, with which I already knew I was both blessed and cursed; second, unconditional positive regard, and third, congruence, which means being properly in touch with what is going on in oneself and giving expression to it when appropriate. I realized that this was what in my untutored way I had been doing in my relationships so far. And I was enraptured with Carl Rogers' writing. His books are like having a conversation with him. There's a purity and profundity about them, and an immediate practical clinical application.

"Then I went into the student counselling service at Keele University. While I was there I wrote with colleagues the first British book on student counselling,[3] and put up with vilification from the psychiatric establishment who thought that no one should dabble in these things unless they'd had at least twenty-three years medical experience ... Then I came to Norwich, where I've been ever since."

We have both been realizing, as we talk, what a high proportion has been concentrated on Brian's early experiences and how little on his subsequent highly successful and influential career. Not to mention how little spent on his work as a counsellor in sensitive situations of conflict in the Church of England, of which there have been high profile cases in recent years (though that of course is confidential). This is Brian's choice. All the more recent story has been a working out of the "God interventions" of his formative years.

I ask him now about Julian of Norwich,* whom he has called "a counsellor for our age."[4]

"She has been my spiritual guide for nearly forty years. I came to Norwich partly, I think, because it is her place. It seems to me that she was doing therapeutic work here six hundred years ago. She tells us that in God's eyes we are 'wondrous creatures,' we

---

* Anchoress and mystic who lived 1342–*c*.1416, author of *Revelations of Divine Love*, a document of religious experience.

are His darlings, we have within us all the properties of the God who made us. Yes, there is sin; we sin inevitably through our shame and grief, but it gives us a wonderful opportunity to be utterly child-like and vulnerable, and in this state to run to our mother God for immediate acceptance."

Family and absences

Family life is something I very much want to ask Brian about. I know that he is still married to Christine, and that he has three adult children. Have the pressures of his profession, and his involvement with the community of the church, meant that they have felt ignored? Brian laughs at the question, and explains that he's laughing because this is such an on-going issue for him.

"But, looking back, I had parents who trusted me to be intimately involved with others. My wife also trusts me to be intimately involved with others. As a therapist you're intimately involved with others all the time, behind closed doors. She copes with me being available to other people all the time. She not only accepts that, but makes it possible. She trusts that I will do that honourably."

And his children? Was he an absent father? "Well, I have asked them, and they tell me that that was not their experience. I was sometimes missing, but when I was there I was really there. Their memories, they say, are full of my presence. One of the tremendous aspects of my step-mother's funeral was all of us being together, walking behind the coffin, and then all being together afterwards, totally relaxed and open with each other."

The church, and angels

What about his on-going relationship with the Church of England? He is a very prominent lay Anglican. Have there been any problems with the clergy?

"Many profound friendships," he replies, "but also some problems, yes. There has always been in the Anglican church a very powerful evangelical wing. Their theology I find extremely distasteful, because it seems to disregard the saving grace of the crucifixion and resurrection and to treat people as if they're still grievously in a state of original sin. As if they still need to be shown how vile they are before they can be saved." *Whereas having himself experienced the reverse, the unconditional love of God* ... "Yes. I know we don't need to grovel. So that theology is so abhorrent to me, and in my life as a therapist I have so often had to relate to people who have been so badly damaged by it, that at times I feel unspeakably angry, and I have to be very careful with that anger. There's another strand too. There are clergy who, even though they may not altogether be conscious of it, are actually on a power trip. When they're on a power trip they can do all sorts of damaging things. And if it turns their priesthood into a power-seeking, career-climbing, ambitious affair, that can be disastrous. If I've been called in to try and sort out some church mess, it is quite often a mixture of these two things: a combination of the degrading of humanity and the lust for power, which results in a sort of malevolent narcissism. It's often intractable, because self-awareness would bring unbearable guilt and might actually lead to self-destruction. The evil must always be *out there* rather than *in here.*

"At times, involvement in these things has made me not want to be in this institution at all any longer. So I retreat, for the sake of my own healing."

At this point I ask Brian about his relationship with his own power, as a professor, as a churchman and as a therapist. "It's always a temptation. It's the most awful question for me." He takes a deep breath. "Going back to that experience in the park, from which the message for me was, 'All that really matters is being loved and loving,' I see my therapeutic task as just that, of loving and being loved. Most people who come to the therapist's door are hurting, feel unloved, often quite denigrated, that they are worthless. So the question is, how do you make them feel that they are lovable and have the capacity to love?

"That process seems to involve, at times, taking the most outrageous risks. In any relationship there is always the possibility that what you feel is a loving impulse may be interpreted by the other person as a power impulse. That what you really want is to have this person somehow as an extension of yourself. And when you move into a real depth relationship with a person, it is very difficult to have sufficient awareness to see what's going on. And even if that awareness is vouchsafed to you, you never truly know how the other person is going to experience it. What they experience as loving this year, they may next year interpret as power.

"As a therapist you should always explore these things with your supervisor, if they're the right sort of person. But it's at these points that God is absolutely essential to me. It means that somehow I have to try and stay as close as I possibly can to God, so that the possibility of my inadvertently succumbing to the power impulse is minimized. If I am out of touch with God, if I can't feel in contact with God, then I am in great danger, and my client is in great danger.

"Having said that, there is no way you can be a therapist without experiencing continual self-doubt. Back to George Lyward, who constantly suffered from self-doubt, and yet was a genius. I follow that path, and I never know from one day to the next whether I might fall into the pit. There have been times, in fact, when I *have* fallen into the pit. And I have been badly abused by clients, too. When either of these situations occurs, it is very tempting to give up. And it's at these times when it is vital to stay close to God, and to Jesus in His Passion."

How does he do this? Stay close to God and to Jesus in His Passion?

"There are two fundamental things, as far as I'm concerned. One is the Eucharist. I don't know what I would do if I didn't have access to the Eucharist for any length of time. It enables me, usually, to feel that closeness to God, a kind of internalization of God, a taking of the divine into me, that is absolutely critical.

"The other thing is the attempt to see in other people that which is of Christ. That is a minute-by-minute discipline. It is the perception of God within others. It also ensures that I am nourished by the food of angels."

So, I suggest, his work is to access, by means of his own nature, the divine nature of others. "Yes. I never suggest any such theology to them, but I feel they are seeking it, whether they know it or not."

Sometimes he feels it is all too much. "I ask God, 'Why have you given me this terrible job, which is trying to love people into being? It's insufferably difficult, impossible. Why can't I have a safer orientation, be psychodynamic and retreat behind transference, be a behaviourist and just take people through behavioural exercises? Why *this* orientation, which depends wholly on the relationship and environment of loving between therapist and client? Why must I always face the possibility of doing something dreadful, of taking a risk which can turn out to be a potentially lethal risk?'"

Does he retreat into the wilderness sometimes? "Not as often as I should. But I do have a facility to cut off. So I can move from one situation to another and leave things behind. Writing, too, is immensely satisfying."

Is there a spiritual movement in him through the medium of words? "Yes, there is. I'm nourished by poets, dramatists and novelists. In my study of languages I became steeped in the works of Goethe, for instance, and the seventeenth century dramatists, particularly Racine, and then there's Wordsworth. There is a sense in which I commune with writers at a spiritual level. I sense a whole company of witnesses. Angels and archangels. When I pass out of this body, that is the company I shall join."

Has he ever seen or felt angels? There seems to be something of an angelic trail through his life. "On a couple of occasions I have heard angelic voices. One was when I was in the middle of an appallingly difficult workshop for therapists, and I heard the most extraordinary singing. No one else heard it. And I knew it would be all right. After all, if all these beings were so jubilant what the hell were we worrying about?

"The other occasion was in Lincoln Minster. I was staying with the Chapter Clerk, and we'd had a number of whiskies, and about one o'clock in the morning he said, 'Would you like to go over to the Minster?' So we went over and turned off all the alarms and went into this amazing building, in the dark. At that time there'd been a lot of problems and someone had suggested that the Minster was evil. It wasn't even spooky or frightening. It was so friendly. A gentle monster. And that was the second time I heard singing. Whether it was the whisky or not I can't tell, but we both came out knowing that this was not where evil resided. I think they were angels singing."

Where are the angels in times and places where evil seems rampant? "The only answer I can offer is that the angels of God are in the pain. In the pain of those who commit the atrocities as much as in the pain of those who suffer."

At the moment, in his grief, Brian is looking into something of a mist as far as his life as a therapist and therapy trainer is concerned. "I'm unsure of my direction. But I know that I must wait. On George Lyward's wall there hung a poem by Richard Church that begins:

> Learning to wait consumes my life,
> consumes and feeds as well ...

It's not always easy to wait, or to know when the waiting must end."

Mehr Fardoonji

"When my brother was dying I shouted at some God that I didn't believe in, 'Don't let him die now! Let him live a few more years, and take those years from my life!' I was talking to the God of my childhood. But at the same time I knew it wasn't possible to add and subtract like that. I was simply shouting in anguish."

"I went into a new village called Shantipuri, which means Peace Village, and lived in a house of bamboo and grass. I became head cook and bottle-washer, started a school ..." Her voice trails off. There was a problem here? *"Yes. I had a sort of breakdown. The thing was, I'd set out to change India. And, of course, you can't."*

Walking through paradoxical gardens

Mehr Fardoonji was born in 1930 in Lahore and grew up in Multan, India (now Pakistan), of Parsee (Zoroastrian) parents. When she was five her father died and two years later the family came to England, where she went to school and then to university at LSE. Then she travelled overland back to India and lived in a Gandhian ashram, spending some time in the land-gift movement with Vinoba Bhave. Since 1962 she has lived in south Cheshire, running an organic market garden and teaching in adult education.

I'm sitting in the living room waiting for Mehr. Beyond the door Nicholas is hoovering (soon Mehr will ask him to stop, not because he's eighty-four but so that he can field phone calls and provide us with herb tea). Beyond the french windows the view stretches over lush market gardens and rolling fields to the far Shropshire hills, and just past the lawn and vibrant multi-coloured flower beds a light spray of irrigation rises like a fan from organic vegetable beds.

In comes Mehr in her gardening trousers. I've talked with her on previous occasions, and now it's crystallizing into this interview. But first I can't resist asking her about clothes. On the various occasions I've seen her, she's sometimes in gardening gear as she is now, sometimes in full Indian sari, and sometimes dressed like a Muslim woman in the shalwar kamiz. *Why?*

"Of course trousers and T-shirts and sweaters are right for gardening. But the rest of the time I like to wear saris, because I'm Indian." *But why the shalwar kamiz?* "Well, partly because it's so comfortable. Half the women of the world wear trousers. But it's partly out of solidarity for Islam. Islam gets such a terrible press over here. I want to work against the hatred in a way that's visible."

This is typical of Mehr: feet firmly on the ground, always aware of the political dimension, working out the path of peace in firmly physical ways.

I start by outlining what I see as the vital parameters of Mehr's life and ask her to say how far I'm right. First, I think, her relationship with her family: her mother, her brother, and now Nicholas. "Yes. Most Indian people have strong family ties, and ours were even stronger because we moved to Europe." *Then her relationship with India/Pakistan? She nods, and we both raise eyebrows about the vexed question of terminology, because the place where she was born and grew up was then India and is now Pakistan. Third, I suggest, her relationship with organic horticulture, and health through natural means. And lastly her Gandhian pacifism, which has run throughout her life. Yes, I'm on secure ground with all these things.*

"But you must understand," she says, "that none of them, philosophies or people, influenced me nearly as much as my mother did. My brother used to call me her 'satellite.' Yet I fought with her, too, for my independence. It's a paradox. When she died, I who am so independent wept and cried, 'When the planet goes, what does a satellite do?'"

Family and education

I ask her to tell me about her mother. "She was the one who brought me to Gandhian ideas. I was born when she was forty, nearly twelve years after my only brother. She'd had schooling only till eleven because her eyes were bad (though they were better than mine) and after that she educated herself. She read and read, secretly at night with a torch: Gandhi, and Rudolf Steiner who showed how children learn through play and imagination and shouldn't start formal schooling till they're six or seven.* What a contrast to her family, who were conventional Parsees.† She brought me up as a vegetarian, whereas my father's family

---

* Rudolf Steiner (1861–1925). Edited the scientific works of Goethe, founded the Waldorf School Movement as well as centres for scientific and mathematical research, architecture, economics, drama and art, and the biodynamic system of farming and gardening.

† Zoroastrianism started in Persia, and those who fled from persecution to India are called Parsee, i.e Persian.

weren't vegetarian at all, they ate meat, lots of it. When I got whooping cough they said, 'It's because she's weak, she needs to eat meat,' but I wouldn't and I got better." *Did her mother actually meet Gandhi?* "Yes, at the Lahore Congress in the 1920s. It was only a brief meeting, but put together with her reading it changed her for life."

Does the Zoroastrian God have a personality, like the Christian God? "No. God's name is Ahura Mazda, the source of light and life and intuitive knowledge. The trouble is, Alexander the Great, wicked man, burnt all the sacred Zarathustran texts at Persepolis. So it was left to the priests to recall them, which is very sinister. It gives them power! So we have no true records of our religion ..."

"We," "our"? Does she still feel like a Parsee?

"Well, I was born one. It's my *jat,* my heritage. I grew up repeating the Zoroastrian prayers, and I was confirmed in London before menstruation, which is the tradition. I wore the muslin shirt with its little inset of special cloth, the symbol of purity, and the girdle of faith. They say their prayers with the girdle, like a rosary."

But did she believe in God? "No, not in God. I've always reacted against organized religion. When I was very young, before my father died, so I was less than five, I was taught that 'God comes first, then Mummy and Daddy, then my brother and the other members of the family ...' But I thought that was wrong. 'Who *is* this God?' I asked. 'I don't *know* this God. Why do I have to love something I know nothing *about*? Mummy and Daddy come first!'

"But the central Zoroastrian theme is 'Good thoughts, good words, good deeds,' and that's what I've kept from it. My upbringing is still within me: I know that because in 1986, when my brother was dying, I shouted at some God that I didn't believe in, 'Don't let him die now! Let him live a few more years, and take those years from my life!' I was talking to the God of my childhood." *Was it part of coming to terms with his death?* "Yes. But at the same time I knew it wasn't possible to add and subtract like that. I was simply shouting in anguish."

Were she and her brother close?

"Oh yes. He threatened to punch my mother's tummy when she was pregnant, but when I was born he adored me. We adored each other. And my aunts all adored my father, their brother, and how do you show someone your adoration? You feed them. We had a general store, so there was lots of food around. My aunts fed my father and he became overweight, and then he got paratyphoid and his heart gave way. No one should die of paratyphoid! But my father did."

Her mother must have grieved? Mehr takes a deep breath. "She was so overwhelmed with grief that I became invisible to her. It had been a love match, they'd met through their love of poetry and fallen for each other, and he'd asked his parents to arrange the marriage. And suddenly, after only eighteen years, he was gone."

Everything changed. The aunts melted away, the shop went down and down, the family broke up. Her mother's brother was in the cloth trade in Manchester so, since Mehr's brother needed a university education, they travelled by boat, sick all the way, to England. "I remember getting off at Marseilles, looking for loos, they were disgusting. Then Manchester, the fog. It was 1937, September. My mother suddenly had to cook: she'd never cooked in her life and she was fort-seven. Instead of playing outside, Steiner fashion, Indian fashion, I went to school."

She laughs. "But I loved school! My mother had always encouraged me to ask questions and I was fascinated by everything I learnt."

How did her brother react to his father's death? "Dreadfully. He was so close to my mother, but she couldn't talk to him. She didn't even tell him how his father actually died. He was frightened of anything emotional." *Why?* "It was his education. He went to a boarding school run by the Irish Christian Brothers, and they flogged the boys when their homework was wrong." *But why did his adoring parents send him to a place like that?* "Because the school got the best results in India. My brother was a sensitive soul, he hated it, but he had to learn to be a man, to be strong, to support us. And he did look after us. He bought me this ..." *She waves a hand round the room and out towards the gardens.* "But I always fought with him. I remember once he told me to pick something up, and I wouldn't, and he bent my arm down towards it: 'I'll break your arm ...' 'Go on, break it!' I said. And of course he wouldn't, he loved me, he wouldn't hurt me. But that's how fiercely we fought."

Return to India, and work with Vinoba

She studied politics and economics at the London School of Economics. "It was international relations really. I travelled a lot: I'd gone abroad in the year after school, and in university vacations I travelled all over Europe. During term-times, with a Jewish boy, I started the LSE Pacifist Society. I've always been a pacifist. My mother gave that to me through the Gandhian philosophy."

Her pacifism took on another dimension one vacation when she worked as a cleaner in a biology lab in Norway. "I'd go in at five in the morning to clean out the monkeys and rabbits on the eighth floor. One day I asked one of the researchers what they did to the animals. He showed me all the processes, the cancers, the amputations ... I couldn't bear it." *And when she graduated?* "My mother would have loved me to work with the UN, but I knew I couldn't, the British government wouldn't have let me because I was Indian. No, I went back to India, to the Gandhi *ashram* at Sevagram.*

"But I spent seven months going there." *In 1953, on her own?* "Yes. My mother was the brave one, to let me go. I'd got lots of connections and I made lots more friends. I went on the Orient Express — I delivered some sort of parcel on the way, heaven knows what was in it — and I worked three months on a kibbutz in Israel. Then Syria, Lebanon, Iraq — I spent two weeks in Baghdad trying to get a passport for Iran, but they gave me one as soon as they heard I was Zoroastrian. I wore my sari all the way through Iran to show that I was Indian ... And finally to Multan, which now of course was in Pakistan. And then to be a village worker at Gandhi's *ashram* in central India, at Sevagram.

"My main work was with Vinoba Bhave and the land-gift movement. Vinoba wasn't perhaps as warm a personality as Gandhi, but he took Gandhi's ideas forward. I'd take his Commentary on the *Gita* to a desert island. Gandhi had advocated *satya graha*† for the community, and when he wanted individual *satya graha* he chose Vinoba to start it, because of his spiritual integrity.

---

* A Gandhian ashram is a community based on simple living and self-sufficiency.

† *Satya graha:* non-violent resistance, demonstrated most vividly in the Salt Marches against British rule of India.

"The biggest social problem was that the peasants had no land, and the communists were trying to solve it by slaughtering the landlords. Gandhi's followers were very much against that, though of course they too wanted the peasants to be able to own the land, and they arranged a big conference in Hyderabad on the direction the Gandhian movement should take. Vinoba had made a vow not to use money, so he never took the bus or train but walked everywhere. He set off to Hyderabad from Wardha months in advance, walking through the villages asking people what their main problem was, and they said, 'We can't do anything because we don't own our land.' The conference didn't achieve very much where landlessness was concerned, and Vinoba made his way back. A landlord who had walked some way with him asked what he'd do if he, the landlord, gave some land to him. Vinoba responded by saying, 'I need time to meditate on that.' At a second meeting he said to the villagers, 'This is God speaking. What would you do with this land if it were offered?' And they said, 'We'd give it to the landless.' So the *Bhoodan* movement started, the land-gift movement. It took off, and the government gave it legal status. Eventually some villages gave all their land to be redistributed."

What was her part in the movement? "I walked with Vinoba in Orissa. We went from village to village, talking to the people about Bhoodan and getting land for them. We'd get up at about 4 AM and say Gandhian prayers (they're sacred songs, recognizing all religions and seeing God in all things) then at sunrise we'd walk to the next village prepare for Vinoba's meeting. But, now here's an irony, I felt that we were slightly parasitical. The villagers gave us food and baths and so on. I didn't feel it was right for me to stay doing it for a long time.

"So I went the foothills of the Himalayas, tiger territory, real rainforest, all totally destroyed now of course. Parts of it were given to Bhoodan by the government to settle landless labourers from the hills. I went into a new village called Shantipuri (which means Peace Village) and lived in a house of bamboo and grass. I became head cook and bottle-washer, started a school ..."

Her voice trails off. There was a problem here? "Yes. I had a sort of breakdown. The thing was, I'd set out to change India. And, of course, you can't. My Cambodian friend Aditia came, and we

built a house together, rammed earth walls and a thatched roof: all
the materials, as Gandhi said, from a bullock cart's distance. But it
was so frustrating. We asked the villagers whether they'd like to
have a house like ours made from earth and thatch, which was perfect in all weathers, or did they want a brick house with a tin roof.
The brick and tin house was baking in summer, freezing in winter,
and sounded like thunder when it rained. But the villagers chose
that one, not ours." *Why?* "Because rich people had brick houses."

Was she in love with Aditia?

"Maybe. With my parents' romantic marriage and my father's
death I was brought up with the idea of romantic love. How could
I marry unless it was like that? Aditia was an artist and an engi-
neer, both. He could do anything with his hands. He built a spinning wheel for me, which I've still got. They used to say he'd got
Lakshmi in his hands.*

*But he wanted to be a Buddhist monk. He'd lived with Lanza
del Vasto, who founded the Gandhian L'Arche community in
France, and he was torn between becoming a monk, and me. I'd
have come second, I knew that.*

"My health simply broke down from all the tension and disappointment. I became weak and weepy, and when my mother suggested we go back to England for a rest, I said yes."

What happened to Aditia?

"He got tuberculosis, and when I was back in England we got
the news that he'd died. I still have his journals here."

Organic gardening and natural health

*At this stage of the Bhoodan movement every family in Shantipuri
was given a plough, a couple of bullocks, and seven and a half
acres of land. Half an acre was for the house and a vegetable garden, but Mehr had a whole acre round her house. She and Aditia
had learnt at Sevagram about growing organically, and from
books by Albert Howard† in Gandhi's library. She was hooked,
and they grew more and more, developing the compost, never
using fertilizers or pesticides.*

* Lakshmi: the Hindu goddess of good fortune.

† Founding father of organic gardening in Britain.

"When Aditia died, my love of organic gardening didn't die. My brother offered to buy me a market garden not too far from him in the north of England, and meanwhile I went off to learn the job in an organic market garden in Bromley, near London.

"Then this place, Oakcroft, came up for sale. The land hadn't been ploughed in living memory and the aspect was perfect. My brother offered a price but the owners wouldn't accept it and said he must go to the auction. But his business prevented him from going. So I thought, well, that's it, it's not mine. Then they phoned: it hadn't reached the reserve price so they'd accept his offer."

Was it "meant"?

Mehr laughs. "Yes! But not meant *by* anyone or anything. Not God. Maybe Nature 'meant' it. Whatever that means. I don't think in terms of 'meaning,' I think of 'trusting in life.' I know that whenever I thought I should leave here because it wasn't making money, something has stopped me. I nearly got a job as a social worker in Crewe, but they said I must have an X-ray every year and I wouldn't. Stupid, maybe, but I wanted to stick to my principles. The Medical Officer of Health said, 'Who does she think she is?' and I lost the job. Crazy. But then the WEA* asked me to teach part-time, so I could stay."

And people with organic ideals come and help in the garden?

"Yes, they live in the flat above. It gives them the chance to learn about organic gardening, and it's learning by doing, very Gandhian. Occasionally there have been disasters, in the hippy era especially, but on the whole it's worked out fine. It gave me Kerry, who was born here because his parents worked in the garden. He always came back twice a year for holidays, and he still comes even now he's grown up and working. He's the nearest to being like a child of my own."

As she describes the people who help in the garden, those who attend her Yoga and other classes and those who belong to the local organic food movement, I get a picture of a network of friends and linkings that seem like an informal community.

---

* Workers' Educational Association, which runs day and evening classes with fees according to income.

Body, mind, philosophy, spirit

I*n adult education she has taught organic gardening, Third World issues, and political philosophy.* "One group of mothers did 'From Plato to Gandhi' and her son still talks about 'the time Mum learnt about Rousseau' and asks what Rousseau would say about whatever they're doing." *Then came Yoga.*

"Yoga was a word that for me was associated with religion, so I rejected it. But when I was ill in India they gave me Yoga *pranayama* exercises, breath control for my lungs, which helped me. So I was interested. When I was learning organic gardening in Bromley I had one day off a week, and I went into London to do three things: I went to the School of Oriental Studies to learn Sanskrit, I did weaving classes and I learnt Yoga. I was fascinated by the philosophy of it, and I realized that it didn't need to have anything to do with religion."

At first it was a personal discipline, and Mehr didn't want to teach it. But so many people asked her that she agreed, on condition that she could teach the philosophy as well as the physical practice.

What connection does Yoga have with Gandhian ideals and growing organic food? "It's about keeping the body healthy. You must care for your body, because if you don't then your spirit won't thrive either. Gandhi felt strongly about that, I feel strongly about that. Yoga connects body, mind and spirit. I don't want to take poisons into my body, I don't want to take drugs, like I wouldn't have that X-ray. The body is the temple of the spirit."

Did she eat meat and go to mainstream doctors when they first came to England in the 1930s? "Yes, we ate meat. But my mother met a herbalist, a Lancashire man called Charlie Abbott who'd been cured of TB with herbs, and he cured my brother of ulcers and he cured me of period pains. He was one of the most wonderful men I've ever met, and he recommended we became vegetarian."

What about pain? Does she take painkillers when she's injured, or antibiotics for infections? "I always refuse antibiotics because I think they work against the body's own system. In India I had malaria, dysentery and typhoid or something like it, and I never took a drug. I fasted, and just drank strained orange juice.

That's the Gandhian way. I accepted it wholly, even though in the ashram they tried to persuade me to take medicines because they were frightened. At one point I was so weak that I thought it would be fine to die. Actually, in the end it was herbs from Charlie Abbott in Lancashire that cured me.

"Later when I broke my arm terribly badly I had to have an anaesthetic when they opened it up. But I don't accept anything chemical or alien into my body unless it's absolutely essential."

She's impatient to tell me something else about Gandhi and God. "I must tell you about my atheist friends. It's so courageous to be atheist in India. These were Brahmans, priests, of the highest caste, but they rejected God and became totally Gandhian. They gave up everything to work with untouchables. Gandhi was thrilled with the work and he told them rather mischievously, 'You reject God, but God is working through you.' Which they didn't like at all! I'm still in touch with them, and the work goes on.

"Another influence from my mother was Vivekananda, who was a follower of Ramakrishna.* I love them both, Vivekananda and Ramakrishna. You'll be interested in this: Ramakrishna said that one day when in *samadhi*† he met Christ, and they embraced, and when Christ had gone Ramakrishna had the marks of the stigmata on him.

"Vivekananda wrote a whole treatise on Yoga. Through reading that I began to see there was a spiritual dimension to life. It came to me through working on the land as well. Still, I was worried because of my dislike of religious practice.

"But then came Jung. A young woman working on the land here lent me a book on Jungian philosophy by Esther Harding, and reading Jungian ideas showed me spirit as psyche, instead of spirit connected to an outside God. At last I understood that the spiritual comes in ways that can't be expressed in words. And Yoga was perfect for me because of the way it balances body, mind and spirit."

---

* Vivekananda (1863–1902), Hindu saint and founder of the Ramakrishna Order; campaigner for Indian independence from British rule. Ramakrishna (1836–1886) preached oneness with the Godhead and with all created beings.

† *Samadhi:* an altered state of consciousness.

Peace and power

*It was in the early 1980s that Mehr's Gandhian pacifism was out-
wardly tested again. She was active in the anti-nuclear movement, and she longed to protest in ways that would have put her
into jail.*

"You must understand that in India, in the Gandhian movement
for independence, everyone who was anyone had been in jail. It
was necessary, it was a privilege. So of course I was ready to go
to jail in the cause of nuclear disarmament. But I was warned by
a lawyer, 'If you get a criminal record and then go out of the
country, you'll never be allowed back into Britain.' So I couldn't
do it or I'd never see be able to travel between India and Britain
again."

Was she at the big demonstrations of women at Greenham? "Of
course I was. It was wonderful, intoxicating. Then I realized that
it was the intoxication of power, and power was what I was
protesting against. We felt absolutely right, we felt invincible, and
that was dangerous.

"I learnt my lesson then. I must beware of power. It's like driving a fast car. When I was young I could have had a love affair
with fast cars, but they're against everything I believe in. In my
work I suppose I could let people make me into some sort of guru.
Here am I in the depths of Cheshire, I'm Indian, I'm a woman,
I'm bossy by nature, so it would be easy to become one. But it's
power. It's wrong."

Extremities of bereavement

She hadn't prepared herself at all for her mother's death. "As I
told you, I was her satellite. When she was dying my brother said
to me, 'You've got to let her go,' and I didn't know what he meant.
Only later, when we sat by her bed, I realized he meant, 'Let her
go into death.' I didn't weep while she was dying: my brother
wept all through it, but I just said my mantra, the first prayer I
learnt as a child, over and over and over. It centred me in myself,
and I wanted to be strong to be with her till she died.

"The morning of her death she said, 'Why are there all these
children in the room?' I said, 'Don't be silly, there aren't any

children here.' But the day after she died all the children came, the neighbouring children, the ones who loved her, and they came with flowers. She must have seen them beforehand.

"After her death, against all British tradition, I kept her body with me for three nights. I stayed in the same room with her and watched the body change. It was almost clinical. That was when I was most aware of my two selves."

"Two selves?" What does she mean?

"I have a way of looking at myself, of asking myself what's going on in my head and my heart. I get completely immersed in what I'd doing or feeling, but at the same there's this dialogue that's always going on inside. There I was, desolate with grief, but I carefully watched the body become less alive and more dead."

Was there any sense of the soul leaving the body?

"In our tradition, the Parsee tradition, you always leave a window open for the soul to leave. I didn't have to open a window, it was high summer and hot, but I was aware of that open window as a symbol."

Has she ever felt her mother's presence since her death? "I know I'll never see her again physically. Or my brother. (Now, I opened a window when *he* was dying, and it was winter, and cold.) After he died I broke my arm on his birthday, shattered the bone into pieces, through grief. I tripped accidentally, of course, but I knew it was through grief. But some time after he died ... I was sitting in the theatre ... these things happen to me anywhere ... in that moment I knew that my relationship with him, with both of them, my mother and my brother, goes on growing even after their death. I can't say '*They* grow,' because I don't know whether they do. But I see them differently because *I* grow."

So these are knowledges, not visions? "I have waking visions, too. One was driving in the car quite near here. It was a series of flashes, and they showed me all the people I love in a visionary way. My father was shown to me as the Himalayas, distant and beautiful and unapproachable, and my mother was a glow-worm to light up my path, and my brother was my 'shadow,' in the Jungian sense. I stopped the car, and I wept and wept. Then, more slowly, it came to me that Kerry was my 'child,' and Nicholas my 'other.' Again, in the Jungian sense.

"Kerry's more distant now he's over twenty, and he gets angry with me, but that's the way it goes with family. Nicholas as the other: yes, he's male and English, and not of my culture or religion. Gentle, tolerant, wise, learned. He shows me sides of myself that I find difficult."

The main purpose of life

It was in 1990, when she was fifty-nine and he was seventy-five, that she married Nicholas Gillett, an old friend who had been widowed two years before, and he came to live with her at Oakcroft. They're obviously very much in love. "You see how we love each other? Oh, I don't like to live alone. I've done it, between my mother's death and marrying Nicholas. But I think to live with someone is like living with a mirror, you have to look at yourself, and that helps you to grow. To me that's the main purpose of life, to grow.

"Sometimes I worry that I'm too happy in this stage of my life. I'm frightened that Nicholas will die before me. Just before we got married I wept over a dear friend and said, 'After my mother and my brother, how can I bear another bereavement?' But then my two-selves come in, the ones that talk to each other, and one of them says to the other, 'You know about pain, you know that it won't go, but it can change you, make you grow.'

"There's a Yogic idea that we're all spiritually lazy. We grab hold of a spiritual belief and we stay with it. We don't grow with it, but we should. The first stage of the spiritual journey is the stage when you revere the great person: like I revere Gandhi, admire him, get ideas from him. Or we can revere Jesus, or the Buddha, or learn about the lives of the saints. This is very nourishing, but you've got to move on. The next stage is the stage of Buddha- or Christ-consciousness, when you make Buddha or Christ or Gandhi part of you. You don't stay with what they said, you make the meaning or the feeling of it your own. That's where some of us remain. The last stage is cosmic consciousness, where there's no you, no ego. You're conscious of the whole universe and the interrelationships within it. That's the journey. That's my journey. My mother always said, 'You can learn to the day you die.'

"The nearest I can get to it is the concept of the *web*. I feel the energy in the universe, and I feel the fine thread that lingers, that we have no knowledge of."

We're into almost mystical realms here. But Mehr isn't mystical. She goes straight on: "Take the issue of animal experiments. I don't argue with people who are in favour of them because they think the experiments help to heal people. Nicholas feels like that. But I remember the experimental lab where I was a cleaner years ago, and I feel the pull of those other consciousnesses. I don't want to hurt the animals because they're part of the web."

She once met Bede Griffiths, the Catholic monk who settled in India. "I was amazed how close I was to Bede Griffiths' ideas. He believed that when the body goes at death, so also does the soul. By 'soul' he meant 'psyche,' in the Jungian sense. I asked him, 'So what happens to the soul after death?' He answered that the individual soul disperses, and all that's left is the universal spirit. That's how I see it. I was a bit unnerved to find that I agreed with a Catholic! I believe entirely that the differentiated psyche is the part that develops and grows so as to become closer to the universal spirit, and the universal spirit is what's eternal."

In Hinduism there are three faces of God: the Creator, the Preserver and the Destroyer. "You can pray to whichever face of God you like. Also there's the Atman, the God within, and the Brahman, the God everywhere. Universal energy is in all things, but it's differently manifest.

"There's a comment by Isherwood on one of the Yoga aphorisms: 'The underlying Reality is by definition omnipresent. If the Reality exists at all, it must be everywhere; it must be present within every sentient being, every inanimate object.'[1] That's what I feel. That's what I know."

Anne Gray

"The soul chooses its own parents." So, I ask, did Anne choose her own difficult mother? She laughs. "I certainly learnt to respect her for what she believed in, for realizing that though she had brought me into this life, I had a different path from her. She got stuck in the past, but she'll have got unstuck by now."

"In a Steiner school, if you have a problem, say a child who has a particular difficulty, you discuss it all together, everyone who has anything to do with that child. By the end of the evening you've gained a different attitude towards that child, and you've come to a better understanding of how you can help them. Now I think that's community."

Awareness of other worlds

Anne Gray was born Anne Connah in 1916 in Savièse,
Switzerland, the only child of a Swiss Calvinist mother and
a British Anglican father. Her Aunt Sal was an anthro-
posophist, a follower of Rudolf Steiner, whose philosophy
Anne at first rejected. She came to England, first to work
and then to study at the London School of Economics,
where the materialism of both the course and the other stu-
dents drove her to re-examine Steiner and his theories and
become an anthroposophist. She married Peter Gray who,
disabled at birth by cerebral palsy, was educated at a nor-
mal Steiner school. They had two children and together they
taught and cared for multiply-disabled children in a Steiner
school in Bristol. Anne is also a member of The Christian
Community.*

I take the bus from Edinburgh southwards to the small town of
Innerleithen, which settles itself comfortably into a fold of hills in
the lush landscape of the Scottish Borders. Anne Gray lives in a
small disabled-adapted bungalow, and her house and garden have
the sense of someone living lightly in this world: comfortable but
with few luxuries, simple food, lots of books and interesting
paintings gathered through a long life.

One painting especially draws my attention: it's unfinished at
the edges, a wild landscape of mountain and lake in wet weather,
its drama arising directly out of the play of strong primary
colours.

* Anthroposophy refers to the body of spiritual knowledge attained by Rudolf
Steiner, which gave rise to practical applications such as science, education, architecture, and many others. Steiner was also instrumental in helping a number of theologians found The Christian Community, a movement for religious renewal.

"That's anthroposophical in style," Anne tells me. "Colour comes first, and your subject comes out of the colours. That painting is one of six by Lady Macleod of Macleod, and the only connection she'd got with anthroposophy was that she once played the piano for children doing Eurythmy, a Steiner form of movement. Curious."

Feet in two camps

Anne's forthright and expressive manner is punctuated with irony and laughter as she tells her story. Her father was a British accountant who went into the family lace and glove business in France, and later into the spring water business on the French-Swiss border. "But he had a passion for mountains, so he took his business to the far side of the lake, the Swiss side, because of the connections to the Alps. There, up a mountain, he met a family with several daughters, and he married one of them.

"My mother's family were originally French Huguenot. When the First World War ended my mother was very keen to leave the narrow Catholicism of that alpine area and get me into a Protestant school, so we moved to Lausanne. She'd been a teacher in the school and her reputation was somewhat at stake.

"From a religious point of view I had my feet in two camps. My father went to the Church of England church in Lausanne — simply to be in touch with the other English people, I think — and occasionally he took me there. But in general my mother took me to the Calvinist State church, the church of that *canton*. In spirit I was much closer to my father, but my mother's values tended to dominate. My mother always insisted I do the 'right thing,' meaning I was to ask permission to do anything at all — which I did not enjoy!

"At about fourteen I was confirmed, and around this time something very sad happened that distanced me from my mother. My father's sister, my godmother who I loved very much, died in England. My mother and I had been looking for pasqueflowers in the Jura mountains, which are limestone. Pasqueflowers are so very beautiful, especially the purple ones that grow beside the yellowing dead grasses and the red box bushes, they're like a velvety egg ... We came back and found the telegram from my father about my godmother's death stuck in the front door. I don't remember my mother's actual words, but she said something like 'Good riddance to bad rubbish.'

"She said the same sort of thing to my father when he came back from England, and he was so horrified that he said to me quietly, 'I think I'll go back to Australia.' I said to him, 'You're not going to leave me with that woman!' So he didn't in fact go. But that was the extent of the rift."

This hardness in her mother, did she attribute it at all to her Calvinism?

"No, I think it was personal. One problem for my mother was that I exchanged letters with my godmother. My father was unusual for his time in recognizing that letters to a child were for the child's eyes alone, and she and I had a wonderful correspondence. I think my mother was jealous.

"With this rift, I realized that my relationship with her was in effect dead.

"I was determined to go and live in England when I left school. I could do that since I was of British nationality, and I had taken all the necessary exams. It was 1935, Hitler was just around the corner. But when I discovered I was like hundreds and thousands of refugees and they wouldn't recognize my qualifications, I did a shorthand typing course, then I took the English 'Matric' and got a job as a student leader with the YWCA in the UK.

"I went back and told my mother, who of course was upset. She'd had a fantasy of marrying me off to some nice Swiss man.

"Then when I was 21 I inherited the money that my godmother had left me seven years before. I could afford to go to University, and I applied to the LSE to study Economics and Social Sciences."

Resisting and accepting the spiritual path

In 1937, then, she could complete her education thanks to her blessed godmother. How did university go?

"I discovered a completely different side of life: politics. Being twenty-one by then I made friends with the older students, and a lot of them were politically involved. But I wasn't a Tory, and the left-wingers were mostly Stalinists who were trying to organize the students into little cells. I hated that sort of materialism."

So for Anne the meaning of life didn't lie in politics. Did it lie in religion? Had she come across anthroposophy or Rudolf Steiner by then?

"I'd dismissed it! My father's other sister, my aunt Sal, came to stay with us every other year. I could relate to her. When I was about twenty she pulled out a book from under her pillow and said, 'I haven't told your parents but I'm reading this book, it's very interesting.' It was by Rudolf Steiner, either *Occult Science* or *Knowledge of Higher Worlds and Its Attainment,[1]* I forget which. I took one look and didn't want anything to do with it. She didn't comment at all."

She just waited? "Exactly. If I went to stay with her for a weekend in Birmingham we didn't talk anthroposophy. Then ..."

Anne pauses. I prompt her. Then? "I got engaged to an older man. He was from the Caribbean, he'd been sponsored by his government for a year and then he was to go back, so I would have gone back with him. But Aunt Sal was absolutely against my marrying him. She said my parents would die of grief."

Why? On racial grounds? "Quite possibly. And it would take me away from them." *Did she resist the arguments?* "At first. But Aunt Sal was so insistent that in the end I accepted, and gave up the engagement. It was horrible. He went back to Trinidad and he never married again."

Was she angry with Aunt Sal? "No, actually. I was unhappy, but not angry. I understood why she did it.

"Then, early in 1939, I went to stay with her and for the first time we discussed anthroposophy. By this time I was ready. I was going on to her about how materialistic my course was, and LSE in general, I couldn't stand it, and she said, 'I did mention Rudolf Steiner to you in 1936 but you weren't interested ...' and we got talking. It was just a year later that I joined the Anthroposophical Society, and I've been a member ever since. The first thing I joined was a youth group. I loved it all, youth group, study groups, everything. What I loved best of all about it, and I've loved it ever since, was eurythmy. That is the expression in movement of the sounds of speech and music. In Steiner schools it's part of the curriculum and it can also be used curatively, but you can do it for pleasure. Think of 'a,' think of 'o,' think if 'i'." Anne is making gestures here. "Sounds which arise

out of your own soul being, not from outside. It can be very
beautiful.

"I carried on my studies at LSE, I was going to get my degree
as planned, but I'd found what I wanted. Life was not materialistic. It was spiritual. I had read Edouard Schuré, who linked
Orpheus, Ramakrishna, Plato, Moses, Pythagoras, and Jesus. I
even used those things for my LSE essays. And got away with it!
Schuré was acceptable, Steiner was not.

The wisdom of other worlds

"Outside LSE, the intellectual side of anthroposophy fascinated
me. I began to realize that life without reincarnation made no
sense. It was an evolutionary theory of spirituality, and I saw that
it needed reincarnation to make it work. Steiner says that you can
accept his views because they make logical, intellectual sense. If
that's not possible for you, you can develop your spiritual understanding as a half-way stage. But he's talking about facts rather
than beliefs."

*In other words, science? How does this "occult science" relate
to what we think of as the "scientific story of creation," the Big
Bang and so on?*

"Ah," replies Anne, smiling. "Not very well. Not really. It's not
a question of one being right and another being wrong, it's that
you're looking at it from different angles. In anthroposophy,
unless you get away from the purely materialistic interpretation of
the universe you're not going to get anywhere. The heavenly bodies are not only water, gas, etc. They're spiritual entities, which
you learn to understand by developing the spiritual senses within
yourself. So you're in a different realm from modern scientists.
Though I think that now some of them are coming round to thinking that the material is only one aspect of the universe."

Back to the anthroposophical youth group. "It was there I met
the man who was to become my husband.

"Peter was born with cerebral palsy because of mishandling at
his birth during World War One, when all the experienced per-
sonnel were at the Front. His parents sent him to a state school for
the disabled, and even though he could read fluently, he couldn't
write and so he wasn't allowed to progress up the school. A

School Inspector said to his mother, 'I suggest you look at a school that's just opened near here which might possibly welcome him.' That was the first Steiner school in this country."

I pause in Peter's story to suggest to Anne that many people hear of anthroposophy mainly in connection with Steiner schools and communities for children and adults with disabilities. What is it about Steiner's philosophy that means that people with all sorts of difficulty and disorder, who are often rejected or reviled by other systems, can be educated in this much more positive way?

"Because, in Steiner's view, as you grow up through childhood the outward education of a child must help its inner development."

That means its spiritual development?

"Yes. Because the spiritual organism is whole. And if the physical organism isn't suitable, you have a difficult problem between the person inside and the instrument that they're using. Someone like Peter, born with cerebral palsy, is locked into their body. I once asked Peter what happened as he woke up from sleep, and he said, 'Oh, I'm free for a few minutes. Then I go back into the cage'."

Why did Steiner think the physical organism is born with such difficulties?

"They choose to enter this incarnation so that they can develop further. The soul chooses its own parents ..."

So did Anne choose her own difficult mother?

She laughs. "It's to do with destiny. It can seem like punishment, but that's not the way it's intended. It directs you in the future on account of what has happened to you in the past."

Does she know why she chose those parents? "No. My father and I were very connected, and that's still there. But I certainly learnt from the experience with my mother. I learnt to respect her for what she believed in, for realizing that though she had brought me into this life, I had a different path from her. She got stuck in the past, but she'll have got unstuck by now."

An anthroposophical education

Peter's education, though he was very bright, started in a school for disabled, then continued in a normal Steiner school. How does Steiner's rather different system fit with the mainstream exams for the able-bodied?

"The Steiner curriculum is a complete system of education, with all the subjects studied every year, and you go through it with the same class teacher for eight years. You take one subject every day for four to six weeks, then you might not touch it again for a year. All the other subjects then relate to that subject. Say, if it's science, then art and music and literature will come in as they relate to science."

Does the school day differ from the day in a mainstream school?

"They always start the day with a poem, or a meditation, something the class teacher has chosen to fit these particular children, relating to their own inner life and introducing the children to the subject. The teacher knows the children well and respects their individual destinies. The teacher will always connect the subject they're studying to the children's development, as Steiner sees it, in what's called Main Lesson. Main Lesson contains what each child needs for their mental, soul, and spiritual development." *Whether or not they're disabled?* "Yes."

Can she give me an example of how it works with disabled children?

"In St Christopher's in Bristol I worked with children who individually had many disabilities. Once, I remember, I taught them for three weeks about the Geography of the Mediterranean. I wrote on the board, they made pictures and so on. With some of them I didn't know if any of it had gone in. At the start of the following term the parents of Gwen, who could speak only with a great deal of difficulty, said to me, 'Gwen's told us about how the oranges and olives only grow in certain areas, and which has flowers and fruits when ...' They were amazed, and so was I. She had come out with words and concepts that they didn't even know she knew. That's the proof of the pudding. It actually works."

Love in an unusual climate

How did Peter's disability affect their relationship? Did people think she was throwing herself away?

"Oh yes. Though he wasn't in a wheelchair, he walked with an irregular gait, and you could understand his speech when you got used to it. Aunt Sal got on with him like a house on fire. When Peter and I were booked to run a study group together, on Shakespeare, she'd insisted on asking him round for tea so that we could get to know each other. Yet, like with the other engagement, she was against me marrying Peter, too. 'Your parents won't stand for it' and so on."

Aunt Sal, this closest and wisest of aunts, didn't want Anne to marry yet another man she loved?

"But by this time I'd got wise to her, and resisted." *And how did her parents stand for it?* "I'd made it clear that I was going to do it, and that was that."

I can imagine.

"Then there were Peter's own parents. They loved him, and helped him to eat, drink, shave, everything. But they didn't realize he needed training in independence. They taught him that he would never marry and have children."

And this was all going on during the war against Hitler?

"Indeed. Aunt Sal had moved to South Wales because having been shell-shocked during the First War she couldn't stand the V2 bombers. I'd made an undertaking to look after Aunt Sal should she need it, but she said, 'I must go to somewhere where I can be looked after during the day, and you're working.' So I was let out of that commitment. That's when I suggested to Peter that when he was up in town, he'd better have the key to my flat. I put a mug, with tea and sugar in it and milk beside it, in the sink so that he could make himself a cup of tea without it mattering if he spilt it. Then came the time when he had to make his way over London through the bombing, and I said, 'Do take care.' I realized that I cared very deeply whether he lived or died.

"I ragged him a bit about not writing me love letters and he said, 'Well I can't exactly get my mother to write them for me!' So I set him up with my old typewriter and hour by hour (and it did take hours) he banged out letters to me.

"I had three rather astonishing escapes from death. The first was in 1940 when a German plane came overhead and went b-b-b-r-r-r-r, machine-gunning directly at me when I was walking on the South Downs, the second was when I was night-watching at Rudolf Steiner House and a piece of shrapnel nearly hit me. And in 1944 when I'd been to a cafe in Kingsway, there was some delay over the bill and I realized there'd been a huge V2 just on the spot where I'd have been if the bill had come straight away. I said to myself, 'Three times. What have I got to do in the future to make sense of being saved from death three times?'"

What was the reason?

"I needed to be there for Peter. He and I must have met in a previous life. It was obvious I had to be with him."

The effect of past lives

Has she herself any inklings of past incarnations?

"One or two. Seven years ago I went on a cruise to Greece and Turkey, and I felt at home in Greece as I'd never been anywhere else. I belonged. That kind of belonging is a memory from the past. Though, strangely enough, when I was especially drawn to visit Delos to see the great Avenue of Lions, a storm blew up and we couldn't land. So I didn't find out what the Avenue of Lions meant to me personally. On Olympia, where the war-like Greeks had to stop fighting for two months before they had the Games, I found the greatest peace of all.

"I know that I was involved with the Dominican monastic movement in the south of France, too. It's so clear that I don't have to query it. I don't want to do anything about it. Steiner tells you to wait until you're wise enough to discover what connection any particular instance might have with your present life."

Does the sense of having other lives make you more relaxed about this life? There are more chances, so to speak?

"Yes. There's definitely more time. I feel that quite strongly with my mother, that I've probably got quite a lot to work out with her later.

"Steiner's theory of reincarnation matters particularly when it comes to disabled children. The anthroposophical awareness is that we're all on a journey, individually and collectively. When the physically disabled child or the child with learning disabilities chose to be born into that body, they made a decision to do this in order to develop further. So their journey is difficult, and the journey of the family too. When you work with them, the family bring you their worries, and gradually you get them to see that there is some kind of sense in this, that the child has some special gift to give them."

But what about the very real suffering these families have? It seems a bit hard to say this is a gift?

"You share in that suffering. You only talk about the possibility of it being a gift when they know you and trust you."

What is the gift that the child brings?

"It brings them the feeling that they're beginning to know what life is all about. Take a Down's Syndrome child. They're wonderful children. I remember a group which wasn't gelling together at all, and I asked for a Down's Syndrome child to join the group because they have such an ability to get other children react together in a group, to make them sociable. A Down's child came, and he was mischievous and delightful, and it made all the difference, not only to the child but to the parents. The mother said, 'You're the first person who has ever told me that you *wanted* my son.'

"There was an autistic girl who I'm sure was an Egyptian in another life, because she was mad about cats and stars in a ceremonial way. But I didn't mention it. You don't go into these things. You touch on them only if it's appropriate. It's the awareness of what this individual brings with him or her into their life that matters."

Physical and spiritual bodies

Over lunch Anne has talked about our life when asleep. I bring her back to the subject later. What does she mean "life when asleep"?

"According to Steiner we're made up of physical body, etheric or life body, and soul and spirit. When we're asleep the first two stay in bed, but the soul and spirit (which some people see as the same thing) go to the world of the spirit. They are

somewhere in the world of God, and when they come back into
the physical body they'll understand better what their life's purpose is.

"Steiner thought that if you want to keep contact with someone
who has died, make a picture of that person in your mind before
you go to sleep. If you've had a question to address to that person, it can be that you get an answer when you wake up."

Are we talking dreamland here?

"No. We're talking of a spiritual state of being. This is very
important in bereavement. Immediately after the death it's important to keep the contact with the person who has died, so that the
bereavement becomes something you work your way through in
conjunction with them. During the first three days the soul and
spirit gradually leave the body. It was like that in Egyptian times:
during the period of priestly initiation, the priest would only be
allowed to remain in the 'mystery sleep' three and a half days, or
he would die. And there's the three days between Jesus's death
and his resurrection."

*Then was Jesus actually dead during that time, or was he in a
state of mystery initiation? Anne says that question, for her,
hasn't been resolved.* "Christ had a particular task to do when he
'descended into hell,' in that he helped the souls of the dead who
had lost their divine nature. That is hell, to lose your divine
nature, your divine purpose."

The Godhead and the experiencing of death

*We turn to Rudolf Steiner's own development. He began as a
theosophist, taking some of his ideas from faiths such as Hinduism and Buddhism. Then what happened?*

"He then had an experience of Christ. He called the Incarnation
'the turning point of time.' He realized that, historically, human
beings gradually incarnated into self-consciousness, but they
needed help to go back to the divine of their own accord. We need
Christ in order to do that."

*Presumably Steiner turned his back on his previous ideas.
Didn't he?*

"Yes and no," Anne replies carefully. "He certainly broke
with Theosophy and founded Anthroposophy. But even though

he had changed, he didn't repudiate his previous writings and lectures. And even though he founded the church he called the 'Christian Community,' he didn't give up the theory of reincarnation."

Given that he had changed so much, why didn't he reject what was past? "Because it's all a question of spiritual evolution. Everyone's evolving, and that includes Rudolf Steiner."

I notice that she doesn't refer to "Jesus," the man, but to "Christ." Steiner seems to have had a very specific idea of the role of Christ?

"Steiner said that Christ needed to incarnate in order to experience human death. The Godhead, and all the angels and archangels, they don't experience death. Christ was the only one."

I find that startling, that the Godhead had to experience death. Why?

"I think it has to do with human freedom. Human beings were made in the likeness of God, but during history we had gradually cut ourselves off from the divine, and death became frightening. It was no longer a transformation but a hard fact. I've a friend who's a priest of the Christian Community and also a scientist, and she says, 'You can't talk to people now about birth and death being gateways. There are walls now, and you can't get through.' If, through your sharpened spiritual senses, you're aware of other lives, you can go on developing."

What about her own experience of bereavement? Did her belief in reincarnation mean she was any the less grieved when Peter died?

"Oh no," replies Anne. "Oh no! I was distraught. I was glad for him, because he was out of his distress. He took three, three-and-a-half days to die, to get out of his cage.

"When he was first dead, it seemed to me that he was here, with me. But then I was distressed beyond words because he had gone."

Has she been able to picture him before going to sleep and find an answer in the morning?

"Very occasionally. Occasionally I know that he's there. I went to the Alps again this year, with Peter in my pocket so to speak. The first time I took him, in 1946, he stood on the glacier — in my mountain boots! — and this time, in the year 2000,

Peter was with me again. But there's no relief from the bereavement."

*Has she any sense of what Peter might have learned from the
experience of being in that cage of disability?*

"It's a lesson in humility."

*I laugh, because that was the answer I expected, and she
laughs too. Does she, I ask, have a picture of God the Cosmic
Organizer, ordering 'This one for this incarnation, that one for
that'?*

"No, not at all."

Then does the individual soul know what they need?

"Each individual soul, according to Steiner, has to go through
experiencing their life backwards, from the time you die to the
moment you were born. Experience your life through other people's eyes. That's what the Catholics call purgatory. All the rest of
the time between incarnations is a development within different
spiritual worlds, where you can let go of your negative baggage for
a while before you pick it up as you go into your next incarnation."

Community and reconciliation

*This sense of relaxation, this awareness that there'll be other
chances to do what needs to be done: is that helpful when it
comes to being in community?*

"Yes. If you find a person difficult to get on with, the reason
may be that in your lives so far you haven't developed the ability
to deal with some quality or relationship, and here's your chance."

*Anne has told me she has never wanted to take part in a live-in
community. Wouldn't that, I ask her, be a particularly concentrated form of learning to get on with people?*

"Indeed. But, to my mind, in a live-in community you've either
got to have strict rules and a hierarchy, or you've got to accept all
the people who belong as they are instead of as you'd like them
to be. Steiner didn't believe in hierarchical rules, but in the ability of everyone to come together for a decision.

"In a Steiner school, if you have a problem, say a child who has
a particular difficulty, you discuss it all together, everyone who
has anything to do with that child. By the end of the evening
you've gained a different attitude towards that child, and you've

come to a better understanding of how you can help the child. Now I think that's community. Not in the sense of, say, the Camphill communities,* but in the sense that you bring all your individual understandings and come to an understanding that is more than the sum of the individual parts. I think that is the real way of having a community, whether you live in or whether you don't. But the response has always got to be an individual response, it can't be a community one. Unless individuals are doing what they feel is right, a community becomes another kind of tyranny.

"In St Christopher's, Peter played a very special part in the community. He belonged to the children in a way that I didn't. He was the granddaddy of them all, they adored him. I was a bit of a dragon, but they went to him instinctively. He was disabled, he was one of them."

There's another aspect of Steiner communities that I've noticed: wholemeal bread, homeopathy, contact the with natural world and so on, what I'd call a wholesome environment.

"That's a very important part of Steiner education. Mind you, we expected a bit too much from our care staff, mending the children's clothes and doing all that parental sort of care as well as looking after the children outside school hours, especially if the child was, say, soiling themselves three times a day."

When there's a death in a child's family, would she offer them any sort of idea that the person has come from God and has gone to God?

"No, we'd leave that out, unless the parents wanted to bring it in or if an individual child asked a question in that area. It doesn't do to push forward your own ideas. Steiner was quite against evangelization. Within a community or a school you discuss it where it's relevant. But not otherwise."

Anthroposophy seems to me very different from the mainstream Christian faith. Do the adherents ever have run-ins with mainstream Christian theologians? Do primates and patriarchs denounce Anthroposophy as evil?

"No," says Anne firmly. "We don't threaten them. There's room for all of us."

---

* Residential Steiner communities for people with learning disabilities or mental health problems.

The tape and the time is almost at an end and I turn off the recorder. Have I got everything I wanted? asks Anne. Yes indeed, I say. But has she said everything she wanted to say?

"There is something," she says. "It's about peace of mind. I've reached a kind of peace now. There was a problem with Peter, which was that he took up an evangelical sort of Christianity. That was okay, I drove him to any church he wanted to go to and I was happy to do that. But I wasn't happy that he never came to my Christian Community services in Edinburgh. I put that to him quite firmly one day, and he said, 'Very well, I'll come.' So he came, and afterwards he didn't say anything very much, but later I heard him talking to one of his evangelical friends. What he said was, 'I could disagree with them in every aspect of their theology. But when I am in their service, the Act of Consecration as they call it, Christ is there.' And I was content with that."

There's one more question I want to ask, and it's about Anne's anthroposophical mentor Aunt Sal. It has been clear that Anne's relationship with Aunt Sal had its tense moments. Did they manage some sort of reconciliation?

Anne's answer is wry but confident. "No, reconciliation wasn't necessary. We'll sort that out next time round."

Rediscovering a sense of the sacred

Rose Hacker

"I have a kind of dialogue with the alabaster. I'm not thinking, I'm meditating. I ask the stone what's there, then I allow it to emerge. See that dark soapstone piece? I did it to get away from Mark when he was ill. It's an injured vulture, of course. But look. The wing, it's an arm, paralysed. The head hanging on the chest ... It's Mark. I was trying to get away from him but he came out of the stone."

At the age of ten she might have said "I wish I was dead," but she doesn't wish she was dead now, in her nineties. "Life is good, I'm reasonably healthy, my mind's clear. I'm not afraid of death. It's part of the order of nature. I'm ready to die." Does she believe in any kind of afterlife? "No, I don't."

Socialist in the quantum soup

*Rose Hacker, born 1906, daughter of a Polish Jewish father
and London Jewish mother, worked as a junior in her father's
tailoring business in London's east end and eventually
became his designer, went to Paris fashion shows and dined
at the Ritz. A radical socialist in the 1930s, she travelled to
the Soviet Union on the same boat as Beatrice and Sidney
Webb. She joined the Co-operative Correspondence Magazine for Women in the thirties and became a Marriage Guidance Counsellor in the fifties. She was the MGC's first
broadcaster, and wrote books on teenage sexuality. In the seventies she was an elected member of the Greater London
Council. She is now President of the Progressive League, and
also spends time sculpting and dancing.*

It's mid-June, but the wind's so biting when I arrive at Euston Station that I buy a coat at a charity shop. I wait for a bus to Highgate Village: it takes forty minutes to arrive, then comes in a posse
of four. I lift my bag to get off the bus at the other end and feel an
agonizing wrench in my already injured shoulder.

I'm on my way to meet a woman in her nineties about whom I
know almost nothing. I'm cold, I'm in pain. For all I know the
woman may be batty, or dead, or have forgotten I'm coming.

But Rose Hacker opens the door, gives me a hug, sympathizes
about my shoulder, feeds me on avocado, pasta, strawberries and
cream, and offers me cool white wine. Then, surrounded by her
sculptures, we talk into my tape recorder till I'm exhausted,
though she isn't.

Poverty, riches and socialism

Rose's long life has so many threads through it that we try to deal
with them one at a time. But they tumble over each other, and we
butterfly-hop from one to another (and mix our metaphors) as the
links between them become clear. Her Jewish family comes first.
"Jews in Russian Poland were persecuted by both the Russians
and the Poles. My father was apprenticed to a bookbinder, he slept
under the workbench and ate scraps thrown to him by the family.
Of course they were all afraid of pogroms, and lots of them fled.
My father counted himself lucky to fetch up in London and it was
the tradition to go into the tailoring trade. He worked hard and he
made quite a lot of money. He went into partnership with an English Gentile, and they went on doing well. By the time he moved
to Hampstead, when I was a child, they had a nanny and a maid."

I ask her: in this Orthodox Jewish family, what kind of a child
was she? Did she believe in God? "No. I was a very nasty child. I
queried everything. I asked my mother why she was lighting candles on Friday nights, why my father cut the bread and prayed over
the wine. She said, 'Because my mother told me to, and that's what
you must do. You must never question anything.' God was used as
a reinforcement. If Mother didn't know what you were doing, then
God would punish you. When I was afraid that God would punish
me I'd say the Twenty-Third Psalm to comfort myself.

"But my father was a free thinker. He kept all the festivals, but
he was a bit of a hypocrite about the outward observance. He
encouraged me to read anything. He bought me H.G. Wells and
Bernard Shaw ... When I was eight or nine I wrote an essay proving that God was Nature, and my father carefully kept it.

"When I was a teenager I decided to test God. I went to tea with
a friend from school, and the mother said to me, 'Now I know
you're a Jewish girl, and you don't eat meat with milk, so I've
made you some nice ham sandwiches with no butter'." Rose
laughs. "Ham! The most forbidden of all food for Jews! I thought,
'Well, I'll eat it, and let's see if God strikes me down.' I ate it all
up, and nothing happened."

What about her education? "We were sent to a small private
school, but I never got a proper education. I'm an auto-didact. I
was bright, and there was talk of a university education, but

my mother wouldn't hear of it, she thought nice Jewish boys wouldn't marry a clever girl, a 'blue-stocking.' My father wanted me to go into the business, and he sent me to Business School and to Art School, so I became his designer."

Rose's autobiography is not called Abraham's Daughter *for nothing.[1] In her Highgate flat she keeps a glass-fronted cabinet full of Jewish treasures.* "You could have called my father bourgeois, he played the game according to the capitalist rules, but he never forgot his poor Jewish roots, he wasn't ashamed of them. He and his partner ran a business on Oxford Street, and when I was about eighteen I could see the Hunger Marches from the top floor of our workshop, and the striking tailors who were starving because they only did piece-work and were laid off from the sweatshops ... There was an organization called the Bread, Meat and Coal Society who gave people a bit of bread and meat and coal every week.

"One of the highlights of my life was the General Strike, 1926. That turned me into a true socialist. I went to meetings, listened to Fabians like Bernard Shaw, H.G. Wells, the Webbs, G.D.H. Cole ... There were Harold Laski, Aldous and Julian Huxley, Bertrand and Dora Russell ... Oswald Mosley, too, he called himself a socialist before all his dreadful anti-semitism."

Rose adored her father, and the image of his outstretched arms reaching towards her from his death-bed is her most poignant memory. "But I knew he had a harsh side. My brother wasn't very academic, he was quite easy-going, and my father was so horrible to him that he ran away from home. My father had a dreadful temper at work. He'd rage against our employees. I thought his rages were an injustice, so eventually I decided I had to defy him. He was in one of his rages, and I stopped him and said, 'You're behaving like a child!' That silenced him. He hadn't any answer. He just turned and walked away. It was terrifying, but I knew I was right." *Maybe it wasn't God who was powerful, but Rose herself?*

Jewishness versus idealism

In 1930 Rose married Mark Hacker, an accountant (and also, ironically, a "nice Jewish boy"), and they had two sons. It was a happy marriage, though with strains that were to emerge later.

What does she think about the Jews being "the chosen people"?
"The Jews *were* chosen. But not chosen over other nations: chosen to give God's word to the rest of the world." *And the prom-
ised land?* "Oh, dreadful! That land was owned by other people!
Look what's going on in Israel now, it's exactly the same as five
thousand years ago!

"Maybe Jesus brought back the original idea of Judaism. I
think he was one of the prophets. Like all the prophets he said,
'Turn from your evil ways, and repent.' Jesus didn't invent 'Love
your neighbour as yourself,' you know! It comes from Leviticus."[2] I didn't know, but I looked it up later and she's right.

*During the war Rose took into her home a Jewish child from
Berlin called Ruth. Ruth's family, who had died in the Holocaust,
had been Liberal Jews, but she had been rescued by a family who
were members of the ultra-orthodox Jewish group Agudah Israel.
They taught her that God had sent Hitler to punish Jews for not
being religious enough. Ruth wouldn't eat at Rose's table,* "or
even at my mother's table, and she ate kosher food. But it wasn't
kosher enough. I was appalled. It went against everything I
believed in." *Ruth couldn't, wouldn't, stay in their home. But they
found her a suitable ultra-orthodox alternative, and Rose has
kept in touch with her ever since.*

*Eighteen months after marriage, wanting adventure, she and a
friend heard there was a boat going to the Soviet Union with tick-
ets for £25 for a three-week tour.* "It was the boat with Beatrice
and Sidney Webb and other socialists on it, who were going to see
the glories of Stalin's Communism. But of course they weren't
shown all its tyrannies.

"I was a real socialist. I was a pacifist, too, before Hitler
came along. I never joined the communist party because of my
pacifism. The communists believed the end justifies the means,
but I've always believed that means *are* ends. My religion was
the brotherhood of man." *Rose joined The Progressive League
(PL), a left-wing group founded by the Russells and other radical intellectuals, who campaigned for a World Federation and
on issues such as divorce law reform and abortion law reform.*
"A whole lot of these things have come about since those days,
but they were quite revolutionary at the time. We really
believed that Man was becoming more rational, that Utopia

was possible. All that meant far more to me than church or synagogue."

Rose was active not only in the PL but also in the Co-operative Correspondence Magazine for women. "Some of the correspondents were quite anti-semitic, and I challenged that. That work went on through the war. But I took my children out of London, to Letchworth in Hertfordshire, for safety. Some people were offering lodgings to Londoners specifying 'No Jews or foreigners.' But there was one woman, Eve Shannon, who wanted to make her protest and advertised rooms to let for 'a family of any race or religion.' She took us in and our two families lived as a community, and we became lifelong friends.

"Where Judaism and Christianity and Islam have gone wrong, I think, is the idea that 'we are the goodies, they are the baddies.' So we all preach love and pacifism and forgiveness, but we've still got the right to kill people who disagree with us. Crazy! I didn't understand this till I studied psychology and psychiatry. I realized people aren't rational after all. There's always the dark side. The Buddhists know this. And that wonderful woman, Nawal el Saadawi,* who understands globalization and human rights. Human rights are my religion, too. And they call this communism! You remember Dom Helder Camara? 'I give food to the poor, you call me a saint. I ask why the poor have no food, you call me a communist.' That's it, exactly."

But where does she think communism went wrong? "Human greed for power, that's the problem. 'The dictatorship of the proletariat' never happened. It was simply the rule of thugs."

Knowledge about marriage and sex

Back in London after the war, Rose became one of the earliest Marriage Guidance Counsellors. In a few small rooms in central London, with a chemist's shop below and a brothel above ("How appropriate!"), she'd sit alone, unpaid ("Yes, I know, bourgeois ..."), and accept all comers. Her socialist public speaking gave her the experience to be one of Marriage Guidance's

* Dismissed from her post as Egypt's Director of Public Health in 1972 for writing *Women and Sex;* author of many subsequent books including *The Hidden Face of Eve* and *God Dies By The Nile.*

travelling lecturers. This in turn led to sex education in schools, and in 1957 she wrote Telling The Teenagers, *one of the first books on sex education for use by teachers and youth leaders.[3] It went into many editions, and in 1960 was followed by* The Opposite Sex *for teenagers themselves, which was also published in Holland and the United States.[4]*

Telling the Teenagers *and* The Opposite Sex *seem amazingly enlightened for their time. The blurb advertises information on*:

> "your first date, loving and being in love, the illegitimate child, promiscuity and disease, petting, sexual responsibility, homosexuality ..."

Even today's teachers and youth workers, embarking on a programme of sex education, might welcome Rose's advice. "Children will show off and seek to embarrass the speaker with smutty remarks. But all contributions should be dealt with seriously. A ready wit and a judicious touch of humour are often successful. What is hopeless, and likely to ruin all chance of further discussion, is sarcasm. Behind the cheeky or impudent or offensive remark there is always a genuine desire to know the answer." *Listen, as she still says, to the children. In* You and Your Daughter ("A total fraud," she says as she hands it over, "because I only had sons") *she recommends self-defence classes for girls who go out on their own, and advises mothers not to pressurize a pregnant daughter into marriage.[5]*

Flicking through the books while she answers a phone call from one of her many friends, I recall my first summer job, working in a bookshop after leaving my all-girls' boarding school. Frighteningly innocent, hungry for hidden knowledge, I'd slip upstairs in the lunch hour and sniff along the shelves for possibilities. I could swear that one of them was — yes, the cover stirs memories — The Opposite Sex *by Rose Hacker.*

When Rose comes back, she tells me that her interest in sex started when she was ten. "I found a book by my parents' bed wrapped in brown covers. I was a very curious child, so I looked at it, and it was all about the human body, and there were beautiful pictures of babies growing in the womb. I told my little brother and sister about it, my mother found out, and she got my father to smack me. I never forgot it. The first sentence of my autobiography is, 'I wish I was dead!' That was what I cried after my father beat me on the bottom. But I wondered why were we not allowed to know these things? Why was I *beaten* for finding out?"

Long after that childhood beating Rose learnt about another side of her mother's life. "The three of us, my sister and my brother and myself, were born only about eighteen months apart, and then my mother got pregnant again. She induced a miscarriage by jumping downstairs and drinking gin and having hot baths ... She was very ill afterwards and couldn't have any more babies. I was horrified. I knew there had to be a better way."

Her own early sexual experiences were ignorant and unhappy. "The men I went out with were inept, and I was afraid. I had a few of these non-relationships and then I came across a novel called *The Hard-Boiled Virgin*. I thought, that's exactly what I am! I was determined to take some notice of my body, to listen to the messages it was sending me. I vowed I'd only marry a man if I was sexually attracted to him. And Mark did attract me sexually."

When she worked in sex education through the Marriage Guidance Council, her socialist ideals came into practice too. "We went into schools in the roughest areas. Deprived children, enormous young men in youth clubs — they didn't want lectures, they wanted to be listened to. No one listened to children then. We did group work, we practically had to cuddle them to get them to open up. They're no different now, however much sex they've had. They do it over and over again, it's a pastime, but they're often broken-hearted inside."

She was the first marriage counsellor to broadcast on radio, and the first to appear on television. Always she worked anonymously and unpaid. "But I could afford to do it. I'm almost ashamed now, all that paid home help I used to have that allowed me to get out and do this work. But my helps weren't skivvies, they were friends. We weren't left alone to do everything like mothers are today."

Many years later a Church of England colleague on the MGC, Gordon Dunstan, later Professor of Theology at King's College, London, invited her to help train Anglican clergy. "What, me, I said, a renegade Jew? 'Yes,' said Gordon, you must help them to unlearn what they've learnt at college, all that preaching and teaching. Get them to learn to listen.'

"So we invented role play. Like the children, these clergymen needed education in relationships. You know Martin Buber? I-and-Thou. Relationship. You can call that God, if you like. Not I-and-It. I-and-It is exploitation. Sin. I-and-Thou is God."

Political involvement

In the 1970s came public service of all sorts. Rose sat as a co-opted member on Labour local councils, she was governor of several schools and hospitals, she helped to set up local Mental Health Centres (one of which was named after herself and her husband), and in 1973 she became the sixty-seven-year-old member for St Pancras North on the Greater London Council (GLC). "Mrs Rose Hacker is not mad," wrote The Guardian *about her ideas for the River Thames becoming an aesthetic resource for rich and poor alike, with parks, seating, walkways and open spaces. "A visionary perhaps, but not mad."*

She was also involved in setting up special schools for children with learning and behavioural difficulties. "I was involved in schools just at the time when the severely handicapped were coming out of Health and going under Education. These children were in hospitals, in cots, rocking and banging their heads. We brought them out into special schools, we gave them enough staff, and enough training for the staff, so that each one could get the help they needed. Often they'd got a talent for art, or music, or sport. Now, oh, it's all back to the Three Rs, 'we don't need art, we don't need psychiatry.' I could cry my heart out, I really could."

A friend of Rose's, Barbara Low, translated Anna Freud's first book. "Long out of print, but d'you know what it was called? *Psychiatry for Teachers*! That's what we need. Teachers have to teach, yes, but they need to understand, too. Counsellors as well. When I first went into Marriage Guidance I thought, 'Amateurs can't do this. I need some psychoanalysis.' So I went and had it, for eighteen months. It was just when my father died, it was very helpful."

Her interest in gender and sexuality was never very far away, even in her political life. "When I was at County Hall I suggested that there were women who wanted to be firefighters. The Tories laughed in derision and went off to the bar. So I got it through! The next meeting they reversed it. They said there wasn't enough money for the lavatories."

We both laugh, and agree that they always use lavatories as an excuse. I tell her that I once knew a transsexual who was sacked because of the muddled issue of lavatories. We fall to discussing transsexualism, and that leads Rose on to the spiritual value of androgyny. "In the Kabbalah the ideal human being is androgynous. The masculine and feminine are on different sides of the body. Intelligence, that's male, on the right, Wisdom, that's female, on the left. Now there's all this talk about how we need to use both sides of our brain!"

Then back we go to the women firefighters, how when they eventually won the right to the job they were subjected to the ghastly initiation ceremonies like the men forced on each other. "Men say they're so strong, they never cry, they're so brave. Yet they're beginning to admit they suffer terrible stress, they need someone to talk to, they need to cry. I call that progress."

Then back to the GLC, where she was on the Film Viewing Board deciding whether or not films were obscene. This wasn't an easy matter for Rose. "I used to think there should be no censorship. In Marriage Guidance I used material some people might call obscene to help liberate people from their sexual guilt, to take them into tenderness. But I've changed my mind. Not completely, but a bit. I think some things should be censored. Exploitation of children, the degradation of women. It's the Martin Buber thing again, treating someone as an It, not as a Thou."

The feminine and the Goddess

The tensions of Rose and Mark's long and mainly fulfilled marriage arose because he was "like so many men, armoured." One of the tragedies of their last years was the loss of the intimacy of full sexual expression after his stroke. "There's a huge need for kissing and cuddling in old age. People don't realize." *Mark died in 1982 after an eight-year illness, and during the Thatcherite eighties Rose resigned from public work because the main item on the agenda was cuts in the budget. She took up sculpture and visited California to see Eve Shannon's daughter, Professor of* *art history Moira Roth. Through the writings of Riane Eisler and Elinor Gadon,* and through the Five Rhythms Dance of Gabrielle Roth she began to see the workings of the "once and future Goddess" in life. At the age of ninety-one she travelled to Crete to dance goddess dances.*

I tell her I'd have called the child Rose an incipient feminist because she devoured her brother's adventure books rather than the sissy tales intended for girls. But Rose says she stood aside from early feminism. "It was just too fierce. Too anti-men. SCUM, the Society for Cutting Up Men, that sort of thing." *Politically, though, her feelings would come under a feminist banner. She has no difficulty in naming patriarchy.* "The Jews and the Arabs, they both traditionally see women as possessions. You know, the Ten Commandments, 'his ox, his ass, his wife.' You can call it patriarchy, you can call it oppression.

"Monotheistic patriarchy, I think it's all to do with abolishing the Goddess. The first thing the patriarchs did when they conquered the territory was to tear down the temple and stop them 'whoring' after the Goddess. They call it whoring because those people worshipped womanly things. The Goddess needs the God, so she creates a God who is Father, Son, Lover. She must have a lover because love is beautiful. It's all in the Bible. It's all in the Song of Solomon."

When Princess Diana died in summer 1997, Elinor Gadon was staying with Rose. "Elinor said all that reaction to Diana's death was a sign of people's longing for the Goddess. People aren't satisfied with just having the masculine in religion. And in life. It's not the whole of reality." *Were they worshipping Diana, I asked?* "No! They worshipped the compassion of this woman. They were accepting Diana as Virgin, Wife, Mother, Whore, but one who could never be Crone."

One of the greatest revelations for her was the discovery that History didn't start with the ancient civilizations of Greece, Rome and Egypt. "What we consider ancient is actually quite recent. Before that there lived other cultures that weren't patriarchal. They weren't matriarchal either. They were matrilocal," she says.

---

* Riane Eisler, author of *The Chalice and the Blade* (Harper & Row 1987). Elinor Gadon, author of *The Once and Future Goddess* (Harper & Row 1989). See also Ann Baring and Jules Cashford, *The Myth Of The Goddess,* (BCA / Penguin 1991).

"There was no hierarchy. Nature was good, the body was good. Sex was good, it wasn't sinful."

Relishing the goodness of the body took Rose into massage (though in fact she did massage long ago, on her father and on her husband when they were ill) and she has had massage from a shamanistic healer who says that the movements of her hands come from God, the God of no distinct religion.

How did Rose start to dance? What made her go to Crete to find out more about the ancient Goddess? "I've done the Alexander Technique and T'ai Chi for many years. Then an old friend from the Progressive League told me that her daughter runs these holidays. I thought, I'm ninety-one, but I'm mobile and I'm quite healthy, and I want to be in one of the places of the Goddess. In any case my passion is archaeology. I love museums. So I said to a friend who'd just lost her husband, 'You need to go somewhere you never went with him. Come with me to Crete.' So we went, and explored all the sites, and swam, and danced."

If she could write a book now it would be about the liberation of men. "Women seem to have everything now: jobs, houses, cars. What do they need with an old-fashioned man? Men need to be liberated into their own feelings. Mark and I both used to think it was I who was dependent on him. But in the last eight years of his life, when he was ill, he was like a baby. He wouldn't let me out of his sight. I'd go to my sculpture classes — I'd never leave him alone, there was always someone with him — but he'd ring me up and beg me to come home. Men need to learn not to be dependent on women for their feelings. That would be liberation."

Sculpture

It's perhaps through sculpture that Rose now finds her deepest spirituality. I asked her how she approaches the stone. "It's a kind of dialogue. Alabaster's my favourite. I'm not thinking, I'm meditating. I ask the stone what's there, then I allow it to emerge."

Sometimes it speaks back astonishingly clearly. "See that piece, the dark soapstone? I did it when I joined the class to get away from Mark when he was ill. When I'd finished I stood back and looked at it. It's an injured vulture, of course. But look. The wing, it's an arm, paralysed. The head hanging on the chest ... It's

Mark. I was trying to get away from him but he came out of the stone.

"On a conscious level I want to sculpt women with all their soft lines. But when I look at that one" — *she points to one of her softest, most feminine forms* — "I can see that it has an over-arching female arm, but within it, can you see? there's a crouched and cowering phallus. Sometimes, with other pieces, the Goddess emerges. Look, there's that most Goddess of symbols, the snake."

One of Rose's most beautiful sculptures is Consummation, *a pale alabaster piece of two figures in close embrace. The figures are without age or gender: they could be parent and child, friends or lovers.* "They came out of that stone without my will. The Israeli archaeologist Uzi Avner noticed it and pointed out to me how strikingly similar it is to a Natufian figurine of *c.*10,000 BC. in the storage vaults of the British Museum.* Look, it's two people together, responding. It's I-and-Thou again."

Old age and death

Rose says in her autobiography that she has:

> "experienced personally the rise and fall, the hope and disillusion, of Marxists, Freudians, Humanists, Internationalists and the Welfare State."

At the age of ten she might have said "I wish I was dead," but she doesn't wish she was dead now, in her nineties.

"Life is good, I'm reasonably healthy, my mind's clear. I'm not afraid of death. It's part of the order of nature. I'm ready to die."

Clearly she doesn't have a belief in a "God out there." Does she believe in any kind of afterlife?

"No, I don't. I had a friend who knew that her husband would be waiting for her, with the dog and the favourite armchair. I don't believe that. I sometimes wish I did, it'd be a comfort.

"I don't want to lose my mind, like so many of my friends are doing. It's such a grief to be with them. Sometimes I just can't bear it. I wonder if people hang on for a long time if there's some-

---

* The two pieces were exhibited together in the BM not long after this interview.

thing in their lives they haven't come to terms with? There are some people who just seem to decide to die. They're ready to die, and they die. But my mother suffered for five years with cancer and all the time she prayed 'Please, God, take me. Please, God, take me,' but the doctors saved her life over and over again. It was terrible.

"These things are clearer now. I'm a member of the Voluntary Euthanasia Society. Mark used to get so depressed but he wouldn't talk about death or euthanasia. I really wanted him to die beautifully and peacefully. I felt terribly guilty about it. I went to a counsellor and expressed how I felt, this great evil in my soul. That's when I learnt that we have to accept all the evil as well as all the good in ourselves. The evil we have to fight is within ourselves, not outside. The Buddhists know that the real battle is within. It mustn't be projected onto other people. I get out my aggression and resentment in exercise, or art, or gardening.

"The Jewish thing is that God is in us all, God is in everything. That's all right. But have you read Deepak Chopra? He talks about 'quantum soup.'[6] That's where we all came from, that's what we all go to. I believe in the quantum soup. We're all a part of everything."

Next day, when Rose has left to take a friend to an opera event at the Coliseum, I stay on in the quiet flat among her books and sculptures. It seems as far from the fashion houses and the Ritz as it is from the hungry Jewish boy sleeping under the bookbinder's bench. Rose lives alone, but her work is present with her, her friends are present with her, her realized goddesses are all around. The "quantum soup" may be a question of genetics, or physics, or ideas, or the transmission of awareness in an unknown form. Whatever it is, a small part of it has emerged through Rose's hands in a form like the two sculpted figures in close embrace: I and Thou, in relationship, with the spirit moving between.

Eric Maddern

The elders told us their concern that their young men didn't want to go through the initiations into the Dreaming any more. They were more interested in town and cars and alcohol. This meant that the whole of their 40,000-year-old culture was threatened with annihilation within a generation. It was as if they were standing on the edge of an abyss.

Soulfulness is to do with small experiences in the day. It's to do with the relationship with the heron, with that tree, between you and me. It's to do with the song I'm learning, with what happens when I go into the Round-house, stir the fire, sit back, take a deep breath and begin to speak, not quite knowing what I'm going to say ...

The land, the dreaming and how to be a man

Eric Maddern was born in 1950 in Whyalla, South Australia, where his father was working in the iron mines. The family came to Britain, where his mother died from polio when he was six. After graduating in social psychology he made a ten-year journey around the world culminating in community arts work with the Aborigines in Central Australia. Since 1986 he has lived on a five-acre site in Snowdonia on which he has built a Celtic roundhouse, and has pioneered storytelling at historic sites, men's rites of passage and telling the Universe Story.

The day seems propitious for interviewing Eric Maddern. The North Wales coast road has been grey and foggy, but now the cloud vanishes and I have a stunning view of Snowdon from the foot of the lake. While Eric goes down the slope from his house to check how the latest building's going (the turf-roofed straw-baled hogan is getting a floor) I go over to the barn and admire its beautifully curved doors of local oak. Then into the darkness of the thatched Roundhouse to imagine it lit by candles and a log fire. I use the composting "loo with a view," surely the most organic pee I've ever pee'd, which (says the notice) will in due course fertilize the apple trees on the slope nearby. The rush of the stream down towards the lake pervades everything on the site.

In his study, Eric leans over the microphone and ponders. "Talking about a life inevitably involves taking experience and memory and turning it somehow into a story: selecting, shaping, finding a beginning, middle and end, characters, plot, climax and so on. Making stories about ourselves is how, I believe, we make meaning in our lives, and meaning is at the heart of most spiritual projects. Having said that, I think I'll flout convention. I'll start where I am and work backwards."

He shows me a leaflet he's been writing for a workshop. "This is on promoting the spiritual dimension in outdoor education. In reflecting on spirituality I've been remembering a couple of recent experiences.

"Last week the heron, who often feeds on my river, appeared beside me as I stood near the barn. It walked past me and down into the river. Until now it's always flown away whenever I've appeared. For the first time in thirteen years it showed no fear. I was able to watch it closely, see its grace as it half hopped, half flew from one place to another, its clumsiness as it slipped on stones in the water. It was one of those special moments of awe in the presence of natural beauty. I felt honoured, as if the heron had finally come to trust me. It's these kind of feelings which are a central thread in my spirituality.

"Of course you can also have uplifting experiences with other people. Last week (it was a good week!) there was a group of young people here on an environmental camp. They wrote poems and together we composed a song about their time here. Their suggestions included phrases like: 'So, there is a place ...' 'sacred', 'a way to continue ...'." *He reaches for his guitar and sings a few verses.* "They were touched by their experience of being here and I felt moved in return. There was a chemistry between me and them and this place which brought about a trans-formation in us all."

The storyteller

So what does he think is at the heart of that "chemistry" which moves people?

"Well, it has to be many things. But for me perhaps the role of storyteller encapsulates much of it."

For ten years Eric has made a good part of his living as a sto-ryteller, telling tales from the oral traditions of Britain and around the world. Why is storytelling so important to him? "Partly it's simply the stories themselves. Because they've been passed down over the centuries and filtered through many minds, they contain the essence of humanity, 'the wit and wisdom of the people' as we storytellers are fond of saying. All of life is there, so many extraordinary and meaningful creations of the human imagination. Perhaps you could say the same of literature and some of what's in the media. But there's a key difference, which is the other reason I love doing it. Oral storytelling is a personal thing. An intimate exchange takes place between teller and listener. It's a reciprocal act, a tool for conviviality. So, as listeners and teller journey together in the imagination, magic happens. It's this kind of quality that constitutes the chemistry. The paradox is that even though these tales are age-old, each time they're told they are made new.

"For me it's a privilege to be, to a small degree, a tradition bearer, a carrier of ancestral gifts brought fresh to modern ears. I love the originality, raw power and magical transformations of the creation myths. I'm continually discovering more in the old legends of Britain, and I delight in all the dark, whacky folk-tales that abound in every culture. I also love singing old ballads and unaccompanied folk-songs."

He does a lot of work in schools with children of all ages. "It's great to see the way kids get completely absorbed by the stories. Teachers often notice in the children a quality of attention they don't normally have. They are literally 'entranced.' One of the pleasures of being a storyteller is that I can be outrageous, I can become all the characters in the stories, I can express the full range of emotions and qualities that are found there. For instance, in the Aboriginal story of *The Rainbow Bird*[1] there's a moment when the old man realizes he's surrounded by fire. He remembers there's a billabong not far away, so he gathers his strength and runs through the fire, and as he runs he turns into ... a crocodile! When I tell that story I *am* that man becoming a crocodile."

How did he actually get to be a storyteller?

"Well, I'd long been involved in 'arts in education.' But my work as a storyteller proper really took off in 1989 when I was asked by English Heritage to tell stories at historic sites. I don't think it had been done before. The idea was to tell the kind of tales told by those who once inhabited these ancient places as a way of bringing the bare stones alive. So I traipsed about the country visiting some of the most wonderful sacred and historic places: Tintagel (telling the legends of Arthur), Stonehenge,

Avebury, Maiden Castle (stories about the Roman invasion), Battle Abbey (the saga of the Norman Conquest). I've now worked in about fifty sites, everywhere finding tales to bring the place alive."

The Roundhouse and Cae Mabon

"When I think about those young people last week, there was another ingredient that affected them and that's this place. And especially the Roundhouse." *We can't actually see the Roundhouse from where we're sitting in the study because it's hidden in a clearing at the foot of the hill, but again I imagine the dark space under the thatch and the eyes of listeners lit up by the central fire. How did the idea of it first come to him?*

"The very first place I told stories for English Heritage was in round-houses at Chysauster near Penzance. They had extremely thick walls but no roof. I thought, wow, how amazing it must have been to live in a place like this. A few weeks later I met Jake Keen who'd built a roundhouse — the kind of dwelling people lived in for about three thousand years before the Romans came — at the Ancient Technology Centre in Dorset. Then I knew it was possible and that I had to make one on my own land. It took three years to build the stone wall, just a week or so each summer. The thatched roof went on in 1994."

Surely it must get smoky inside, from the fire in the middle?

"No, the smoke seeps out through the thatch. With candles and lamplight, rugs and cushions on the floor, it has a magical atmosphere, and people come from far and wide to tell and be told stories. For me it's my home patch so I'm relaxed, and very much enjoy playing spontaneously with tales and audiences."

How did he find this special place?

"When I finally felt ready to settle down I found myself gravitating to North Wales, probably because we used to come up here for holidays on the other side of the mountains with my Nain and Taid.* I stumbled on this place by chance when I was looking at houses in the area. I fell in love with the setting at once, then realized I wasn't in a position to buy anywhere at the time. But a year

---

* Welsh for Granny and Grandad.

later, at the end of a meditation retreat, I had a powerful vision of what I could do here. So I came back — to discover someone else had bought it. Then I really had to let go of it. Months passed and I came back to look again. Again by chance, I discovered that the house had been put back on the market just a few days before. This time I knew I had to go for it. I still had no money, no job and no accounts, but I did now have determination and eventually I managed to get a one hundred per cent mortgage.

"But the day before signing the contract I was beset by doubts. I looked at the house from over the lake, under a sullen cloud (it was June!) and I thought, 'God, what am I doing?'"

He'd come from sunny Alice Springs!

"Exactly. But that night I went to a singing group and someone had brought a song for us to sing: 'Sleep, sleep tonight, and may your dreams be realized. And when the thunder cloud passes rain, oh let it rain down on me.' After singing that over and over I didn't mind about the rain. Next day I signed the contract with a clear heart."

How has the place grown? Did he have a clear plan for it?

"I've never had a blueprint. It's more that the place has evolved organically according to what's been offered, what's been possible, what's been needed. I've tried to learn the right thing to do from the place itself. Sometimes I sit with my back against a particular oak tree to try and work something out." *And the answer comes from the tree?* "No, the answer may come from my own mind, but with the perspective of the tree.

"For the past ten years I've been growing what I call the Cae Mabon encampment, centred on the Roundhouse. By now it's much more than a camp. You've seen the renovated barn with its beautiful windows and doors? And the state-of-the-art composting loo?" *Yes, I tell him, I used it, and look forward to tasting the apples and cider that I've fertilized.* "There's a tinker's bow-tent, a thatched shower hut by the river and an exquisite straw-bale and turf-roofed hogan. I'm currently working on a pagoda-like garden shed!"

Many different groups use Cae Mabon as a venue for spiritual, creative or therapeutic workshops and retreats. The ones that particularly appeal to me are Singing, Woodland Survival Crafts, Zen Adventures and Five Rhythms Dance. Eric also organizes events himself. He shows me his three-year millennial pro-gramme. It starts with 1999 as "The Year of Memory," goes through 2000 as "The Year of Vision" and finishes with 2001 as "The Year of Action." "This year," he tells me, "I organized a series of workshops under the title 'Ancestral Voices.' I thought we could look back through the stories told in different human epochs, seeking out the valuable nuggets worth taking forward into the new millennium."

One of the most successful focused on the Middle Ages. It was entitled "The Gifts of Wonder and Mercy" and was run by Alida Gersie. * "Alida's incredibly adept at stimulating creativity and we had a wonderfully inventive time exploring the meaning of images like a bundle of sticks and a piece of cloth. We looked at the story of the Pied Piper from different angles and discovered extraordinary depths of feeling in it. The whole three days was a succession of little miracles.

"The place itself plays an important part in the magic. It has a naturally healing and inspiring effect on most people who come here."

The Men's Work

Where did the impulse come from to run courses especially for men?

"The first event we had here in 1989 was a 'men's rites of passage.' The idea for it arose from a feeling a few of us had that many men today are struggling with issues of identity, purpose and meaning. They want to change. We felt that men who feel like that could benefit from focusing on their particular transition within a group, where each would have his passage marked by a ritual created specially for him."

And what are the issues that come up? "They go from being born to facing death and everything in between. Parents, adolescence, relationships, work, being a father, being an absent father: all the things that men have to deal with in their lives. By framing them in a 'rites of passage' context we've found that it adds potency to the changes men make. In our society we don't have

* Director of Therapeutic Arts at Hertfordshire University and author of such books as *Storytelling in Bereavement* (Taylor & Francis 1991).

adequate substitutes for rites of passage, so many men get to adulthood without learning how to deal with difficult emotions, without really knowing who they are and what their lives are about. Their adolescences get stretched out to mid-life, when they stop and think, 'Is that it?'

"One thing men find powerful about the rites of passage is that they can speak their truth and be heard. That can be very challenging. But when men speak what's in their hearts amazing stories are told, and a lot of compassion is felt. At the beginning of the week you might think, 'God, I've got nothing in common with these blokes,' but at the end you feel respect and admiration for everyone." *Are these events still going on?* "Yes. The form has gone on evolving under a new leadership team, and it's now regarded as very effective and transformational by the men who experience it."

How does this compare with the rites of passage that women make?

"Traditionally I think it was felt that women are, to a significant extent, initiated by Nature — through menstruation, childbirth, menopause and so on. Their rites of passage ceremonies weren't as involved as those set up for boys. It's as if something had to be devised for males which would equate with those physical experiences. And some people say that the energy of young men — which can be aggressive and destructive — needs to be tempered and redirected towards the furtherance of life. Of course now the world is increasingly different, and young women probably need their own specifically designed ceremonies too. This year for the first time we had an experimental mixed rites of passage for men and women. I made a special effort for that one and marked it by installing a proper kitchen with units, beautiful oak work tops, a fridge and a brand new full-size gas cooker!"

Lessons from Aboriginal Australia

So why has he done all this? What was the motivation that led to storytelling, doing rites of passage, creating the encampment?

"I think it goes back to the time I spent working with the Aborigines in Central Australia in my late twenties and early thirties. I went into communities where people still live on their own land, speak their own languages and conduct some of their traditional ceremonies. I realized that whereas whites are always desperately trying to 'civilize' blacks, perhaps there was a need for us to be 'aboriginalized' by them. I became interested in finding out what we could learn from indigenous cultures.

"Altogether I spent four years working in about fifty Aboriginal communities throughout South Australia and the Northern Territory. Initially I was simply a community artist, then later, based in Alice Springs, I worked as part of the Araluen Bush Arts Team. We performed specially devised shows — we found that music, humour and strong visual material crossed the culture gap — we also worked with the children in the schools and supported the creative endeavours of the men and women, which included providing them with materials to paint and record their stories.

"Near the end of our time there we were summoned to a men's meeting at a place called Tara — known to the whites as Neutral Junction. These men, the elders, wanted to know what we were doing and whether we'd stolen their paintings. After much careful discussion they were reassured and turned to a deeper concern. Their young men didn't want to go through the initiations into the Dreaming any more. They were more interested in town and cars and alcohol. This meant that the whole of their 40,000-year-old culture was threatened with annihilation within a generation. It was as if they were standing on the edge of an abyss.

"I was very moved by this, and I vowed to do what I could to get their voice heard. So when I returned to Britain I took a show about Aboriginal life to school and community venues around Britain, trying to promote a better understanding of their history and culture."

I'm not sure that I understand "the Dreaming." What exactly is it?

"For Aboriginal people the Dreaming is a multi-layered complex of stories, ceremonies, relationships and the law which connects them with the shape of the land, with the origin of plants and animals, with their ancestors and with each other. Through rituals at specific places they keep the spirit of the Dreaming alive, draw spiritual energy from sacred ground and bring each generation into full adulthood. Just before leaving Australia I came across the saying 'White Man got no Dreaming,' a quotation from an Aboriginal man who felt that white Australians had no spiritual relationship to the land or with their ancestors. I found myself thinking: But if there *was* a white man's dreaming, what would it be?

"So, when I finally contemplated coming back to Britain after ten years travelling round the world, I reflected on what I — and we — could learn from Aboriginal culture." *And what was that?* "For me it boiled down to three things. One was to do with the Dreaming, the stories that connect them to spirit, land and ancestry. The second was to do with the initiation rites that bring about the maturation of boys into manhood and maintain continuity and stability through the generations. And the third was simply the notion of sacred land, and the respect and care due to the earth. It was these three lessons that led me to storytelling, rites of passage and Cae Mabon."

Facing death

This "going backwards" method of Eric's gives me my next question. Why was he in Australia in the first place?

"Well, I was born there, as were both of my parents. I came into the world in a dusty town where the desert meets the sea called Whyalla, which means 'water hole.' My parents took me and my sister to Britain when I was three years old and we lived in London, my Dad bricklaying and shop-stewarding on building sites. He had strong radical political views in those days. My mother looked after us two small children and was also a teacher. After three years she contracted polio — she'd had it once before — and died within a week. It was an utterly devastating blow to all our family.

"Fortunately for my father, my mother's best friend who was a teacher in the same school came round to help out. Within a short time, realizing there was nothing he could do to bring my mother back and desperately short of money and family support, they were married. My step-mother was from North Wales and when I was taken to her parents' farm I took to it like a duck to water. Later, when we returned from another four years in Australia, I told them I wanted to live with my Nain and Taid. I loved the timeless life of the farm, feeding hens, cutting wood, milking cows, digging potatoes, going to the mart and so on. But it was decided that I should go with my parents and my sister to keep the family together. So we went to Windsor, and I went through my secondary schooling there. I did well enough in sport, exams and as a prefect, but always I felt an outsider."

So why did he go back to Australia as an adult?

"Partly to find out about my mother. Not much had been said about her after her death. I also wanted to get to know my extended family and especially my two ageing grandmothers. I'd had a premonition that I needed to experience something of death, but what or how I didn't know.

"Almost as soon as I got back to Adelaide.I was spending each evening with a cousin, trying to talk her out of suicide. I saw her several nights in a row and I knew what she had in mind. I tried everything I could to persuade her otherwise, but in the end I had to say, 'I don't want you to do this, but if you do, God bless you.' Next day she drove north, walked off into the woods and shot herself. It was grim. I vowed I'd never be so helpless again, and soon afterwards I took a job as a psychologist with the Department for Community Welfare, where I learned some counselling and therapeutic skills.

"Then, two months after my cousin's death, my father's mother, my Nan, also died. She was ninety and this was a good death. She even hinted that she'd been waiting for me to return. I suppose I was like my father who, it was said, had been her favourite son. There were an extraordinary few days when we shared the depths of sorrow and the heights of joy. She told people who came to visit her later that she'd had 'a service.' On her final day I made up an improvised last rites. I thanked her for her life, for all she'd given to her children and grandchildren, and finally I said goodbye. Then I left. Two hours later we got a phone call saying she'd died. I went to run on the beach, and as I came back to the car I saw a white bird come out of the sky, circle round my head a few times and then fly off into the coming night. My Nan's departing spirit, I thought.

"Those experiences with death, along with seeing photographs, paintings and letters and hearing about my mother's life from close friends and family (I discovered that she'd been an actress, and had taught in an Aboriginal community just before I was born) helped me to finally and fully grieve for her and come to terms with her death. Only then did I feel really able to get on with my life."

Journey round the world

What about his ten-year journey?

"I'd come back to Australia after a social psychology degree at Sheffield University and four years 'dropped out' and on the road in North and Central America and the Pacific Islands. I can see now that during this period, my late teens and early twenties, I went through a series of remarkable but nearly always unsupervised initiations. The first was a six-week expedition to Arctic Norway when I was seventeen. The following summer I went to the World Youth Festival in Bulgaria and met young people from all over the world (including the Vietcong — I remember treasuring an aluminium ring made from a shot-down American warplane) and engaged in the heated debates of the time. When it was over I hitch-hiked back through Eastern Europe and was in Prague just days before the 1968 Russian invasion. After leaving school in 1969 (I'd struggled through science A levels because I thought I wanted to be a vet, though really I'd have been happy as a farmer, like Taid) I dropped in unannounced to see my adopted Welsh grandparents. Two nights later Taid died in my arms. Everyone said I'd been sent.

"In what's nowadays called a 'gap year' I hitched down through Europe and had a romantic spell with a Canadian lass on a Greek Island, then went to Lebanon for an International Work Camp digging up a Byzantine ruin. When that was over I hitched to Damascus and was one of the first English-speaking people allowed into Syria since the 1967 Arab-Israeli war."

How was going to university after all that?

"A bit of an anticlimax, I have to say. I'd chosen psychology and sociology because I wanted to understand what it meant to be a human being, and their emphasis on statistics and experimental behaviourism wasn't my cup of tea. But I stuck it out, and I did relish the acting and directing that I did in the Theatre Group. The next summer I hitched across Canada, down the west coast of America and by Greyhound bus went from Los Angeles to New

Orleans and New York. I may have missed San Francisco in 1967 but I wasn't far behind!

"My final thesis was on 'Educational Change and Identity,' but after I completed it I realized I had no idea what 'identity' really was. So I set out on a quest for it. I went off to North America with very little money, and deliberately shed my roles, my qualifications, past history, family and social circles, and threw myself naked into the world. If this doesn't work, I thought, nothing will."

"Work?" In what way?

Eric frowns. "There are many tales I could tell from that time. It's difficult to convey briefly the depth of what happened. But — " *and here he gets back into his stride* — "I learned that if I took risks and had faith I would survive. Later, in the San Francisco Bay Area, I educated my body through dance and gave my mind a rest. I lived alone in a cabin for six weeks and read William James's *The Varieties of Religious Experience.*[2] I went to Mexico and had a series of deeply expanding experiences. But, when went back later to Central America in pursuit of more, I crashed into a soul-splitting low. That was the darkest time really. For a while I felt lost, alone, shattered to pieces, as if I was wasting my life. But bit by bit I began to love myself again and to value my moment-to-moment experience."

How did he pull himself out of the depths?

"Partly by repeating to myself regularly: 'Each day I'm learning new ways to love.' Then finally I was in Hawaii, watching the sun set, when I had something like a divine revelation. Suddenly I could feel the distance between me and the Sun. Then I had a sense of the space of the solar system, the stars and the planets, and that the Earth is the most extraordinary planet of all. I imagined billions of years and an immensity of space as if it had all acted as a lens with the Earth as its focus. For this Earth is the one place we know where Life has taken off and evolved. And Humanity is the cutting edge of that Evolution, and here am I, a living human being. It was tempting to feel 'Yes, but I'm nothing compared with the great people who have lived.' But then I realized that I am alive now, and they are all dead. My task, it seemed, was to put my shoulder to the evolving wheel of Life.

"Once I'd had a glimpse of how extraordinary the gift of

human life is, and how it comes at the end of the long journey of the evolving Cosmos, I could never sink so low again. Once I'd truly realized that, everything changed. It was like a conversion experience, only without God. Soon afterwards I spent a month in paradise on a tiny island in Western Samoa. It felt like a reward for getting so far. Then I returned to Australia."

Rites of Passage for Youth

Could it be that Eric's own journey has something to do with the work he's now doing with young people?

"Well, not many young people get the chance to go on such an extended journey of discovery as I did. So, drawing on my personal experience, plus my understanding of early peoples and what we've learned in the men's rites of passage, I'm interested in developing a contemporary rites of passage perspective for work with young people. We draw on outdoor and adventure education, youth work, creative arts — music, storytelling, drama, sculpture — and on environmental education. On psychological and spiritual approaches, too."

What would he say are the functions of traditional rites of passage that are relevant today?

"In a nutshell, spiritual awakening, developing emotional intelligence, giving a sense of identity and purpose, realizing responsibilities, involving the community ... Most of these things aren't done well by our educational system. Everything is so pressured and complex in the lives of young people that we — and they — often don't see the wood for the trees. And in the absence of genuine, guided rites of passage, the need for initiation often breaks through anyway. All too often it's in the shape of a painful and humiliating induction rituals into a public school or a gang."

But surely there's a huge difference between tribal societies and the society of today?

"Of course, but some things, like the essentials of growing up, don't change."

And what about the older men who are needed to lead the young men through this transition?

"Yes, the cry does go up, where are the 'elders'? Where are the men who have, as they say, 'dealt with their stuff,' who've looked at their own cycle of negativity and broken it? Sometimes it seems like an uphill struggle, but I think there's more radical change on this front than we generally realize."

I wonder, with a smile, whether Eric feels that he's broken his own 'cycle of negativity'?

"Work in progress, I'd say. I still desire things I can't have. I'm still scared of speaking truth in relationships. And I probably have other deep-rooted problems that I haven't sorted out yet. But being aware of these shortcomings is half the battle. I feel I've come far enough to be able to work constructively with young people. In any case, the 'crisis of youth' means it's essential to try."

Evolutionary leap

He pauses, and from the crisis of youth he begins to ponder the broader crises of the twentieth century.

"The last century has been a period completely unprecedented in the history of the Earth. For example, the growth rates of speed, consumption, knowledge and waste have been exponential. I've got a layman's sense of the evolution of Life in the Cosmos and to my mind we're potentially poised on the threshold of an evolutionary leap. It could even be that humanity is about to go through its own transition from youth to maturity. For the first time it seems that evolution no longer depends on apparently random genetic mutation and environmental change. In many ways — and I'm not just referring to scientific genetic manipulation — we have the reins of future evolution in our hands. We can decide how we want it to be. The creative 'God' power has come down to us.

"It isn't easy. The moral choices are complex, often contradictory. But if we step back and relax a bit we can see that the sweep of evolving Life has brought us greater and greater diversity, flexibility, variety, sensitivity, complexity, integration, self-organization, beauty, freedom ... It's as if this is what Life offers us, this is what Life asks of us. I suppose," he says, leaning back, "you could substitute God for Life, and Love for everything else."

I can feel that at this significant point the interview is coming towards its end. "But there's something behind and below all this," Eric says slowly, "and that's to do with soul. I'm not sure what that word means, but my intuition tells me that cultivating soulfulness is important. It's what Alida was fostering on her workshop. It's not a single, one-dimensional thing. It's to do with the small experiences in the day: with the relationship to the heron, with that tree, between you and me. It's to do with the song I'm learning, with what happens when I go into the Roundhouse, stir the fire, sit back, take a deep breath and begin to speak, not quite knowing what I'm going to say ... It's, yes, that fire, that healing water in the lake that flows off Snowdon ...

"It's to do with finding your gift, with as Joseph Campbell says, 'following your bliss.'[3] I think I've followed mine, and I've been lucky. What I'm looking forward to now is more time to think and to write, to sing and tell stories, to explore this wondrous world. And to love and be loved! What more could I ask for?

"That really sounds like The End, doesn't it," he says, laughing. *I switch off the tape and, leaving Eric to make soup and ponder his next course, I walk down past the Roundhouse, climb the stile over the slate wall, and make my way through the oak forest down to the lake for that healing swim.*

Kathy Jones

*It was the first time I'd heard it, the Spirit as "She." And —
this is my mythology — how wonderful it was for me to
sing the Spirit as She. It had always been He. Spirit had
always been He. Earth now, Earth could be She. But not
Spirit. Now, for me, Spirit was She, She, She.*

*When my hair began to fall out with the chemotherapy I
decided to have my head shaved, so as to take my power
rather than have it taken from me. We made it a death and
rebirth ceremony. And two friends shaved their heads, too,
so that I wouldn't be alone.*

Embodying the Goddess

Kathy Jones was born in 1947 and brought up in Gateshead, County Durham. She went to Methodist Sunday School, and in her early teens chose to be baptized. After university and doing research for BBC scientific programmes she lived alone in rural Wales, meditating and studying theosophical texts. In the seventies she moved to Glastonbury, Somerset, where she discovered goddess stories in the legends and the landscape and found ways of expressing a Goddess spirit in ritual and drama. She has co-founded several community institutions which include the Goddess and feminine spirituality in their constitutions, such as the Isle of Avalon Foundation, Bridget Healing Centre and the Library of Avalon, and in 1996, while recovering from breast cancer, she organized the first Goddess Conference.

I approach Kathy Jones's house with varied preconceptions about the sort of home the founder of the Goddess Conference will live in: an upmarket cottage announcing modestly that this woman is a princess of heaven, maybe, or an airy stone house draped like a temple with esoteric works of art. In fact Kathy lives in an ex-council house in a crowded Glastonbury street. Only the view from the back garden of Glastonbury Tor's shapely cone and the tendency of surfaces to transform into altars give clues to the spirituality of the owner. Kathy lives here with her teenage son and daughter and her second husband, Mike.

She glows with health, but the day after our interview has to go for her six-month cancer check-up. I phone a few days later, and she tells me she's clear.

The Sergeant Major and the Methodist

"My parents were not religious at all," she begins, "but they sent me to Methodist Sunday School, I think to make me a good girl. My mother was very affectionate, but my father was a very Victorian man, very strict. In my teens I hated him. He wasn't a violent man physically, but he was emotionally. Very controlling. It was very frightening. I never knew what mood he was going to be in when he came home from work, angry, or ... Horrible. He'd been a Sergeant Major in the Military Police. When he came out he had to start again from the bottom. He was intelligent but he'd had no chance to go to university, and at home here were his wife and two little girls. What do you do? Do you shout at them like you're in the barracks?" *What did this do to her?* "It strengthened me, I think, to be myself, not to be trampled on.

"The Methodists were very plain, no incense or candles or alcohol. But when I was about twelve I really fell in love with Jesus. It was a very passionate thing. I would go to church three times a Sunday. Sang a lot of hymns, loved it. I hadn't been baptized as a child, and I got baptized then. Standing up, as a teenager, in front of everybody, getting sprinkled with water: it was very visible thing to do. I went into quite mystical raptures.

"At home I was fighting all the time, fighting for my freedom. I knew that I couldn't be part of their limited way of looking at things.

"Then, around sixteen, seventeen, sex came along. Where the church was concerned you weren't allowed to have sex. But it was the sixties, the sexual revolution, and I'm afraid Jesus lost out. It wasn't that I jumped into having sex, but I have a passionate nature, and it was the sexual energy that arises in you in your teenage years.

"Fortunately I was intelligent, and I could leave home by going to university. I went to Nottingham and studied psychology and physiology. What interested me was people. Not that I learnt anything about people in my degree, it was all human beings as machines, how many times are you going to press the button ... But in the rest of my life I found out about relationships. I smoked a bit of dope, but I once took something that must have some opium in it and it was horrible, so I stopped smoking dope. When

I graduated I did bits of research for writers and then I got a job with the BBC doing research for *Horizon,* the scientific documentaries.

"I had a great time with *Horizon,* they sent me to America and I met people like Carl Sagan* But I didn't really like the people I was working with, and the relationships I was having were always going wrong, I was always getting hurt. The scientist in me, where you could explain everything in terms of molecules and DNA, had taken over."

A lone development of spirituality

"Some friends of mine had gone to Morocco on a spiritual journey and I went to visit them. Something happened when I was there. I was looking at this mountain, and at the pilgrims walking up it, and I realized that there was more to life than what I'd known. There was this whole area of life that I knew nothing about. All these people, following so many traditions. There were books to read and things to explore. It was like a door opening.

"So I came back and I began to meditate. I read Mouni Saddhu, who taught exercises in concentration like setting a pin on the top of some water and getting it to move just by the power of your mind. All sorts of spiritual books, east and west. Then I got the chance to move to Wales."

She was willing to leave this very good job? Not for a sexual relationship, just for an exploration of the spiritual? "Yes. There wasn't enough air.

"It was autumn, and very muddy, and the house was across two fields. But it was so beautiful. The green, and the water, the wet ... It was back to the earth, self-sufficiency. I dug the earth, planted vegetables, chopped wood ..." *This was a huge change, surely, from earning lots of money and interviewing illustrious people?* "Yes. But I loved it. When I had to move out of that place, I found a farmhouse across the valley and I moved into it on my own. I can remember the first night. It was the first time I'd ever been completely on my own. I was in the middle of

* Carl Sagan (1934–96). Director of the Laboratory of Planetary Studies at Cornell University and author of books such as *The Cosmic Connection, The Dragons of Eden* and *The Demon-Haunted World.*

nowhere, I was so scared, and I was so lonely. This owl went by, hooting. And it was full moon! I was terrified someone was going to come across these fields and kill me. There was no one else. I had to do everything on my own.

"So I began to develop a spiritual practice. I'd read the Abremalin magical rite, which is a six-month exercise where you get to meet your guardian angel. But that wasn't really what I wanted to do, so I developed my own spiritual practice: so many hours of reading, so many hours of meditation. I did it for six months, several times over. There was no one to ask, how do I do this, no one to query whether it was a good idea. I just felt I had to." *No contact with family? No relationships?* "I was celibate for most of those years. My parents came once to see me towards the end of the five years, but they couldn't understand what I was doing." *Earning a living?* "There were some job creation schemes, and for a time I wrote brochures about Welsh places of interest. But I was pretty self-sufficient. If I did earn money I gave it away. It seemed a plan by the universe to supply anyone who needed it. And I wrote a book about living in the country[1] It got published, and it seemed to sell quite well.

"I'd read Taoism, Buddhism, those sort of things. Before long I started to read Alice Bailey.* Her writings were very esoteric, very obscure. They're like a jigsaw, you get one or two pieces from one or another book and then you have to go back and read them again. It's about the journey of the soul into incarnation, and the different energy bodies we have and the way energy moves in the chakras.† She asks what we are, physically and spiritually: how spiritual energy precipitates, how it comes into form, how it appears in the world. I would read, and then I would meditate." Not looking for a guru? "No. I've always been anti-guru. I was driven to do it myself. I'm not so much like that now. Now I know that I sometimes need help. I learnt to think for myself, which I'd never done before."

---

* Theosophical writer who followed Madame Blavatsky in the USA.

† In Indian spirituality, the seven points on the body where the spirit enters most readily.

Towards Glastonbury

How did she come out of isolation and live in the sociable world again?

"In the middle of this I went to Findhorn.* I went to a conference, and it was so wonderful. It was a time of great energy for Findhorn. I'd been alone, and the only people I'd known who did this sort of thing, meditation and spiritual study, were a few friends. Here were all these hundreds, and so much happening!

"The friends who'd been in Morocco were now living in Glastonbury, and we started to do full moon meditations. Alice Bailey recommends you to do them, with a prayer called 'the Great Invocation.' I wouldn't say it now but it was very precious to me then. I'd travel from my home near Brecon down to Glastonbury every month, often reciting the Great Invocation all the way, to do full moon meditations in the Town Hall." *Why the Town Hall? Seems an oddly staid place for such an esoteric event?* "We just hired it. In the seventies Glastonbury wasn't the New Age centre it is today, there were signs up in pubs and shops saying 'No Hippies.' We wanted to give what we were doing respectability. We gave a little talk, did the meditation, said the Great Invocation. Then I drove back to Wales.

"We dabbled in other things, like Co-Freemasonry and the Liberal Catholics, that were started by Annie Besant.† The Liberal Catholic Church was a form of Christianity that involved working with the angelic forces and knowing what was happening energetically. I would do the communion for myself at home in Wales using their liturgies.

"But still I was almost always alone. I was very peaceful. I got lonely because I didn't see anyone, I'd forgotten how to talk to people except to the farmer about swedes, but I was incredibly calm. I'd transcended my emotions ..."

We laugh, Kathy uproariously, because we both know what's coming next. And then ...

* The spiritual centre founded by Eileen and Peter Caddy and Dorothy Maclean near Forres, Inverness, Scotland.

† Annie Besant (1847–1933), theosophist, social reformer and campaigner for Indian independence.

"And then ... A young woman called Melanie turned up, and she stayed. She was like a young version of me and she made me laugh. There'd been this incredible contrast to how I was feeling spiritually and how I was feeling around people, and Melanie introduced me to people again.

"Then one time, when we were here in Glastonbury doing the meditations, it was Beltane* and a full moon, lots of energy around, I had a dream. I went underneath the Tor, and I saw all these strange creatures, like I'd never seen before, like teddy bears with long noses, and fluffy things, fluffy animals, and they all lived under the Tor. I got up in the morning and I felt as if I'd spent the night under the Tor." *Did she know at the time about the mystical land of Avalon?* "No! When I first came, a friend took me up on the Tor and it was covered with cow-shit. I thought, what *is* this? Why are people going *on* about this place? But gradually the energies drew me in.

"So I decided to move here. I went back to Wales, and my garden was looking really beautiful, the whole place was radiant, it was sunny all the time as if it was doing its last thing for me. Within a couple of months I'd moved."

Discovering Goddesses

Did she have a job in Glastonbury? "I worked in shops, little jobs to keep me going. I stayed with those same old friends who'd been in Morocco. There were a whole group of us who moved into Glastonbury at the same time, spiritual explorers, we'd all done the Alice Bailey stuff. We called ourselves The Inner Plains Trucking Company. We came to Glastonbury to clean the energies up." *Get the cow-shit off the Tor? She nods.* "Clean up the psychic cow-shit." *And then?* "And then, within a very short space of time, our group had been completely torn asunder."

Ah. How?

"It's the arrogance of us human beings. People today still come and say they're going to clean the place up." *Great laughter again. Then, very serious:* "We have so little influence on these spaces, these energies."

* The pagan festival around 1 May.

So what happened? "All our friendships, all our relationships fell apart. I'd gotten into a relationship that was just a disaster ... And I thought, how could I have come from that sublime state to *this* state? What was all that spiritual stuff *about* if, when it came to it, in a human relationship, it meant nothing? It was like, it was meaningless. It didn't work in the place where I needed it to work, which was in loving someone else.

"So I thought, what happens if I give all this up? If I give all this spiritual stuff up, if I drop all the spiritual practice and the structures and the belief systems, is there anything there?"

This, I feel, is the real question. Did she give it up? "Not instantly, but gradually. Yes, I gave it up.

"Then a Women's Group started in town. A big bunch of women, and it had a really big effect on all of us. It was very exciting. We started off with the seven demands of women's liberation, abortion on demand, free contraception, equality of opportunity, a whole list of things. Each time we'd take a different topic and debate it. It was an exploration of who we were as women."

The Spirit as Woman

Had she completely given up the spiritual practice at this point? "It overlapped, me giving it up and me coming into the women's movement. I'd been arguing in the Co-Freemasonry circles about why it was always 'He' and 'Him,' and they wouldn't listen. Liberal Catholics, the same. The structure was so rigid, it couldn't incorporate the new feminine consciousness. I was reading all the feminist books, Mary Daly in particular.* I began to understand how the patriarchy functions. All my spiritual life so far had been in masculine terms, but now my life was in the feminine. The place of my enjoyment was in this women's group.

"When Greenham Common† happened, we were there. There were several actions and a bus load of us would go up there, join in, stay overnight.

* Author of e.g. *Gyn-ecology* and *Beyond God The Father,* Beacon Press.

† The US Cruise Missile base in Berkshire where women set up peace camps in the 1980s.

"I remember one time — now this is where it becomes mythology — it was dusk. We'd lit candles. The women were all outside the fence, in the woods. And there was the fence. Beyond it, policemen. Barbed wire. Soldiers. More barbed wire. More soldiers with guns. Protecting this thing. Protecting death.

"This contrast, the feminine and the masculine ... Whoah.

"Then what happens is, we begin to sing. *You can't kill the Spirit, She is like a mountain, Old and strong, She goes on and on.*

"It was the first time I'd heard it, the Spirit as 'She.' And — this is my mythology — how wonderful it was for me to sing the Spirit as She. It had always been He. Spirit had always been He. Earth now, Earth could be She. But not Spirit. Now, for me, Spirit was She, She, She."

Dramatizing the goddess energy

"Some of the women from Glastonbury had left their families to go and live at Greenham. I wanted to do something to celebrate what they were doing, and I found the story of Demeter and Persephone and I saw the parallels: how man takes the woman and rapes her, takes her into the underworld, and after a while she gets to quite like him. In terms of Greenham it was: here come these guys, they rape you and they rape the earth, they destroy the earth and take you to the underworld, but then they give you washing machines, television sets to keep you quiet, and you come to quite like them, and you agree that what they're doing, destroying the world, is keeping you safe. That's how we collude.

"That was the dynamic of my play, and we did it in Glastonbury. It was very exciting, we had the fence on the stage, and we did it in a very short space of time and it was very strong.

"Afterwards I thought that was that. But I'd been reading Diane Wolkstein's book on Inanna* and I just loved the language of it.[2] [The book is co-written with Samuel Noah-Kramer, who translated the original story from the Sumerian.] So I made a drama of that. These amazing people came together, actors, singers, musicians ... We did this staggering performance. The whole thing was

---

* Inanna, the Sumerian goddess who goes into the underworld to her sister Erishkigal.

sacred drama. We experienced the Goddess energy. We experienced Her.

"After Inanna there were more sacred dramas, and I began to experience different goddesses. One of them would come and speak to me: 'Hey, here's me, what about me?' I'd trip up against information about one of them I hadn't heard of. For instance, Green Tara. Green Tara is the Tibetan goddess of compassion. Someone had given me a poster, an image of Green Tara. I'd had it for years, I'd just bunged it on the wall. I had a desk underneath this picture, and it was like someone tapped me on the shoulder and said, 'Look at me.' I turned — 'Did I really feel that?' Then I looked again and it was as if Green Tara was sitting on the wall in 3-D. I heard her say, in my head, 'I am Green Tara. Find out about me, write a play about me.' I knew nothing about her but I went away, got a lot of books about her, wrote a play.

"I brought the knowledge of the past into the present. In fact for me, with Green Tara, it's more than the past: I've been a Tibetan Buddhist monk, I know it. I don't want to be a Tibetan Buddhist now, I'm in a twentieth-century woman's body. But I know I've been there.

"People's lives were changed by these sacred dramas. Many people's lives, mine as well." And she tells me the long story about how, after a fraught marriage to the father of her children, she met Mike who already knew about the Goddess and with whom she's now been together for ten years.

"I wanted the audience to experience Green Tara's energy. She's the goddess of compassion and she helps people — she helps me — to overcome fear. The same with the Ariadne play, *The Beauty In The Beast*.[3] I'm not telling the patriarchal story. I want to tell myth but I want to change it to create the future."

She's not fazed if people say "That's not historically accurate"?

"Oh, they do say that! No, I'm not trying to repeat what's been said already. I think there's a mythic layer to reality. We know how the laws of nature govern the physical world, attraction, repulsion and so on, yes? I think that psychically there are laws, too, and they create the mythic layer. The mythic layer has a substance, and a lot of things that we are driven by as human beings come from this mythic layer. If we're to change human behaviour we've got to change at this mythic level. And to change it you have to know what it is."

To return to the children, and to Mike. First, the children. "I was thirty-three. I'd never thought of having children, but now I got a really strong desire to have a child. But I wanted it within a steady relationship. So I surrendered to the universe. In fact I think it was my daughter saying, 'Hey, I want to be born.' I met someone and got pregnant almost straight away. Very quickly the relationship went *splat*. He went into his shadow side, and it all imploded. But it went on, on and off, for years. My son was born — yes, he went 'Knock knock, I'm here' too — and I was on my own." *When she had cancer and talked about her fear of death, she knew that the worst thing would be to leave her children.*

Then, much later, Mike. How does a Goddess woman at last get together with a bloke and make it work? She grins. It's obviously a very strong relationship, and she's already mentioned how complete was the support he gave her when she had cancer. "We met when we were doing Green Tara, when he came along as a musician. In the rehearsals, if I went *ding!* on my Tibetan bells, he was going *ding!* too. We seemed to be on the same energy frequency. We discovered — after about three months! — that we both had the same surname, that our mothers were both called Eileen, and we saw that our lives had been brought along parallel mythic lines. He knew about the Goddess. That was the great thing, that I didn't have to teach him about the Goddess. I'd been asking for an equal partner and so had he. I got through my karmic struggle in my first relationship, and I won't have to do it again. He's very secure, he's not put out by me being strong because he's strong too. And he teaches me lots of things." *Like?* "Like it's all right to be wrong. I'd learnt from the patriarchal system that you had to be perfect, that to say you were wrong meant death. From Mike I've learned to say, 'I'm sorry, I did that and it hurt you, and I'm really sorry.' And I don't die."

How to worship Her

What was the journey towards the Goddess Conference?

"I'd found out about the goddesses of other cultures. Now I had to find out about the goddesses around here. The signs of divinity in Glastonbury were all male: Joseph of Arimathea who brought the thorn from Jesus's crown, King Arthur, St Michael whose tower is on the Tor, though the rest fell down in an earth-quake in the 1300s ... They'd cornered the market! I thought, if the Goddess is everywhere then she has to be here. Philippa Bowers was around, doing goddess sculptures in the High Street, and Marion Zimmer Bradley had written *The Mists of Avalon*.[4] I looked for all the goddesses in the British Isles, and started vis-iting ancient sites all over the country, getting steeped in the landscape and in the times when the Goddess was revered. Robert Graves was one of my heroes.* Brigit, Cerridwen, Ana, Dana, Mab, Vivienne, the list is endless. Then in the women's peace movement we found women's sacred things to do, making spider's webs to block the road, pinning children's clothes to the wire. We were bringing the Goddess into expression. The God-dess has always been scrunched up in a corner and I thought, we have to get Her out.

"But if we want to worship the Goddess and tell her stories, how do we do that? To worship the God you have churches, syn-agogues, mosques. We have no buildings, no paid priests, no structure. Most of us don't want any of that anyway. How do we express Her in our daily life?

"So I thought, we're all scattered all over the place and we have to get together. We need to have a vehicle, we need communal rit-uals to honour the Goddess. In the summer of 1995 the Goddess spoke to me and said, 'Now's the time to create a Goddess Con-ference for next Lammas, a gathering like the Conference of the Birds.' Then, within two weeks of making the decision, I found I had cancer. I'll tell you about that later ..."

And did it work, the Goddess Conference? Has it continued?

"It was wonderful. I'd had visions of it for a year, and it came up

* Poet and author of many books, especially in this context *The White Goddess*, Faber 1948.

to it and more. There were two traumatic moments. Some women came from outside to protest about it being a gathering of rich people excluding the poor — which it wasn't, a lot of low-income women were working their ticket. And a couple of the contributors attacked me and Tyna for not giving them enough recognition. I thought, 'No! This sort of conflict is what gives me cancer!' But for the first time I managed to express my anger in public, to stand up for myself, to stop taking the crap into myself like I did with my father. It was a turning point for me. My leg was sore and I hobbled over to the women and hugged them. At the same moment a sliver of light shone through the Goddess banner, connecting the rose at Her heart to the stone of Sophia, the Philosopher's Stone, at her belly. It was a moment of synchronicity that sent shivers through the room, a profound message of reconciliation from the Goddess.

"Yes, the conferences are going from strength to strength. They just get better and better. We're preparing for the fourth now. I see the goddess as returning inexorably into people's lives. Nothing can stop her.

"We don't need to fight the patriarchy, it's just crumbling into dust. They don't need to fight us, either. Patriarchy isn't just bad for women, it's bad for men too. I don't need to convert anybody. The Goddess will speak to people when they are ready to hear her. Or they'll just die out. Kids born now are coming in with more consciousness than we had. My daughter doesn't see limitations to who she can be, in the way that we did. There will be limitations but she doesn't see them. It's a long term process. The Goddess is coming back. And when She is back, recognized in consciousness, then God can come and take his proper place. In a proper balance."

Hanging on by a red thread

Guiding a walk round the labyrinth of Glastonbury Tor at Lammas, 31 July, 1995, Kathy felt a bit detached and decided to dedicate herself once again to Ariadne, to whatever transformation She willed. At the time she had had a slight pain in the side of her right breast. "Mike said, *Go and get it looked at.* On 25 August a surgeon told me I had a malignant cancerous tumour and all he could offer me was a complete mastectomy. Mike and I clung to each other and cried and cried.

"At one level I couldn't understand why I'd got cancer. I was happy, I was creatively fulfilled, I'd been vegetarian for twenty-five years ... I'd asked Ariadne to transform me but I didn't mean like this! At another level, talking to wise loving friends I could see that what I was and did, bringing the Goddess in, tended to provoke lots of anger and I couldn't deal with it. My astrologer friend said I had to set aside my missionary zeal and learn to love myself, and I realized I didn't know what that meant, to love myself."

What treatments did she have? Orthodox or complementary?
"Both. People who choose only complementary medicine nearly always die. I wanted passionately to live. I had surgery, chemotherapy, radiotherapy, spiritual healing, Bach flower remedies, acupuncture, visualizations ... And counselling from my doctor, Phil Jackson. He was wonderful, I could talk to him about my fear of dying, all my other fears, my fear of mad drivers, violent men. My fear that someone would come across those fields in Wales and kill me ... But I remembered one night someone did come, a friend came in and woke me up in the middle of the night and I felt no fear at all. I saw that at the root of all those fears was my fear of dying. I could see how wonderful it might be to die surrounded by the love of my family and my friends. I was in the labyrinth" *(Kathy pronounces it, and spells it,* labrynth) "and, like in Ariadne's story, I was confronting the Minotaur not only of my fears but of my animus, my shadow figure.

"One night Ariadne showed me a room that was deep pinky red, where I could sleep with rays of light from her hand pouring into me. I prayed to the Morgens, the nine transforming powers of the Isle of Avalon, for help and healing. We know very little about them, but I felt them caw-cawing to me through the crows and hiding behind tree trunks in the apple orchards."

When her hair began to fall out with the chemotherapy Kathy decided to have her head shaved voluntarily, so as to take her power rather than have it taken from her. "We made it a death and rebirth ceremony. And two friends shaved their heads, too, so that I wouldn't be alone." *She shows me the photos in her book.[5] They look like a group of very happy, very loving Buddhist monks.*

The chemotherapy was especially horrendous. But in the end, she says, it was an alchemical journey. "The disease took me through a process of radical change on all levels, which I couldn't resist. It was a case of transform or die. Our Lady Wisdom called me to transform my life. I've had a great realization of the oneness of the soul. Our soul is expressed through all sorts of personalities, but in essence it's one. I am you, you are me, we are one. I am doing or learning this bit for you, you are learning or doing this bit for me. In the middle of the cancer someone told me, 'You're doing this for all women' and I said, 'I'm not, I can only do this for me, I can't be responsible for anyone else.' But I'd missed the point. I have done and am doing this for me *and* for you. It feels extraordinary to know that we are really one."

Eventually, after nine months, the treatment was over and she was on the road to recovery. "It taught me so much. For instance, about healing. In my early thirties I used to be a healer, but I lost my faith in it when spiritual healing failed to heal my newborn first baby and she had to have major surgery at six weeks old. But now I see disease itself as a form of healing. It's the soul's attempt to awaken us to an inner imbalance, forcing us to expand our limited horizons and consciousness."

Walking on fire

"It was amazing when I had energy again, doing what I love, speaking about the Goddess, feeling her energy flow out to women and men who are only just beginning to know her. It's a lovely life.

"I wondered if I wanted do another fire walk — walking on live fire. I'd done it four or five times before, in the spirit of proving to myself and everyone else that I could do it. Now I didn't have to prove myself any longer.

"In May 1996, when I was better, the others were doing it in the fire-walking workshop and I joined them. I felt very calm, with no pressure at all to do this thing. As we circled the fire, I waited for my intuition to say *Yes* and it kept saying *No*. But right at the very end the voice said, *You don't have to, but you can do it anyway.* So I walked across the fire."

Gordon MacLellan

There's a group of us who work together, and I'm the only one who's human. Some of them have been with me for thirty years, some just come visiting. There's a core of about five of us. Most days I'll stop for an hour or so, just to be with them, to meditate, perhaps to dance. We're bound by love.

As a shaman I work with vision. In your life there's a spirit that's you, that inspires you, that gives you character. And it's trying to live out a particular pattern within the universe at this time.

Dancing between worlds

Gordon MacLellan, or Creeping Toad, works as an environmental educator and follows a shamanic spiritual practice. Born in 1959 of Scottish parents who were "gently Presbyterian" he grew up in the new town of Cumbernauld. After studying Zoology at Glasgow University he taught for three years in Malawi, where he almost died of malaria. Returning to Britain he became a country park warden, and now works freelance in educational and environmental situations. He is the administrator for the Sacred Earth Drama Trust and writes extensively on shamanism.[1]

"I'm an environmental educator, that's my job," says Gordon. "I work in National Parks, Wildlife Trusts, schools. On the surface that might seem completely divorced from the belief that inspires and guides and directs me. But to me they're reflections of the same thing. My life isn't a series of set choices, it's a way of being in the world." *Great, I say; that's what the book's about. But why does he live in a tiny terraced house in un-green central Manchester, with no garden and hardly a tree in sight?*

The answer is simple and twofold. "I can't afford leafy suburbia, and I like this place with its dynamic mix of cultures living together."

Gordon tells me more about his job, which he clearly loves. "It's to help people explore and appreciate the world they live in, to whatever depth they want to take it. We'll find ways of expressing what they've found and maybe have a celebration of the experience we've all been through. No way do I ever say to them, 'Now we're going to have a spiritual experience.' Essentially I'm helping them to have a good time. But for me as leader, as facilitator, my job is a spiritual one. I don't tell them I'm a pagan, a shaman. That would just get in the way. What they do belongs to them, not to me."

How does that work?

"I'll give you an example. A few months ago I was in Kent, sixty or seventy children each day, creating a celebration for the opening of a community woodland. I asked the children what might be looking at them in this woodland — birds, voles, insects, leaves even. I got them to see it as a place where adventures might happen. They made giant toad-stools, puppets big as themselves, pheasants to wear on their heads ... Two boys made eerie ghost figures that sat on a log, back-lit by the sun, looking like spooky woodland police. So when the visitors came for the celebration they entered a wood that had just woken up. Strange creatures were going about their strange-creature business. Giant toadstools watched them from the shadows. A dragon and some bluebells wandered around, a princess with her pet crocodile.

"The children had decided on the point of it all: it was that the wood wanted to be respected. A collective story emerged about an offensive little girl called Natalya who went riding through the wood crushing bluebells. At the end the other creatures followed her and swallowed her up. That was the children's idea, not mine, and we danced it in the final performance.

"Now, where am I in all that? Where's my spiritual practice?

"As a shaman I work with *vision.* In your life there's a spirit that's *you,* that inspires you, that makes you who you are. And it's trying to live out a particular pattern within the universe at this time. Discovering that pattern is vision."

By "vision" does he mean "purpose"?

"It's not that definite. 'Purpose' smacks of fate or predestination. It's more like, 'This time round, this is what you're trying to do.' My vision is that I'm a patterner because I work with groups, where a healer might work one-to-one. And my job is to help people explore their relationship with the living world. There are no pre-determined outcomes. My task is to set the exploration in motion. A lot of it is getting people to have the confidence to do things themselves."

The web of connection

This word "vision." What precisely does he mean by that?

Gordon ponders how to explain. "In the shamanic world everything is connected. Every action we take reverberates in the world around us. If we're drinking tea here, obviously we have a connection with a tea plantation somewhere else in the world. In a shamanic sense there's more to it. In sitting here, our breathing affects the plants. The fish in the fish tank associate me with food, so we're raising their expectations. We bring heat into the room, we make sure that the mice won't come in here while we're around."

That's a physical connection. Is there also a connection in a psychic sense?

"Yes. We tend not to separate the two. Tonight I'll be sitting here on my own and the house will be echoing back, 'We had a visitor here today. We saw this and this, tell us more about what went on.' In the shamanic world everything has the possibility of communication, though it may choose not to. I sit in the house and listen to what it's feeling, what its energies are like. I've lived in this house ten years now and we've worked hard to build up a house consciousness.

"For the shaman, our world is entirely alive. And the shaman needs to be open to that communication, to be able to listen to and to speak with that world. But that can mean you're in danger of spending your time being bombarded by the living presences of that world. In fact a lot of your training is to enable you *not* to have to do that — otherwise you'd be swamped, you'd never get the hoovering done.

"These connections comprise the 'web.' At any one time, we as individuals and communities move along those lines of connection — we follow the paths of our lives through the web of the world. For me as an individual, living inside or upon the web, there's a way of moving along my line that causes least disturbance in the web. Disrupting the web is wrong. There might be ways of justifying it to yourself, but if you're a shaman you'll soon be called to answer for it. We try to find movement with harmony. Finding that movement — that's what vision is.

"Vision is you surrendering yourself to the infinite. It's an awareness that comes both in the deepest levels of yourself and from the universe around you. It seems to give you the tune: like, if we're all playing these notes together, this is resonance that works for you."

The shamanic role

Did his shamanic training let him know what he ought to do with his life?

"Yes, it took me into environmental education — but that was also because of the physical skills that I've got. As a shaman I could just as easily have gone back to being a teacher. Vision doesn't make you say, 'I'm a shaman.' That could be your ego talking. If you come out of your vision wanting to be a healer, you don't have to be some shamanic crystals healer, there would be just as much respect and honour and power in being a doctor or a nurse or a care-worker. Vision is empowering, but it also needs to be humbling. You might have to give something up. One of my teachers once said, 'You can never doubt whether someone had a vision, but you can question how they're living it.' The test is not what you saw, but what you do with it."

Is he saying that the vision may reveal in you the ability to be a shaman but, unlike the ordained priesthood in monotheistic religion, there may be times when you have to step down from the role?

"Exactly. You don't get to wear the frock for life. Often, in traditional societies, the shaman is also a hunter or a mother or a fisher. I think the best shamans in our society are often invisible. As a shaman you're owned by the community you serve. My community is the group I'm working with at any one time. My job is sometimes to protect them from other people, like teachers who say 'He can't do that because he never speaks in public' or 'That one can't read.' Stuff it, when they're with me they can do whatever they like. I'm the clown out front, and that helps people to do the most outrageous things. And sometimes, for them, the most courageous things."

His spirit family

I've noticed that he often says 'we.' Just who is this 'we'? Gordon laughs. "Oh, that's me avoiding the word 'I.' Quite often 'we' are simply the people I'm working with on a project. There I'm talking about my human community. Or the community I live among here in Old Trafford, they use me as a friend, which is another shamanic role.

"Often by 'we' I mean my own spiritual community, the community of spirits that I owe allegiance to. As I said, for a shaman all the world's alive. In that plethora of possibilities, you make friends. Just like human friends, only the pattern of friendship reverberates in the non-human world too. There are spirits of animals, spirits of plants, spirits of stones. You might meet a fox spirit who is spirit of an individual fox, or it might be the generic Spirit of Fox. There are spirits from myth and folklore, and there are the bigger spirits who are gods. Some spirits remain passing acquaintances, some become friends, a few might become totems. There are also spirits of place, like the ones I meet in Manchester itself. The city spirits are new, in the sense that haven't got any folklore around them yet. Folklore gives you a language for what's going on. The spirits need someone to develop that language, so I try sometimes to create a magical space where I can meet them."

How does he communicate with them?

"Well, you don't just go up to them and demand 'Which spirit are you? And what's your history?' That would be incredibly rude. You forge relationships all the time, and if in doing that you find out what and how and where they are, then you do. Much like human friendships. There maybe something they want to tell you. Stones, for example: if you touch a stone you're into time-scales that are outside our comprehension, so we tend to pick up surface stuff, human things that have washed across the surface of their lives. In the magical landscapes I work in we've still got wolves. A few hundred years in the landscape's memory — 'What's that? Nothing!' say the hills. They're still remembering when we had wolves."

Ceremony and totem

What might the spirits be saying to him?

"They might say 'We want a ceremony.' They might say, 'You're the first person we've had in a while who's going to listen to us. We want you to do ... *this.*' And here's where I have an obligation to the non-human spirits. The city spirits once asked me to go and dance in the centre of Manchester at two o'clock in the morning. Oh bugger, I thought, I don't want to get arrested. But I had to do it."

Are ceremonies particularly important?

"Yes, but not in the sense that other magical orders see ceremonies, the ones that do ceremonies for the full moon and so on. We tend to do ceremonies because spirits ask us to do them. A healer might do a ceremony because she's talked to her human client, and to her own spirits and her client's spirits, and she's decided that there's a ceremony to be done here. I usually have some sort of ceremony at Samhain.* Maybe I'll stay up all night in the dark. The place tells me, or my own spirit family tells me, what ceremony is right. Sometimes I just know, 'We've got to do this now and this is how we've got to do it'."

Could he say more about totems? And about his "spirit family"?

"Again, there's a difficulty with pronouns here," says Gordon. "'I' and 'we' and 'they' tend to get confused. But let's have a go.

"There's a group of us who work together, and I'm the only one who's human. Some of them have been with me, as a conscious connection, for thirty years. Others have been twenty, a few or more recent. Some just come visiting. There's a core of about five of us. Most days I'll stop for an hour or so just to be with them, to meditate, perhaps to dance. I slip out of this world and into the spirit world. My spirit family are there then as a conscious, definite presence. The rest of the time they're there but not so consciously. We work better together than we work alone. We're bound by love."

Do other shamans work like this? "Yes, most of us have

---

* Samhain: pagan festival on 31 October/1 November, which Christians call All Hallows or All Saints.

connections like that. And a lot of us have one spirit, usually just one, who is ... best wording is, 'right inside you.' That's your totem. Your totem is *the one who makes you complete.* In societies with a more extant set of traditions you might have a personal totem, and you might also have a family totem or a magical totem, but in modern white western cultures we've lost those."

In popular awareness the only totems tend to be 'totem poles.' "The north-west coastal American, or Polynesian: they're the most dramatic and they're family totems. There are lots of different readings of totem poles, but mostly it's a magical family lineage."

Can he describe his own totem? Or is that private?

"No, for me it's public. My totem's a toad."

So that's why he calls himself Creeping Toad?

"Yes. When I set it up in about 1986, Toad had to be in there. And it had to be in progressive mode, and Dancing Toad seemed just silly, so ... Creeping Toad."

Developing awareness

How did he first encounter Toad?

"That's hard to say. He or she (gender is difficult) has always been there. I've got childhood memories of always bringing home frogs or toads in yoghurt pots. I'd *have* to go to the pond, it was a kind of fixation."

I wondered what his parents said. "Oh, they were very tolerant." *His parents belonged to the Church of Scotland?* "Yes, Presbyterian Church of Scotland, in Cumbernauld, an incredibly bleak new town in the middle of Scotland. Before that, Glasgow suburbs. Before that, Surrey." *Never in the countryside?*

"No. I suppose I was about ten when I realized that more things were going on than I was being told about. Nothing very dramatic, I was just aware of things that didn't fit in with what I could see with my ordinary eyes. Somewhere I'd got friends who were special people to me. If I was out in the woods Toad was, if you like, turning over inside me.

"Then I read a couple of books by Alan Garner.[2] I'd read C.S. Lewis and that stuff, but that's always detached, it's not present. Alan Garner's writing was wonderful because it gave me a language. Almost an acceptance that said, 'All those magical things, it's all right. It's possible'."

Did he talk about it to anyone about it?

"No. I was a very secretive child in many ways. From a very early age I knew there were things I wasn't going to talk about. I also grew up gay, and in central Scotland that combination of pagan and gay was not a 'nice' one in the sort of huge comprehensive school I went to."

How early was he aware of his gayness? "Probably from about ten years onwards I was beginning to try and find ways of accessing what I was feeling, ways of exploring it. I remember waiting and waiting for the age of thirteen, because thirteen was such a magical age that the fairies were bound to come and take me away." *To where?* "Oh, just away! Vanish! In Scotland the folklore is full of fairies taking you away.

"This was the beginning of me growing into who I am, rather than who society expected me to be. And the beginning of me getting the strength to hang on to it, because I wasn't living in an easy world.

"But my parents were good at supporting their children to make their own decisions. They wanted us to be ourselves."

Does he feel that he chose his spirit family? Or his genetic family?

"No, I think it's much more random than that. I don't recognize ancestry much ... Having said that I'm beginning to explore my MacLellan lineage, right back through the Highlands to their origins in Northern Ireland."

In folk tales, isn't the 'blood line' often very important?

"Yes, but in modern society depending on the blood line can be very disempowering. We have so little contact with our grandparents and beyond. I've been up in Argyll recently and the MacLellan stuff has come at me demanding 'Look, do something about this.' So I am doing. But I've the right to say to it, 'I've got enough on my plate, go away just now. Make an appointment or something'."

Togetherness and aloneness

There's a big question that I want to ask at this point. It's about the company he keeps, and whether he's lonely; about how much his friends, lovers, colleagues and so on have to know about his relationship with the spirit world if they're to be close to him and work with him.

"That's a very difficult one to answer." He takes a breath and taps his fingers. "One of the things I've noticed about the shamanic network is that we're all outsiders. Maybe that's because we're socially dysfunctional! But maybe it's because we're walking between worlds, on the edges of worlds. We're talking to the spirit world and the ordinary world all at the same time. So we're marginalized just by who we are and what we do.

"And that makes for a lot of loneliness in our lives. It can be very hard for other people to understand what motivates us and how we move. People can appreciate what I do, which is fine, but they still don't understand what it's like to keep on meeting things that they think aren't there, or get instructions to do things they think are appalling."

Appalling, like ...?

"Like, dancing till I bleed. I trance-dance, and one of the signs of trance is that you come out of it finding that you're bleeding. I have to make sure there are no knives nearby. I dance with a spirit, and it's her who's doing the leading."

'Her'? Is he talking about possession here?

"Yes. Again, the terms we use tend to be very loaded. The 'she' I'm thinking about at the moment is a big cat, a lynx, and she and I will dance together as an 'aware lynx.' One thing that I bring to the spirit family is an awareness of rhythm, so I'm able to let them dance with rhythm. You have nothing to give but yourself, in the end, and I give dancing. And sewing. In that too I give blood. I'll always prick myself when I'm sewing leather."

He uses leather? Animal campaigners might be horrified by that.

"If I'm working with it in a magical context I have to get permission. Say someone asks me to make a leather cloak from water buffalo skin. Before I start sewing I have to go before the Water Buffalo Spirit and dance the death of that buffalo. I have to dance until the spirit is convinced that my actions are honourable, that I respect the lives that have ended to give us this leather, and that their use will feed energy back. If I'm not convincing enough, then I have to roll up the skins and accept that I can't make the cloak."

Would that Being be a god water buffalo?

"No, 'god' is the wrong term. Maybe 'master spirit,' but that's not really right either. There's the spirit of an individual water buffalo, then there's a bigger spirit of the whole of that herd, and beyond that there's the spirit of all the water buffalo there have ever been. That last one is the one you've got to convince.

"It's the most difficult thing I ever do. That great thing's just looking at you, with dribble drooling down its face ..."

It's that physical?

"Oh yes! You have to prove to it how much you're prepared to give away. In dance, you're prepared to dance till you drop. Yet the next day you'll wake up feeling invigorated."

Does he use drugs as an aid to trance? "I don't. Quite a lot of shamanic traditions use quite heavy ritual drugs. There's an academic bit of me that says 'That'd be interesting,' but I don't think it's respectful for me to use drugs magically just because it might be interesting."

Is this a moral system in which he might be punished if he did?

"No. We're each responsible for ourselves. If you decide to do something like getting totally pissed, and you don't hurt anyone else, then it'll come back to you next day saying, 'You made a mistake there, *didn't* you!' You're making choices not in fear of retribution, but in terms of actions that ought to be done. If there's an action you feel shouldn't be done, then you shouldn't do it. I was once asked by a friend to work with the spirit of Bear, but though it was fine for my friend it wasn't right for me or my family. I had to go back there with my spirit family and explain to Bear that there were times when I couldn't help, but I'd try to find someone else who could."

It sounds extremely demanding. Does he have a spiritual practice to help him?

"There are rituals and ceremonies, for instance to seal the boundaries, so that I can more or less keep under control the times when I am or am not 'available for work.' And experience helps. I've been doing this for a long time now, and I know how to walk on my path in such a way that I can control what happens and other spirits can't get in to divert me. The Bear sort of incident happens very rarely.

"Shamanic control is control of yourself, not control over other things. It's not like a magician conjuring up things to do his will. I may move over and let something else move in for a while, but that's my choice. With the spirit family we're very tightly woven together, but within that I'm still Gordon the Toad. My moral principles as a shaman lie in respect for who I am, and in respect for who you are and who everything else is and is trying to be. I'm working with spirits who have no physical grounding themselves, so I have to be very self-reliant and very strong. Because we don't work in churches or temples or magical spaces, the only thing I'm carrying around all the time is myself."

It does sound very lonely.

"It is. That's where we came into this section, isn't it? It's lonely. But it's also very passionate and very joyful. We shamans live a long way apart, but we network a lot. We live in a joy that other people don't seem to."

Does anyone ever tell him he should see a rather good psychiatrist?

"No one's ever dared! But yes, people can get incredibly threatened by what we do. I can see that people could call us schizoid. But if we're schizoid then we're the most integrated schizoids I've ever met. We're leading the lives we choose to lead, and if that defies convention then it's not our problem."

Surrounded by life

Now we turn to his education, which Gordon tells me was very mainstream.

"I spent my teenage years trying to be a witch. There was a New Wave of witchcraft at the time, witch teachings and rituals were more accessible than ever before, and that was how you seemed to do magic. People around me were going to church and I was looking for a substitute for that. On reflection, what I think I was looking for was a way of consciously belonging to the world that was talking to me. I wanted the equivalent of being in touch with God. I lit candles and did ceremonies, and none of it seemed to work. But by the time I met real witches, years later, I was already on my own shamanic path and had my own relationship with the gods."

When he says it didn't "work," what does he mean by that? "Times when it's *there*. You're sitting in a room and the colour changes. You're sitting in a magical circle and you realize there's something else sitting there with you. You're not alone. It's like the air you breathe. Enchantment, magic ... You can't see it, but you know it's there because you're alive.

"The shamanic world isn't revelatory, it's about flows and changes. People are usually looking for something much more dramatic than that, but the strongest stuff is often the stuff that simply reminds you that you're a living being and that you're surrounded by life."

I bring him back to his own history. His university education was in fact scientific. Did he enjoy studying Zoology? "Oh, I loved it! I specialized in ecology, and that was a scientific slant on my spirituality. I wasn't at all fazed by the grizzly bits. The shamanic way can be quite grizzly itself. I've sat in a meeting with my Cat spirit, and there are other animal people around. It's like sitting next to someone who's whispering, and she's whispering to me, 'Hares are really *crunchy*!' There's no preciousness there at all. Look at this house, it's full of skulls."

Indeed it is. There are skulls and other animal bones, and feathers and skins, all over the place. But is he vegetarian?

"Yes I am, because I disapprove of how animals in this country are kept and are killed."

Back to Zoology at Glasgow University. What came afterwards? "I trained as a teacher in Durham. Then I didn't know what to do, but my mum saw an advert for a teaching job in Malawi, and I applied for it and got it, and a month later I was standing in an airport in Africa not knowing quite where I was. I'd never been out of Britain before! I do tend just to jump off a cliff and see what happens. But I settled into the school, Kamuzu

Academy, and it was great. Very academic in a western way, it prepared pupils — some of them straight out of the bush — for taking part in the national and international community, and to be doctors and nurses and lawyers and so on." *What was it like spiritually?* "Oddly enough it was Church of Scotland territory, Livingstone territory. I had to be very careful about my spirituality there. I caused all sorts of trouble just by being me. The head threatened to send me home because I was wearing earrings in public." *What did he teach?* "Biology, chemistry and geology. But I was very ill, I nearly died of malaria, and then I got very depressed, which often happens after malaria. Maybe I needed to get that close to death.

"In Malawi there were some very public expressions of traditional culture. The one I remember best was the Gule Wa M'Kulu, the amazing masked Nyau dancers. They're probably the oldest expression of their culture, they can date it back hundreds of years. One of our students was an ex-Nyau, he took me to his village one New Year's Day, and I had a lot of time to talk to him about how those societies worked and what they believed in and to watch dancers in their own community rather than at a big public spectacle. He told me that a Nyau couldn't be tried for what he did when he was masked because he wasn't a human then, he was spirit. I recognize that better now than I did then. It's not community drama, it's spirit possession. They can only dance when the drummers drum, and when the women are singing the songs that release the spirits. Like us as shamans they can only act when the community allows them to. For all their presence, the magic that surrounds them, they're still at the mercy of the villagers who are their community."

Did he have re-entry problems when he got back to Thatcherite Britain?

"Oh, awful. I tried secondary teaching in Dumfries, nice little comprehensive, but I loathed it and one day I just walked out. At the same time my sister was ill with a terrible wasting disease and eventually she died.

"But the web unfolded, and I landed a job as a warden of a Nature Reserve with Durham Wildlife Trust. After that I was a Countryside Warden in the Mersey Valley, and eventually I became Creeping Toad and started to work as I do now."

What do his family think of his way of life? "We get on really well. They've kept up their principle of letting us be who we are."

God and gods

Is there a God in Gordon's universe? "Not a single omnipotent Presence. A shaman works with the gods who choose to turn up. There was a moment, I can't say when, when I met a Mother Goddess figure, the mother of living things, and a Hunter God, a big man with big antlers. These don't change for me. I try to encounter others, like other pagans do, the Goddess in this aspect or the Goddess in that form, but my Mother Goddess and Hunter God say to me, 'What're you doing that for? You've got us!' The gods seem to me to embody parts of the web. They're the force of the web moving onwards. They're bigger than me, with huge amounts of energy, and without any doubts or reservations at all I've given a lot of myself away to them because I have complete faith in their expression of unconditional love.

"There are times in a shaman's life when the spirits involve you in a dismemberment. In the spirit world you can choose a different shape, though you can return to your physical state at any time. You can be hunted by a pack of dogs, for instance, and be caught and torn apart, and you have to get through the shock of that and then return to who you physically are."

At some point in this last section I've caught sight of one of the many sculptures on the crowded surfaces of Gordon's terraced house, and we've both creased with laughter. It's a massive penis beautifully moulded in black rubber. "It was given to me by two lesbian friends of mine," says Gordon. "They said they saw it and thought of me."

Does he think that being gay has made him more open to the world of spirits? "I think anything that makes you question the labels that people offer you is good for opening you up to all sorts of possibilities.

"I know that the body I've got is here to be celebrated. It's the physical expression of the web, and it's holy. Going to the loo, eating a meal, changing a baby's nappy, they're all holy if you choose to see them that way.

"It's about joy. That's what keeps me going, through feeling alone, through feeling 'Oh my god, it's raining again, and I've got no money,' through all the loneliness and the struggle. You can touch this heart of joy. We care, we try to work towards harmony and we recognize that even when people are making a shitty mess of this world, it's still a wonderful place. Being a shaman is about celebrating being alive."

Afterword

a personal response

"If the doors of perception were cleansed, everything would appear as it is, infinite." William Blake

The absurdity of knowing God

When I had almost finished work on *Living in Godless Times* I went to the valley of the Vézère in the Dordogne region of France, where works of art of between 9,000 and 21,000 years old have been discovered. I found that it wasn't the replica at Lascaux that left the most lasting impression on me but the smaller caves farther down the valley, where only a few people are allowed in at a time but the original paintings and carvings are visible to the naked eye.

Our party of six was the last that day to be taken into Les Combarelles. The guide led us deep into the hillside and, with her small red-beamed pencil torch, helped us to read the more difficult, heavily over-scored drawings. Horses are a particular feature here, with some antelope, reindeer, ibex and mammoth, and occasional signs of human representation. I tend to claustrophobia and the tunnels are very long, but I felt no fear. At the farthest point the guide shone her larger torch into a tiny tunnel that only expert pot-holers crawling on their bellies could enter. "See down there?" she said. "In Neolithic times that tunnel was half that height. Down there are hundreds more paintings, some of them the most beautiful of all."

So came the question *why*. Why did these early human beings, whose daily struggle for survival against climate and predator and natural disaster surely took up all their energies, crawl into these dark spaces with their animal-fat candles flickering on small bowls of chiselled stone, not to hide, or eat and sleep, nor to make their homes, but to create works of art that still shock with their raw beauty? The cave painters themselves surely had their own answer, but they left no record except the art itself, the naked experience, the mystery.

A few months later, in Cornwall, I crawled into a stone-lined underground *fogou,* one of the Neolithic end-blocked tunnels which, useless as an escape tunnel or for storage, can only have been created as a ritual space. Crouched in its final airless wedge I experienced a choked, bound, trapped feeling of passage, as if I were about to be born or about to die, and that those two moments of transition were one and the same. I don't know whether this experience was the original purpose of the fogou. That purpose has been lost, and probably I was making my own meaning out of my modern need.

When the painters were busy in the Vézère valley and when Cornish Celts crawled into their fogous, all times and all spaces hummed with divine presences. Now, in the West in the twenty-first century, the times and the spaces we live in are unavoidably godless. This can feel like a huge relief: away with outmoded world views, out with rules and guilt, let's arrange our destinies according to our heart-felt needs and desires. Yet, for those of us who reject both the materialist and the fundamentalist roads and opt for that shadowy path we call the spiritual, there remains the age-old "mystery of the more," which we experience but can never truly define.

One of the most striking aspects of working on this book, for me, was the extent to which the participants acknowledged what they did not know. "This insistent claim to *know* God and his ways, it's absurd. We don't even know ourselves. We can never know the Word, and if we hear it sung with faithful ear we cannot communicate that epiphany to anyone else" (Raficq Abdulla). A key concept on my own journey has been *Negativity Capability,* a phrase John Keats coined to describe "when a man is capable of being in uncertainties, mysteries, doubts, without any irritable reaching after fact and reason."[1] Not that fact and reason don't have a primary place. If we love what is true, then we must start from what actually happened, what people actually did, how they felt, what we can see and hear and prove. But there is more to life than outward truth. The inner truth of any situation is subtle and difficult to find but none the less real. The truth is our destination, but we have to wade through uncertainty and doubt if we are to arrive at it. I particularly like Keats' use of the word "irritable." *Irritable* is a demanding puppy, pawing and clawing until it gets the beautiful bone, only to realize it didn't want the bone after all, it wanted a walk. The truth we need may be different from the truth we seek.

Presence, attention, response

All these people acknowledge the absence of a provable, intervening divinity.

— Only fools believed in God. He was a way of getting you to toe the line.
— As the Hindus say, *"Neti, neti,* God is not this, not this ..."
— There's a void in me which Jesus left, and the void is all right.
— Some people are very certain of being "guided," but I don't feel certain.
— I don't believe in an afterlife. I sometimes wish I did, but I don't.
— I begin to speak, not quite knowing what I'm going to say ...

But side by side with that absence lies a presence. During the three years of *Godless Times* I was working out a new theology for myself. The process is still too convoluted and shadowy to articulate, but I felt as if I was making an outline round an empty shape — drawn, it seemed sometimes, by a pen other than my own — and the space within it filled with a wash of colour, or a texture, or even the bump of granite or the squish of wet clay under my hand. When Anne Gray said, "Colour comes first, and your subject comes out of the colours," I understood what she meant.

For the seeker aware of some *mysterium tremendum,* the starting point is to be sensitive, open to the movement of the Spirit from wherever it may come.

— In my early teens there were stirrings of something beyond the given.
— I heard an inner voice: "Now is the time to look to your inner life."
— I kept asking questions, like "Why isn't God a woman?"
— I saw my Jewish faith through the eyes of someone coming new to it.
— I was pursuing Buddhism in my own rebellious way.
— At first I rejected Steiner's ideas but a couple of years later I was ready.

There's a quality of attention involved in this openness. Adam Curle emphasises the necessity of alertness, Brian Thorne knows the need to wait and to stay with the waiting, Jocelyn Bell Burnell is sensitive to the movement of the Spirit in the gathering of Quakers. Rudolf Steiner says that we can cultivate this attention:

> "Preparation consists of a very definite cultivation of the life of feeling and of thought, through which the 'body' of the soul and spirit is equipped with higher instruments of sense ... The first step is made by directing the attention of the soul to certain happenings in the world around us ... and following what the soul has to say [about it]."[2]

He goes on to suggest that our attention will be most effective during this time of sensitization if we suspend our preconceived categories, our likes and dislikes, and simply do what an artist does: look at and listen to things as they are.

After the sensitivity, openness and alertness, there is the response to what they have experienced.

— I don't know what sense it is you're using, but something clicks.

— The love was free but compelling. Responding to it was the only thing that mattered.

— Even if I'm afraid, I still take it seriously. I don't always say yes, but I respect the leadings.

— I found my own answer to the question, "How do you go forward from a position where your family were herded into ovens like vermin?"

— The response has always got to be an individual response, it can't be a community one.

The response is not to something already defined, but to whatever has come and in whatever form. Adam Curle couldn't tell where the power of the dervish came from, but he recognized it as spiritual power. Brian Thorne had no proof of George Lyward's insights into work with disturbed children but he heard the truth spoken by this stranger. Jocelyn Bell Burnell didn't understand why her assistant clerk nudged her to call the woman in blue, but she acknowledged the authority in the voice and acted on it.

Contradiction and integrity

As someone who naturally sides with sceptics and muddlers-through rather than with born-again believers, I was heartened by the way a whole-hearted spiritual response, for these seekers, didn't need to deny contradiction and paradox. However clear their calling they can still cry out to a God they don't believe in, turn their back on their vocation the fuller to return to it, recognize a voice from the dead though the afterlife means nothing to them, seek understanding of love through common identity with the hideous and vile. A favourite quotation of mine comes from Jacob Needleman in *Lost Christianity*:

"The soul is not a fixed entity ... It is a movement that begins [with] the psychological pain of contradiction. Whenever there is pain or contradiction, this energy of the soul is released."[3]

And another, from Thomas Merton:

"I have to accept that my life is almost totally paradoxical, to learn gradually to get along without apologizing for the fact."[4]

I enjoyed the way that these sixteen, rather than denying contradiction, allowed a rhythm of engagement and retreat so as to give time for intolerable friction to transform into a paradox they could live with.

Having trusted the experience and their response to it, each of them tested it against the stringent demands of their personal integrity.

— My spirituality must be consistent with the rest of my life, with my integrity. I'm interested in seeking the truth of the situation.
— I was neurotic, yes, but not cracked. I asked for a discernment process.
— I have this other self that doesn't believe anything they say unless it strikes true with me.
— I've got this rational, scientific side that insists on looking into things.
— I stay in touch with whatever it is, not suppress it. And that includes the grief. That's the only whole way forward.

Where does this integrity come from? It seems to me to arise from a refusal to deny uncomfortable realities — even your own wrongness or the partiality of your view. "Everyone's biased," says Raficq Abdulla. "What's necessary is to recognize it and take it into account." This integrity involves humility, such as Adam Curle's when he recognized that all the time he'd been trying to be part of the solution actually he was part of the problem, and Mehr Fardoonji's when she realized she couldn't change India to Gandhian ideals but she could set up a garden run on Gandhian principles in England.

Movement and change

They have lived with paradox and tested each insight against their criterion of integrity. What then? Next I perceived movement.

— It was like a door opening. I came back and began to meditate.
— The vision of wholeness wasn't easy to carry through in
  practice. But I visualized where I should go next.
— I knew I had to be different. I went to London and said I was
  a poet.
— I was getting set in my ways, and I needed to live with
  people again.
— I still had no money and no job, but I did now have the determination. This time I knew I had to go for it.
— You might revere Gandhi, or Jesus, or the Buddha, and it's
  very nourishing. But you've got to move on.

The movement may be into the desert, the ashram or the city centre, to visit or revisit a prison, to dare to look at your traumatic heritage, to dance and swim and sculpt, to marry the person of your choice, to return home. I recognized all these as responses to the extra layer of living which a spiritual awareness gives.

The vision and the path

As I write, the daily tension that serves for peace in the Middle East has broken down into frenzied killing, fury and blame. Naomi Gryn e-mails me from Jerusalem:

> "I came to spend a few relaxing weeks with friends while
> we celebrated the Jewish New Year, but instead it has been
> a month of agony as we watch fear and hatred grip the
> hearts of Arabs and Jews alike ... I've been thinking a lot
> about how people cling to the stories that shape their sense
> of being. For me, belief in God provides a structure for my
> inner world and puts the poetry into my day, but while I
> see reflections of divine creation in every atom and every
> action, there are many who cannot maintain consistency in

their system of beliefs if it contains such an abstract notion. Increasingly I see that each of us create our own reality, but it is not for you or for me to doubt the validity of anyone else's spirituality."

So she still has a vision of trying to "build bridges, to look at the culture of the 'enemy,' understand what makes them smile and what gives them pain." It is a wild and perhaps crazy vision. It entails leaps of the imagination and forays into the feared and the unknown. This kind of path is not a recipe or a system but a process — a process which, as Jocelyn Bell Burnell says, has to be lived experimentally, experientially, checking it all the time against integrity, truth and love. It does not shirk the pain and complexity of present reality, and it embraces possibilities as yet unseen.

A few years ago I took part in a well-organized experiment in trance, based on the work of Felicitas Goodman.[5] The leader described the academic research that underlay the experiment, then told us to take up a certain posture, breathe deeply, and give ourselves fifteen minutes to see whether we could enter into trance and what it might show us.

At first I saw bright colours flying across my vision from right to left. The colours became a mass of rushing animals, probably wildebeest fleeing from a predator. Then I was one of them, a young beast on the outside of the herd as we raced in panic. Suddenly the nape of my neck was seized and I felt my head wrenched backwards. I was caught. But I felt no pain, I didn't experience my own death. The next vision was of the herd bowing in a circle around my bones, mourning my loss and thanking me for my sacrifice. My spirit was in two places: among my bones arranged in the centre of the circle, and at the same time hovering overhead and feeling the gratitude and grief of the herd rising up towards me.

I found this experience inexplicable but profoundly moving. I've put it into the great big cauldron at the base of my soul and left it to stir with more rational experiences and insights, and over the time since it happened I find that I've become more aware of the animal world and my connection with it. On sceptical days I know it could be seen as fanciful, but I don't doubt that some emanation from the spirit of evolution reached me in that trance. It linked with my experiences in the Vézère valley and the Cornish fogou, giving me a hint of those early human beings' integral relationship with the rest of creation, and with their ease of movement between the physical and the spiritual worlds.

Some of the insights and visions in these chapters evoke a profound spiritual response in me, others I can identify with immediately, while others again I respect and put to one side. The same will be true for each reader. There is no need to deny spiritual truth in ourselves or in anyone else. We can be open to all of it, and celebrate its diversity, richness, persistence and strength.

We live in a culture which does not openly value the things of the spirit but at the same time searches desperately for the Meaning of Life. The experience of meeting these sixteen people and listening to their life stories has made me see the futility of a Grand Unified Theory, the search for Truth, or any Meaning Of Life which requires capital letters. What is both necessary and possible, though, is the cultivation of spiritual awareness, so that we can grow more sensitive to every layer and nuance that life offers us and become more able to connect one experience to another and our own experiences to those of other people. So our many worlds more readily become one.

> *You measure authenticity by this, not this by some other*
> *authenticity.*   June Raymond

> *The truth is, we don't have to go anywhere, we're here*
> *already. Our task is simply to know it.*   David Banks

> *You can touch this heart of joy. Even when people are*
> *making a shitty mess of this world, it's still a wonderful*
> *place. It's about celebrating being alive.*
>   Gordon MacLellan

Endnotes

Introduction

1. Poll commissioned by the BBC for its series *Soul of Britain*, May 2000.
2. A N Wilson, *God's Funeral,* John Murray 1999.
3. In an interview with Linda Grant, *Guardian* 25 June 1999. (Slightly paraphrased.)
4. Alison Leonard, *Telling Our Stories: Wrestling with a fresh language for the spiritual journey*, DLT 1995, p.65.
5. H A Williams, *The True Wilderness,* Constable, UK 1965; Mowbray 1994, p.72.
6. In a BBC TV *Soul of Britain* discussion, June 2000, chaired by Michael Buerk.
7. *The Ascent of Man*, BBC, 1973, p.437.
8. See *Unveiled: Nuns Talking*, Vintage, 1993, pp.5-6. (Here paraphrased.)
9. Capell Bann Publishing, 1998, p.4.
10. *Reality through the Looking Glass*, Floris Books 1996, p.12.
11. In a radio discussion on her novel *Fugitive Pieces*, BBC Radio 4, 8 October 1999.
12. In his essay *The Will To Believe*. Author of *Varieties of Religious Experience* (1902).

Jocelyn Bell Burnell

1. On CD-Rom.
2. The 1989 Swarthmore Lecture, published by Quaker Home Service. This quotation from p.36, later quotations from p.51.
3. In *Spiritual Evolution: Scientists discuss their beliefs*, Giniger, Philadelphia and London 1998, p.21. Again, Jocelyn is the only woman contributor here.

Raficq Abdulla

1. *Mohammed*, translated from the French by Anne Carter, Penguin Books 1971.
2. *Words of Paradise*, Frances Lincoln, UK; Penguin US, 2000.
3. Alan White, *Within Nietzsche's Labyrinth*, Routledge 1991.

David Banks

1. D. Hofstadter, *Gödel Escher Bach, An Eternal Golden Braid,* Basic Books, NY 1979; Penguin, UK 1980.
2. Mina Banks, *Not Somehow – the story of a Christian life in nursing,* published by Virtual Angels Press 1995.
3. In *The Phenomenon of Man,* published by William Collins & Son, 1959.
4. Author of *The Way of Zen, The Wisdom of Insecurity* and *The Book: On the Taboo Against Knowing Who You Are.*
5. Author of *A Private House of Prayer, The Case for Reincarnation* and other books.
6. *Four Quartets:* "Little Gidding," lines 239-42.
7. *Four Quartets*: "The Dry Salvages" and "Little Gidding."

Benjamin Zephaniah

1. Benjamin Zephaniah, *Face,* Bloomsbury 1999.
2. "She's Crying For Many." This and other poems quoted here are from *City Psalms,* Bloodaxe 1992.
3. "Dis Poetry."
4. "U-turn."
5. "Overstanding."
6. "The Old Truth."
7. "My God, Your God."

Dayachitta

1. The Buddhist teachings on karma and conditionality are explained in *The Three Jewels,* by Sangharakshita, Windhorse Publications, fourth edition, 1998.

Adam Curle

1. For instance in: *Making Peace,* Tavistock 1971, *Mystics and Militants,* Tavistock 1972, *True Justice,* QHS 1981, *Tools for Transformation,* Hawthorn Press 1990, and *Another Way,* Jon Carpenter 1995.
2. See, for instance, *A Human Approach to World Peace,* Wisdom Publications 1984, and *Universal Responsibility and the Good Heart,* Library of Tibetan Works and Archives, 1984.
3. "The Policeman Calls," in *Recognition of Reality,* Hawthorn Press 1987.
4. "Quakers," in *Recognition of Reality,* Hawthorn Press 1987.
5. *Taming the Hydra,* Jon Carpenter 1999.
6. In *Recognition of Reality,* Hawthorn Press 1987.

Naomi Gryn

1. James Hillman, "Betrayal," in *Loose Ends*, Spring Publications. Hillman heads a psychotherapeutic school that uses mythological stories as a therapeutic tool. He is the originator of post-Jungian 'archetypal psychology.'
2. Peter A. Levine, *Waking the Tiger: Healing Trauma*, North Atlantic Books, 1997.

Marian Partington

1. The letter is published in Olive Shapley's *Broadcasting a Life*, Scarlet Press 1996, p.120.
2. The film has not been made.

June Raymond

1. T S Eliot, *Four Quartets,* "Burnt Norton," 2.
2. New Testament. Paul's Letter to the Galatians, 4:22
3. *Knowing Woman: A feminine psychology*. Shambala, Boston, 1973.
4. *Original Blessing* was the title of Matthew Fox's book, published by Bear & Co in 1975.
5. F. Capra, *The Turning Point*, Flamingo 1983.

Brian Thorne

1. See *Person-Centred Therapy Today* and *Carl Rogers,* both Sage Publications, London.
2. See *Mr Lyward's Answer*, by Michael Burn, Hamish Hamilton, London 1956.
3. *Student Counselling in Practice,* co-authored with Audrey Newsome and Keith Wyld, University of London Press, 1973
4. In *Julian of Norwich*, pamphlet published by the Guild of Pastoral Psychology 1999.

Mehr Fardoonji

1. In *How To Know God, the Yoga Aphorisms of Patanjali,* translated by Swami Prabhavananda and Christopher Isherwood. George Allen and Unwin 1953.

Anne Gray

1. Now published as *Esoteric Science* and *How to Know Higher Worlds,* published by Anthroposophic Press, New York, and Rudolf Steiner Press, London.

Rose Hacker

1. *Abraham's Daughter*, Deptford Forum Publishing Ltd 1996.
2. Old Testament. Leviticus 19:18.
3. First published by Andr, Deutsch, revised and enlarged 1966.
4. Published by Pan Books, price two shillings and sixpence.
5. *You and your Daughter,* Four Square Books, 1964.
6. In *Quantum Healing: Exploring the Frontiers of Mind, Body and Medicine*, Bantam, 1989.

Eric Maddern

1. *The Rainbow Bird,* retold by Eric Maddern and published by Frances Lincoln, 1996.
2. *Varieties of Religious Experience,* William James. First published in 1902, latest edition published by Random House 1999.
3. In books such as *The Hero with a Thousand Faces* and his trilogy on *Myth.*

Kathy Jones

1. *How To Live In The Country*, Wildwood Press, 1976. Out of print.
2. Wolkstein, Diane and Kramer, Samuel Noah, *Inanna: Queen of Heaven and Earth*, Harper & Row, NY, 1983.
3. These plays are published in *On Finding Treasure*, Ariadne Publications 1996.
4. First edition 1983. Now in many editions, including Penguin 1993.
5. *Breast Cancer – Hanging on by a Red Thread*, Ariadne Publications 1998.

Gordon MacLellan

1. See *Sacred Animals*, Capell Bann 1996, and *The Piatkus Guide to Shamanism* 1999.
2. *The Owl Service, The Weirdstone of Brisingamen*, both published by Penguin UK, Harcourt USA.

Afterword

1. Letter to his brothers G and T Keats dated 21 December 1817.
2. *Knowledge of Higher Worlds*, Chapter 2, op.cit.
3. Element Books USA, 1993.
4. *A Thomas Merton Reader*, ed. T.P.McDonnell, Image Books, Garden City NY, 1994.
5. See F. Goodman, *Where The Spirits Ride The Wind*, Indiana University Press 1990.

Index